Praise for *Daughters of the Flower Fragrant Garden*

"Exceptional. . . . *Daughters of the Flower Fragrant Garden* is not a history of Taiwan-China relations, but in telling this gripping narrative of one family divided by the 'bamboo curtain,' [Zhuqing] Li sheds light on how Taiwan came to be—and why China might one day risk everything to take it."

—Deirdre Mask, *New York Times Book Review*

"At last, a profoundly human story that illuminates the staggering personal consequences of China and Taiwan's historic split—from both sides. Rare is the author who can portray war and its aftermath so evenhandedly. This powerful page-turner of a family torn apart—and surviving—is as unforgettable as it is important."

—Nicole Mones, author of *The Last Chinese Chef*

"Li recounts this real-life saga of rupture and reunion in propulsive, poignant detail. The book's gripping narrative reveals the devastating human cost of the Chinese Revolution and will resonate, in particular, with anyone whose family has been severed by political events. . . . The author's perspective, from having lived both inside and outside the People's Republic of China, yields exceptional insight into her aunts' personal histories and the constantly shifting political vicissitudes they endured. She unspools the unexpected, accidental swerves each life took with spellbinding grace. Here, in the pages of her book, she has knit together the family story as it was lived in both Chinas." —Diane Cole, *Wall Street Journal*

"Zhuqing Li has captured the agonizing struggle of late-twentieth-century Chinese history within the microcosm of her own extraordinary family. This is a tale of accidental exile, capitalism and communism, medicine and mercantilism, lifelong nostalgia and willful forgetting, and the breathtaking resilience of two sisters, Li's indomitable aunts. How lucky we are that their niece has the skill and devotion to tell their story so well."

—Janice P. Nimura, author of *The Doctors Blackwell*

"A very personal story informed by a scholarly set of interests. . . . [I]t's a memoir and family history, driven by the author's interest in figuring out the things that the family didn't talk about."　—Jeffrey Wasserstrom, Fivebooks.com, "Best China Books of 2022"

"A heartrending story, beautifully told, about the struggles and triumphs of two sisters separated by the Taiwan Strait, but united in their determination to pursue meaningful lives amid political upheaval. I couldn't stop reading it."

—Amy Stanley, author of *Stranger in the Shogun's City*

"Zhuqing Li has written a compelling book about family secrets, Cold War politics, and the emotional consequences of displacement. . . . By interweaving the perspectives of its two protagonists, Li emphasizes the persistence of family ties in the face of political and geographical distance, and the disappointment and culture shock that can accompany a long-anticipated reunion."

—Tobie Meyer-Fong, *Los Angeles Review of Books*

"In gorgeous prose, Zhuqing Li tells a story that is at once distinctive and familiar, of Chinese families of a certain generation that lived through wars, revolutions, separations, and reunions. I couldn't put it down. A lovely book."

—Mae Ngai, author of *The Chinese Question*

"With sensitivity and sincerity, *Daughters of the Flower Fragrant Garden* takes readers through the most complicated, difficult, sorrowful, and indecipherable years in China's modern history. Zhuqing Li's beautifully narrated family stories are tightly entangled with the wider historical context unfolding on a magnificent scale, and evoke unique feelings of pain and helplessness that belong to that era."

—Ai Weiwei, author of *1000 Years of Joys and Sorrows*

"Beginning in war-torn China, *Daughters of the Flower Fragrant Garden* tells a compelling story about diaspora, root-seeking, and the triumph of familial love and human perseverance."

—David Wang, author of *The Lyrical in Epic Time*

"Beautifully woven family memories coalesce into a vivid history of two very different Chinas." —*Kirkus Reviews*

Daughters

of the

Flower Fragrant Garden

Daughters *of the* Flower Fragrant Garden

Two Sisters Separated by China's Civil War

ZHUQING LI

W. W. NORTON & COMPANY
Celebrating a Century of Independent Publishing

For information about permission to reproduce selections from this book,
write to Permissions, W. W. Norton & Company, Inc., 500 Fifth Avenue,
New York, NY 10110

For information about special discounts for bulk purchases, please contact
W. W. Norton Special Sales at specialsales@wwnorton.com or 800-233-4830

Manufacturing by Lakeside Book Company
Book design by Lisa Buckley
Production manager: Anna Oler

Library of Congress Cataloging-in-Publication Data

Names: Li, Zhuqing, 1963– author.
Title: Daughters of the flower fragrant garden : two sisters separated by
    China's Civil War / Zhuqing Li.
Other titles: Two sisters separated by China's Civil War
Description: First edition. | New York : W. W. Norton & Company, Inc,
    [2022]
Identifiers: LCCN 2022007374 | ISBN 9780393541779 (cloth) | ISBN
    9780393541786 (epub)
Subjects: LCSH: Fuzhou Shi (Fujian Sheng, China)—Biography. |
    Chen, Wenjun, 1923–2014. | Chen, Hong (Pseudonym) | Chen
    family. | Sisters—China—Fuzhou Shi (Fujian Sheng)—Biography. |
    Families—China—Fuzhou Shi (Fujian Sheng)—History—20th
    century. | Fuzhou Shi (Fujian Sheng, China)—Biography. |
    Refugees—Taiwan—Biography. | Taiwan—Biography. | China—
    History—Civil War, 1945–1949—Biography.
Classification: LCC DS797.26.F89 C445 2022 | DDC 951.04/20922—dc23/
    eng/20220217
LC record available at https://lccn.loc.gov/2022007374

ISBN: 978-1-324-06439-8 pbk.

W. W. Norton & Company, Inc.
500 Fifth Avenue, New York, N.Y. 10110
www.wwnorton.com

W. W. Norton & Company Ltd.
15 Carlisle Street, London W1D 3BS

1 2 3 4 5 6 7 8 9 0

To
my two aunts who have inspired me
and
Ed, Dan, and Will, who have sustained me

煮豆燃豆萁 Beanstalks roar as the beans boil,
豆在釜中泣 Weeping in the pot, the beans roil:
本是同根生 Out of the same roots we have grown
相煎何太急 What is the rush to kill one's own?

—Cao Zhi (192–232), a poet in the
Three Kingdoms period

Contents

Prologue

To be separated of course means having been together once, and Jun and Zhen started out from the same place, a home named the Flower Fragrant Garden, a spacious, verdant family compound, one of Fuzhou's biggest and richest homes. It crowned what was called the Cangqian Hill across the Min River from the main part of Fuzhou, like a tiara encircled by a low stone wall. The main building was a grand, two-story red-brick Western-style house rising from the lush greenery of the rolling grounds. A winding path dipped under the canopy of green, linking smaller buildings like beads on a necklace.

Growing up, I knew of the Garden the way one might know of a big old house in town, no more than a noteworthy part of the scenery. My parents returned from their political exile in the countryside when I was ten, and they took up posts at the Teachers College next door to the Garden. They weren't senior enough to be assigned housing there, in the exclusive

Map of Fuzhou City, 1945. (COURTESY OF THE UNIVERSITY OF TEXAS
LIBRARIES, UNIVERSITY OF TEXAS AT AUSTIN)

compound for the leaders of the university, so we lived instead
in a more modest faculty apartment building not far away.

From there I used to go often to visit my maternal grandmothers who lived at the foot of the Cangqian Hill. Yes, I had
two maternal grandmothers, a relic of the Old China, where
wealthy men like my grandfather could, and often did, have

more than one wife. There was Upstairs Grandma, who was Jun and Zhen's biological mother; and there was Downstairs Grandma, my mother's mother. The front door of my Grandmas' home had a large hibiscus tree, and through its checkerwork of leaves we could see pieces of the Garden on the peak of the hill.

The Garden looked down on us like something from a fairy tale, forbidding and aloof, off limits to ordinary people. Guards were posted at its main gate. I didn't know that in times past—when the Chen family, my mother's side of the family, was one of the wealthiest and most prominent in Fuzhou—it had owned the whole compound. Or that several branches of my extended family lived there under the same roof, where they raised many children, worshipped their ancestors, and celebrated the festivals in lavish style. During my girlhood, nobody in my family spoke of the place. But the trail that took me to school ran along the outside of the stone wall that encircled the Garden. I'd walk past a ditch that overflowed in every heavy rain, skirt an abandoned graveyard that always sped me up, and at the last turn, look out on a spectacular view of the Min River below where I'd pause to catch my breath.

So I knew of a hole in the otherwise impregnable wall, and one day when I was seven I went through it, pursuing a runaway ball. I lingered: the cicadas' buzz was especially intense there, so was the mélange of floral and fruity fragrances.

There was nobody inside the wall, only me and my ball. What captivated me was the gigantic and massive front door of the main building, fortified with a rich layer of red lacquer and two fierce lion-face bronze knockers too high for me to reach. It stood tauntingly ajar. My heart beating, I leaned all my weight on it, and it gave way a few inches, emitting a deep, throaty, scary growl. I flinched reflexively even as I peered within. The cavernous hall inside sent out a gush of cool air seeming to threaten to suck me into the vacuum of the house. I pulled away and ran for my life, but not until I paused for a glimpse of the porcelain toilet behind a half-closed door in a small outhouse before making my way back to the hole in the wall.

Nobody spoke of my Aunt Jun either, and this was perhaps even stranger. She was my Aunt Zhen's older sister. The two of them had been nearly inseparable when they were girls, especially during the eight years of war with Japan when the Chen family was forced into an internal exile. But their lives were disrupted again by China's Civil War, and then they were abruptly separated when the bamboo curtain fell between Communist and non-Communist regions of China. Zhen never mentioned to anyone in my generation that she even had a sister, much less a sister whose own life and associations had caused both emotional anguish and political trouble for the family in Communist China. By the time I came along, Zhen had become a prominent physician in Fuzhou, famous as a pioneer in bringing medical care to China's remote countryside, and later the "grandma of IVF babies," in vitro fertilization, in Fujian Province. She was an important, unsentimental person, too busy perhaps to recount tales of days bygone. But none of my other aunts and uncles ever breathed a word either, about Jun or the Garden, to me or to my cousins. Not my own mother, not even Jun's own mother, my Upstairs Grandma, ever told me or my cousins that we had an aunt named Jun.

It was only when I was finished with college in China and my application to graduate school was blocked by my new employer that Jun appeared in my life, suddenly, and out of the blue. My mother told me that I had an aunt I'd never met, and that for the first time in thirty years, she was there in

Fuzhou, visiting her family—something made possible when China and the U.S. established diplomatic relations in 1979.

"Maybe you should meet her," my mother said. Maybe with her foreign connections she would be able to help me go to graduate school, and in America.

And so I did meet her—and she did help me. She was a slender, elegant woman, with a confident manner and an amiable smile, somehow different from the other women I knew, even while wearing the Maoist outfit that she must have picked up from some local store in order to fit in. It was she who talked to me about the Garden. Then, shocked and saddened by my complete ignorance, she started to paint me a picture of the place that she once called home. As she reminisced, I felt as if she were holding my hand and walking me through the gate, pushing open that door that I'd been too scared to go through as a seven-year-old, and unlocking other doors to the past that the rest of the family had preferred to keep tightly shut. As Jun started to tell me her own and her sister's remarkable childhood and young adulthood, questions about Zhen came to my mind for the first time: What was Zhen doing and thinking at the time? What did she see and hear, and what was it like for her? I reached out to Zhen for the other half of the story, and for the first time, learned from her far more than she'd ever seemed willing to tell me before. These two remarkable and pioneering women—sisters from the same family who lived their adult lives on the two sides of the bamboo curtain—had fought and won against adversities that might have crushed less powerful, determined figures. Their separation and gritty determination to succeed, which embodied the traumatic split of China itself as a nation, are what prompted me to write this book.

PART I

The Garden

"But the Garden is an empty hull," I said.
"No," Aunt Jun corrected me, "It is a jewel, and it has come a long, long way."

My Upstairs Grandma Lin Ruike, Jun and Zhen's mother, was born and raised in Sanfang Qixiang, meaning "three alleys and seven lanes," a small enclave for the local elites in the center of the city of Fuzhou, the capital of Fujian Province. There was a saying in the city, "The Chens and the Lins take up half of the world." My grandfather was a Chen, and Upstairs Grandma was a Lin. She had attended a missionary high school, as did most of the city's educated elite, considering these Westernized schools more rigorous and well rounded, as they offered subjects such as world history and geography and physical education while traditional Chinese private tutoring focused on Chinese classics. She had been slated to study in America after graduation in honor of her academic distinction. But the Lin family traded that prospect for a promising marriage to a handsome rising star in the Nationalist establishment, a Baoding graduate,* and a member of the elite Chen clan.

---

* Baoding Military Academy was founded in 1912 and closed in 1923.

Fuzhou, just outside wall, gatehouses, flooded rice fields. (COURTESY OF HARVARD-YENCHING LIBRARY OF HARVARD COLLEGE LIBRARY, HARVARD UNIVERSITY)

My grandfather was the first to break away from a longstanding Chen family tradition of scholar-officials. His name was *Chen Shouchun,* meaning "longevity mahogany." Born in 1895, the second of four surviving sons,* he went to the Baoding Military Academy, China's first modern military training

---

* In the year of my grandfather's birth, China lost to Japan in the Sino-Japanese War. This is one of the major events that set in motion the final decline of China's last dynasty, the Qing. In the Treaty of Shimonoseki with Japan, concluded in the wake of China's defeat, the island of Taiwan was handed to Japanese custody "in perpetuity." China's two-thousand-year dynastic history came to an end in 1911, just as my grandfather was coming of age, and the Nationalist Party founded the Republic of China.

institution. There, he took a new name: *Chen Daodi*, meaning "Chen Who Smashes the Enemy." Aunt Jun remembered her father explaining why he had had two majors, in cavalry and artillery: Having been assigned to cavalry, he was worried that being a southerner who had never ridden a horse, he would never make it to the top of his class. So he decided to complete another major that offered a better chance to compete.

After graduation, he briefly served in the Nationalist Army. Then he returned home to marry, and soon after the first children were born, he bought a villa on Cangqian Hill outside the city walls. Aunt Jun remembered the courtyard of that villa particularly well, because that was where Downstairs Grandma joined the family. "It was a beautiful warm spring day," Jun told me many years later. She was about five years old, and her mother was reading to her in the courtyard. Zhen was just learning to walk, holding on to her nanny's hand. A breeze sprinkled flakes of cherry petals on the ground. The front gate creaked open, and Jun watched in surprise as the doorman stepped through it and announced that her father was home.

The women in the courtyard looked at each other, wondering why Grandfather had come home in the middle of the day, and then, suddenly, they knew. Music streamed through the gate and into the yard door. Grandfather appeared—looking handsome and confident as usual, wearing a light-colored suit for the warm weather, complete with a bow tie. Following him was an exquisite sedan chair, lacquer red, carved with flying phoenixes and draped in matching red silk canopy. It was carried on the shoulders of four footmen, and behind it came another chair only slightly less glamorous. Grandfather gestured to the footmen to set both chairs down and as soon as that was done, a beautifully dressed maid emerged from the second sedan chair and she followed Grandfather to the first.

Jun and the others watched spellbound as the woman lifted the curtain that hung over the front of the first sedan chair. Grandfather reached inside, and lifted from within a bejeweled hand, followed by a delicate young lady. She stood still for a minute, a grave expression on her pretty face. She was wrapped in a splendidly styled and shapely red sequined *qipao*. Her headdress glittered in the sun; her dainty shoes caressed the courtyard speckled with fallen petals. Jun's mother grabbed her and her sister Zhen and handed them to their nanny, who hustled them away. Nothing was said, nothing explained. Jun remembered that her mother's room was moved upstairs later that day. And Jun and her sister were told to call the dainty lady who had stepped from the sedan chair into their lives *Ah Niang*, meaning "mother." They were to refer to their own biological mother as *Ah Nai*, a different appellation for "mother." So Ah Niang would become my biological grandmother, my Downstairs Grandma, who would occupy the lower floor of the various houses that she shared with the other wife, who always took an upstairs room. No one seemed to know anything about Downstairs Grandma's family, except that she came from outside of the city's elite.

At the Confucian apex of the family was Grandfather's mother, a commanding person with bound feet and progressive ideas. She had been given very little in the way of formal education herself, but she was nonetheless a strong and well-respected woman who set a shining example for Jun and Zhen, her granddaughters. Popo, as Jun and Zhen called her, was a talented storyteller. Night after night in the Garden's long summers, she'd hold court in the mélange of gardenia, jasmine, and roses and, to the tune of singing crickets, fill the mysterious darkness with tales of ghosts and demons that gripped the children with fear and wonder. Her incredible memory compensated for her illiteracy. When Grandfather brought in the latest shows—Chinese and Western operas, movies, and dramas—for grand festivities in the family's home, those characters would all somehow resurface in Popo's stories.

And she found in Grandfather, her third son, the best partner in shaping the family's agenda and image. During the years he lived in Fuzhou, Grandfather worked as Fujian Province's salt commissioner, a powerful, ancient position. Smuggling from the salt-producing regions on the coast to the interior was rampant, since there was much profit to be made by evading taxation, and this made Grandfather's job, commanding a flotilla of boats to patrol the Min River to catch smugglers, dangerous as well as prestigious. One year, he held the family's Mid-Autumn Festival on his main boat, so everybody could gaze at the moon unobstructed and at its reflection on the water. The boat was converted into a floating garden, with singsong girls, flowers, and food. Grandfather, standing at the bow, tipped his fedora to arriving guests while helping women get on board.

When his mother arrived on the family sedan, Grandfather promptly got off the boat to greet her at the dock. Great-grandma held on to his arm, her "golden lotus" bound feet pointed toward the boat, an image that seared into Jun's memory. All eyes turned to those feet, Jun's heart pounding in the silence around her as the singsong girls swallowed their unfinished tune, watching Great-grandma reach the gangplank. Her steps slowed. The planks were narrow and set widely apart. They creaked and swayed with the gentle rocking of the boat. The water below was tearing the moon into pieces. All on board seemed to freeze at the sight, and Jun remembered gazing at the two sets of shoes, her father's shiny patent leathers and her grandma's beautifully embroidered three-inch slippers with their pointy tips and pointy heels. But before anyone realized it, Great-grandma lifted her first foot onto the gangplank. Under the intense gaze of all, her golden lotus shoes proceeded surely and resolutely across the water-slicked wood.

As his career took off, Grandfather decided to move to the very peak of Cangqian Hill, "a low eminence . . . along the river bank," as it was described in an English guide to China from 1924, with "foreign consulates, churches, hospitals, clubs, residences, etc., which constitute almost an independent community." There, he built the family compound known as the Flower Fragrant Garden, looking across the Min River into the old city behind the city walls. His own income, added to the Chen family's wealth from its ancestral lands in Luozhou, was considerable. He designed the new home to provide room for all three of his brothers, their families, and his widowed mother, the family matriarch. Grandfather even tended to details such as the proper width of the driveway to accommodate the largest sedans of the time. Crowning the hill, the Garden was a house and garden that proclaimed the Chen family's wealth and stature in Fuzhou.

The Flower Fragrant Garden atop the "low eminence" described in the guidebook was where Jun and Zhen came of age amid their large extended family. It was where the family's values shaped them. In the traditional way, Cang, Grandfather's firstborn son, studied with a tutor who had been hired to give him an exclusive and comprehensive traditional education at home, which was the way princes were raised. The girls would often listen in from the window, and when their mother saw that they were learning faster than their brother, she informed her mother-in-law, Popo, the family matriarch, of the girls' talents, and promptly got her support to let the girls sit in on their brother's private lessons in their after-school hours. Soon Popo sent the girls to the local missionary school, known for the best classroom learning in Fuzhou. Both Jun and Zhen were grateful all their lives to these two women, their mother and grandmother of the Garden, who were united in their belief that girls should be given the best education possible. "We'll pay for their tuition," the girls' Popo said in support of their schooling, "even if it means that we have to take it from their dowry. Girls with educations can marry without dowries."

The girls' education combined modern subjects taught in their missionary school with the Confucian values of the past. Indeed, their own family embodied a similar mixture of old and new. Their Popo was a devout Buddhist, and on New Year's Day, she would take the entire family on a trip to the Xichan Temple to ask Buddha for her family's well-being in the coming year. But she also sent the girls to Christian missionary school and had no problem when their two mothers converted to Christianity, or with her sons' observation of Christmas in their workplaces.

For Jun and Zhen, Christianity was not so much a matter of a religious belief as it was a set of associations that their missionary school brought to them. For Jun, it was a bond with her mother, who also got a missionary school education. It was one of Jun's teachers who gave her mother the Bible that she treasured all her life. Later, both Ah Nai and Ah Niang were baptized in her school's chapel. For Zhen, the association was the Christian value of charity. For both girls, Christianity was part of an educational package that also included Greek mythology, world history, geography, and other subjects in sciences, and of course, English, all of which would germinate through their long years of becoming themselves.

Jun remembered her father's explanation for the different,

contradictory observances of the family. "We don't really know for sure if either Buddha or the ancestors or even God are watching over us," he told her. "But if worshipping them helps us do good and live as righteously as we can, I don't see how there can be a conflict worshipping them all."

And the family did have a long list of ancestors for worshipping aside from Buddha and God. The first member of the clan whose name appears in the imperial records was one Chen Huai, who in 1538 became a *jinshi*, a distinction given to those who placed in the top ranks of China's imperial civil service exam system. In a country where aristocracy was synonymous with meritocracy, that was what elevated the Chen family into the ranks of the social elite.

The family had its origins in Luozhou, a small island in the fertile estuary at the mouth of the Min River, but by the time another ancestor, Chen Ruolin, won the clan's second *jinshi* in 1787, the family had moved upriver to Fuzhou, the capital of Fujian Province. There, they settled in Sanfang Qixiang in the city center. For centuries, the grand homes of the Chens and Lins and a few other clans in the Sanfang Qixiang neighborhood stood apart, their grandeur giving no hint of the humble beginnings of their occupants, who could certainly never have imagined that one day all that glory would turn to dust.

In the final 360 years of imperial China, the Chen family would produce a total of 21 *jinshi* and 110 *juren*, the titles awarded to the winners of the national and provincial exams. That included Chen Chengqiu's six sons, a record of fecundity that earned him an imperial plaque from Emperor Xianfeng himself, inscribed in gold on cobalt blue: "Six Sons Ascending Scholarly Heights." (The plaque was still there when I visited Fuzhou in 2015, stubbornly standing amid the rubble of an ongoing urban renovation.) These top degree holders all held important positions in the bureaucratic system. For all of them, Sanfang Qixiang was their family seat. One of them was my great uncle Chen Baochen, who was the tutor to the last Chinese emperor, Henry Puyi.

• • •

One day, weeks before the Spring Festival of 1937, when Jun was playing chess with her grandmother in the Garden after her afternoon siesta, she heard the housekeeper announce: "The Fifth Master's home!" That was her father, the fifth male of his generation in the Chen clan. He had by then been working in Shanghai for years. Jun only knew that he worked for the Nationalist government.

Jun broke from her game and flew down the stairs, bumping into Zhen who briefly lifted her face from the book she was reading, returned to finish a sentence, and when she was done, closed the book with a finger in it as a temporary bookmark. "I predict you're going to get another pair of new leather shoes," she said.

"I can never figure out how father gets the perfect size each year," Jun said incredulously. "It's like he's got the pace of my growth down to a science. What do you think he's bringing you this time?"

"Father knows better than I do. I honestly can't think of anything that I really need."

"Come!" Jun pulled her sister's other hand, running past Auntie Huang, the nanny, and bolting out the door.

They saw their father (my grandfather) enter the house, followed by streams of boxes and suitcases carried inside, not the one car full that he usually brought home from Shanghai on the New Year but two carfuls instead. Everyone noticed that. The little children froze in awe at the endless procession

of beautifully wrapped boxes. Jun got her annual perfectly fit-
ting leather shoes, Zhen became the happy owner of a small
typewriter, with the stipulation from their father that it should
be shared with her sister. There were bolts of brocade from
Suzhou, China's silk capital, and a box of perfumed French
soaps for Great-grandma. There were gifts for everyone, the
servants included. The excitement lasted for days.

Great-grandma believed that she owed to Buddha her
son's earlier-than-usual return home for the New Year. But
the real reason was his disillusionment with Chiang Kai-shek's
government in which he worked. Six years earlier, in 1931,
Japan had seized the three northeastern provinces of Man-
churia, creating a puppet state called Manchukuo, and ruling
it directly from Tokyo. It seemed only a matter of time before
the Japanese would take another bite out of the rest of China.
But to the consternation of an increasing number of people, including Grandfather, the autocratic Chiang put more
resources into combating the country's Communist insurrec-
tion than he did into the resistance against Japan.

This policy came to an end at the end of 1936 when, in
a celebrated event known as the Xian Incident, Chiang was
kidnapped by the commander of his own Nationalist Army
in China's northwest and forced into negotiations with the
Communists. After a few tense days, during which the whole
country seemed to hold its breath, Chiang flew back to Nanjing, the country's capital, and announced the formation of
a "United Front" with the Communists to fight the Japanese
aggressors.

In fact, the United Front was a smokescreen, covering up
the deadly struggle for power between the Nationalists and
the Communists, which would break out in full-scale civil war
eight years later, after Japan was defeated in World War II. But

for the moment, the country's spirit had been renewed by Chiang's and Mao's agreement to work together, as China faced the inevitable next step in Japan's military conquest of China.

The situation had an immediate effect on the Chen family. Grandfather soon announced that he would stay at home in the Garden for good. He may by then have completely given up on the Nationalists' ability to protect the country and decided to take the safety of his family into his own hands.

Whatever his exact reason, Grandfather's decision prompted Great-grandma to call for an unusually lavish New Year celebration that year. The sliding partitions in the front hall were pulled open to make room for a grand banquet. Every nook and cranny of the house was cleaned to rid it of the detritus of the year past. Tailors arrived to take measurements for new clothes for the entire clan, to be made out of those bolts of Suzhou silk. Grandma set herself the task of sorting the different grades of oranges from Luozhou, the family's ancestral town. The best ones were for the altar, the second best for visiting guests, and the ordinary ones for family consumption.

There was an extra-long dragon dance that year, performed by a famous troupe hired for the purpose. The creature, dressed in bright red and gold, ringed the entire courtyard. It bucked, turned, and twisted, seeming to try to break free of the enclosure, but the drums, gongs, cymbals, and piercing horns kept it in place.

As always, Jun and Zhen's mother took all the children to her parents' Lin home in the Sanfang Qixiang and stopped at the lantern festival on their way back. Jun got a beautiful, translucent, peachy-orange lantern. It was made out of rice paper, decorated with just a few simple brush strokes so the light inside looked like a soft rising sun seen through blades of grass. She paraded with the children in the Garden, the flickering lights like fireflies appearing and disappearing in the deepening night. When they rejoined the adults in the great hall, the lights were dimmed, the children's lanterns illuminated the faces of the ancestors above the altar table. All the new silk gowns glimmered in the flickering light, as Great-grandma began the ritual chant that would bring the festivities to an end.

When Jun made her way back to her room, for some reason her lantern popped and went up in flames.

Expelled

JUN'S DREAM WAS TO GO to the Yinghua High School, the best high school in Fuzhou, and then to the Fujian Teachers College, the best in the province, which was conveniently located right on the other end of a short trail that started on one side of the Garden's gate.

But on July 7, 1937, Japan launched a full-scale invasion of China, attempting to put the entire country under its direct control. It took a while for Jun to realize the vast discrepancy that existed between the world outside the Garden and the world within it, where she would start early each morning by picking fresh fruit for her grandma, who liked it still wet with dew. Then she would begin a full day of study, getting ready for the entrance exam to the Yinghua High School. Her father's announcement that he would stay home for good just a few months before had gotten her hopes up, and she had been looking forward to spending more time with him in his study, a privilege that she alone in her generation enjoyed. But unlike the old days, her father was now often absent. He took frequent trips to Nanping, a small mountain

The Southern suburb of the Chinese city Fuzhou. (COURTESY OF HARVARD-YENCHING LIBRARY OF HARVARD COLLEGE LIBRARY, HARVARD UNIVERSITY)

town upstream on the Min River. When he was home, he looked grave. Often black sedans or jeeps would arrive, disgorging men whom her father would meet in his study, after which he would seem distracted and distant. A war was going on, Jun thought to herself, and, after all, her father was a military man by training.

One morning, Jun went to a giant old longan tree so heavy with fruit that its branches draped to the ground, forming a kind of cathedral where the children played in the summer, accompanied by birdsong. But this morning, instead of birds chirping, Jun heard the sound of digging. A group of workmen was there, and one of them told her they had been ordered to dig a bomb shelter. Jun ran back to the house where her grandmother, looking grave and resigned, told her that it was true; they were building a shelter and soon practice runs would begin. Jun was dumbfounded and indignant: why had no one breathed a word to her that her Garden was being desecrated?

The war had started with a skirmish between Japanese and Chinese forces at the Marco Polo Bridge near *Beiping* (meaning "Northern Peace"; now it's *Beijing*, "Northern Capital"). By the end of July, Beijing and the port city of Tianjin had been captured by the Japanese, and the invading troops marched quickly south down the Eastern Seaboard. On August 13, heavy battles broke out in Shanghai. From Shanghai, it was only a few hours by train to Fuzhou.

Soon, the first practice run in using the bomb shelter took place. Decades later, Jun remembered the adults' nervous chatter and the children's excitement, as women and children were guided by the men in the family along the Garden's paths to the giant longan tree on the edge of the property. She remembered her grandmother hobbling on her bound feet, rushing with Jun's two mothers' help—in an imagined air raid—as they crossed the uneven grounds. When the exercise was over, Jun confronted her father: How would the shelter be safer than the house, especially since it took so long for the entire family to get to it? And what was the need to traumatize Popo? And what if the Japanese bombs caught them midway between the house and the shelter? They would have no protection! Her father listened to her patiently, praised her thoughtfulness, and promised to explain everything later in his study.

Never had Jun entered her father's study with such heavy

premonition. The study had always been a place of wonder for her, filled with her father's collections of books. Jun
had traveled through time and space in this room with her
father, impressed that whatever book they needed, it always
seemed to be at his fingertips. But the study seemed to
darken as her father explained to Jun what was happening.
The Japanese had swept down half of the Eastern Seaboard
in a matter of weeks. Fierce battles were being waged in
Shanghai. Her father rummaged through a pile of newspapers on his usually orderly desk. Pulling out one with
photos on the front page, he reeled off names, numbers,
and dates: Japanese dive bombers and riverboats firing at a
range of sixty yards, amassing tens of thousands of troops
in and around the city, declaring that it would take down
Shanghai in a month, and all of China in three months.
The Chinese army under the command of General Zhang
Zhizhong was suffering heavy losses. On August 17, three
hundred Nationalist soldiers, cut off by Japanese tanks, were
brutally slaughtered. Jun saw the images of carnage on the
front page of the newspaper, and she shuddered. Shanghai
was China's most beautiful city. The Paris of the Orient. She
had dreamed of going there to visit her father one day. She
imagined it as a place of unbelievable glamour, sophistica-
tion, and glitter, but the photographs on her father's desk
showed only devastation.

Chiang Kai-shek, China's leader, the Generalissimo, as he
was called, had wanted the invasion to unfold in front of the
foreigners, her father explained, which was why, rather than
retreating, he had allowed the battle to take place in Shanghai, hoping to move other countries to come to China's rescue. But, Jun asked, was anyone sympathetic to China's cause?

"Thousands of human lives are being sacrificed in Shanghai," her father said. "For what? So we can get the world's

sympathy. But you know, my child, unfortunately sympathy doesn't figure very prominently in world politics. Sympathy won't make countries go to war against Japan for our sake. Refugees are pouring out of Shanghai now, but the rest of the world is not going to help." And as for the location of the bomb shelter, he said, houses were more likely to be attacked than the gardens, so the shelter was under the longan tree rather than under the house.

All of this was certainly very scary and bewildering for a girl Jun's age, but it was what Jun's father told her at the end of their talk that she remembered with a shudder almost eight decades later, words that signaled to her that her hopes and dreams were being shattered, like that lantern that popped in the night.

"I'd like our family to leave here soon before it's too late," her father said, looking straight into her eyes.

To leave? Tears surged as her father sat down next to her and gently explained, holding her hand: "My child, war is something no one can predict, not your father, not even the general in charge. Right now, the situation in the cities is dangerous, and the Japanese are not far from Fuzhou. We have the wherewithal to stay away for a while, so we should take advantage of it. I understand how hard it is to uproot a family, but you know the old saying: 'If we keep the mountain green, we'll always have firewood to burn.' You're still young, and you are bright and hardworking. You'll be able to realize your dreams wherever you are. You know I want you to go as far as you can, just as much as you do, don't you?" Jun nodded, blinking her eyes.

Jun walked out of her father's study. She thought of the Tang dynasty poet Du Fu's famous lines:

The nation is broken
But hills and rivers remain
Deep in grass and trees is the city
When spring returns again
国破山河在
城春草木深

And she heard in her mind, too, the anguished question that another Tang poet, Wang Han, had asked:

Ever since ancient times,
How many have returned
From their march to the battlegrounds?
古来征战几人回

It was on a moonless night not long afterward that Zhen, Jun, and the rest of the family went overnight by boat up the Min River to Nanping. They were lucky to have a small cabin, given that all of Fuzhou seemed to be moving en masse upstream to Nanping. The deck was covered with people and their luggage. Children's cries mixed with the clucking of caged chickens, but still more people pushed their way across the gangway on board, carrying their belongings with them.

As they waited for the boat to get moving, her father told them what to expect when they reached Nanping, and for the first time, Jun understood what her father had been doing on all those trips he'd made there. She listened as he explained that he'd rented a house on a hilltop from a wealthy widow, and there, their world would be replicated as much as possible. Grandma's bedroom would be in the center of the second floor and her Buddha shrine directly across the hallway. He told his wives and children that he had bought the town's

Grandfather's photo among other ancestors in the Chen family shrine, fourth from the right, in a light-colored suit.

best hotel in order to generate income, but as he spoke, Jun's attention began to drift.

Suddenly, the boat's engine sputtered to life, and as it did the commotion on board seemed to give way to a momentary silence. The boat banged once against the dock, shuddered, and moved into the river. The journey had begun. Wordless, the matriarch of the Chen clan looked out the window. Jun saw her eyes dim, her hands gripping a railing.

The boat arrived at Nanping before dawn. Grandfather had arranged for a sedan chair to take his mother up a steep path to her new home at the top of the mountain town. Jun and her father trudged alongside the chair in the dark. When morning came and the mist lifted, Jun found herself standing on her new home's patio, looking down at a confusion of rooftops that tumbled towards the river. The house that would be her home had four wings surrounding a central courtyard. It felt eerily like the Garden, perching over the Min River as it was, except everything seemed shrunken in size, and there was no garden. The front door led to a flight of steep stone steps, tethering the house to the end of the road. Halfway down the mountainside was a broad ledge, forming a kind of town square. It served as the hub of Nanping, a busy, disorderly place heavy with traffic on roads going further inland. The Minbei Hotel, which Jun's father had newly purchased, was the largest building just off the main square.

The Yinghua High School, unlike a few others, had not relocated to Nanping, and Jun, unable to concentrate on her studies in any case, suspended her preparation for the entrance exam there. With that dream deferred, she threw herself into the tasks of settling into the new house. She helped her grandmother make a replica of her Fuzhou bedroom and installed her Buddha shrine across the hall.

There were many children in the Chen family entourage— Jun, Zhen, and their older brother Cang, plus three cousins of similar ages, and Downstairs Grandma's two babies (the younger one was a girl named Xiang, my mother.) All of the children of school age, Grandfather decided, should prepare to take the entrance exams to go to a Fuzhou missionary school called Weili that had resettled in Nanping, the best option available locally. To ensure that all the children got in to Weili, he temporarily delegated his hotel business to his manager and became the in-house schoolmaster to prepare them for the entrance exam, with Jun, the oldest girl, serving as in-house supervisor and tutor. When everybody passed the exam and her father returned to manage his business, Jun took over the children's supervision. Every day, like a pied piper, she led them on mountain trails to and from the school, skirting the busy part of the town which was off limits for all the young ones of the household, because it was too *luan*—disorderly.

Busy as she was, Jun couldn't repress an underlying sadness and anxiety. When her grandmother, who was turning eighty-two, announced that she wanted her normally two-day birthday celebration be reduced to one in keeping with the times, the reality hit home for Jun. This seems now like a very trivial matter, but the two-day event had always been a celebration of the Chen clan's traditions and prosperity. Now, the war had seeped into this cherished private corner of their lives. Grandmother was surely right that it would be futile in the bleak landscape of the present, in this unfamiliar home, to try to sustain the glory of the family's past.

• • •

One day in mid-December 1937, Grandfather returned home from his hotel looking ashen. He plunked down in the chair in the hall to take his tea, which was prepared for him every day at this hour, rattling the tea set on the stand, and exploded. "This gang of beasts, these wolves!" he muttered, speaking, apparently of the Japanese. "These sons of bitches deserve to become extinct without any descendants!" He stormed into his study, leaving everyone in the anteroom speechless. Grandfather never lost his temper, much less spoke with such vituperation in front of the women and children of the house. Something terrible must have happened, Jun thought.

So, as soon as she could get her sister Zhen to take over the duty of watching the children, Jun flew down the hallway to the kitchen, where she asked the cook, a small man who, for some reason, was called "Third Sister," to lend her his work clothes and his hat. In a few minutes, dressed in man's clothing, Jun was walking down the steep steps from the house toward the hotel.

In all the time since arriving in Nanping, she had never

even been near the hotel. Now, approaching it at nightfall, she began to hear bits and snatches of conversation, Shanghai accents and Mandarin accents, distinctly different from the local dialect. Under dim lights, the hotel patio was crowded with people, many of them old, looking weak and exhausted. Others whom Jun took to be hotel workers were passing around steaming hot food. Beyond the patio she could make out a crowd, undulating in the darkness, and she sensed its anger and agitation.

Near the hotel entrance, a young girl was shrieking, "Let me die!" Some men tried to calm her down. Jun learned what had happened from some women around her. The young woman, they said, had been gang-raped by Japanese soldiers, and her uncle had risked his life to drag her away from what the women called "the pack of hungry wolves." Her uncle had been stabbed. Nobody seemed to know if the woman had any other direct family members. Shivering, Jun followed a trail of cigarette smoke, trying not to cough, to listen in to what the men were saying, information that might help her understand what had so troubled her father.

The Japanese started to bomb Nanjing, the capital of Nationalist China, on December 9. Soon thereafter, thousands of troops marched into the city. By then, Chiang Kaishek, his family, and his closest confidants had fled. The defending general, Tang Shengzhi, radioing from an American ship moored on the Yangtze, pleaded for reinforcements, but Tang not only did not get any help but also the American ship from which he had sent his telegram was fired on by the Japanese. Tang's troops broke ranks and fled—many of them disguised as civilians. The whole unarmed civilian population was now at the mercy of the Japanese troops, who looted, burned, raped, and killed at will.

It was getting late, and the crowd began to disperse. Jun's oversized man's clothes flapped in an icy, misty breeze creeping up from the river, and she began to shiver uncontrollably. Her knees knocked against each other and she had to keep her teeth clenched tight to keep them from clattering as she made her way home, her heart pounding in her chest.

The news of the Nanjing Massacre, which went on for six long weeks, soon became known all over China. While the number of those killed is still hard to gauge today, ranging from forty thousand to three hundred thousand by various estimates, the brutality and its horror have been seared into the collective national memory. Anti-Japanese fervor rose to a fever pitch, only to intensify as the year 1938 began and the war took on a series of dramatic turns. Tragedy and destruction continued in the wake of the Japanese troops' advance. City after city reported atrocities similar to Nanjing's.

In a rare bright moment, Grandfather returned home one early April evening, and announced a piece of good news with excitement in his voice. The Guangxi general Li Zongren had scored a victory over the Japanese at a place called Tai'erzhuang on the eastern plains near the city of Xuzhou, a strategic crossroads of the four provinces of Shandong, Jiangsu, Hubei, and Hebei and a crucial railroad hub, and it looked like the enemy would be held back from the interior of the country, at least for the time being.

But by the end of May, Xuzhou fell, and the ground gained with Li's victory just a little over a month earlier was lost overnight. In a last-ditch desperate effort to gain time for a retreat from the Japanese troops now charging south, Generalissimo Chiang ordered that the dikes on the Yellow River at a place called Huayuankou be breached. The hope was to stop the enemy's advance, but the water unleashed from China's mightiest river—not by accident called "China's sorrow"—inundated thousands of villages. The destruction of lives and property was astronomical, yet it only deterred the enemy for three months. By August, Japanese troops were driving toward Hankou on the Yangtze River, chasing the retreating Nationalist government deeper into the mountains of Sichuan in the Southwest. The Yellow River region was lost, the country's leader was on the run, and more people's homes were destroyed in the paths of the advancing war. Jun, like millions of Chinese, was in deep despair.

Jun became haunted by relentless nightmares. She never told anyone of that night's scouting trip down the hill. But she sought out her father for updates on the war, engaging him in conversations almost like the history classes that they used to have together in his old study. She learned that the Yinghua High School had finally relocated to Nanping. But this news, which she had anxiously waited to hear, now only fueled Jun's conflicts: The dream of college seemed to her not just hopeless, but obsolete. Who could care about college when everyone was just trying to escape the wartime brutality, hoping just to survive?

Her sister Zhen had a different reaction. Unlike Jun, she did not see the war's trauma firsthand, and her education was not disrupted. She had one singular goal in life, and that was to become a doctor, and secondhand stories of war only made her more determined to become one.

Another Spring Festival was around the corner, but even word that her two sons who had remained behind in Fuzhou would join them for the festivities failed to cheer up Great-grandma. Her arthritis was worse than ever and her spirits were suffering from being uprooted from her home for the first time in her long life. On New Year's Day, Great-grandma came down from her morning prayer in the Buddha Hall and

Cast members in Zhen's high-school production of "Five Generations Under One Roof," 1945.

announced that she was returning to Fuzhou no matter what. No amount of persuasion was able to make her stay. Safety was no longer an issue for her, she said; whatever happened to her, she would handle it in her own home, the Flower Fragrant Garden. She needed to appease her ancestors, she said, in this unsettling time of war. Seeing that further persuasion was futile, Grandfather eventually reached a compromise with his mother: Instead of returning immediately with her two other sons, she was to stay until the Qingming Festival* in the begin-

---

* This is a day when every family visits the graveyard of their ancestors. The families bring with them stacks of paper money and many symbolic objects—colorful paper replicas of luxury household objects—as well as carefully prepared foods to visit the graves. Once there, they clear the area, present the sacrificial food, burn the symbolic objects and paper money for the use of the ancestors in the netherworld.

ning of April. That was as long as Grandfather could keep her—with the hope that he'd still be able to change her mind.

Qingming—the time to sweep the ancestors' tombs to reaffirm the continuation of the family line—arrived with no sense of the usual gravity of the occasion. Jun walked with her father to the dock alongside her grandma's sedan chair. She tried to put on a brave face by recalling happier times and other Qingmings years before. But her grandma, though she was returning to the Garden as she had determined, remained sullen.

Jun left her grandma to her thoughts and turned to her own memory of the only Qingming trip she made years before. She had always been indignant that tomb sweeping was an exclusive privilege of the male members of the family. When she appealed to her father to be included that year, she got this non-committal response: "When you come see us off, make sure you wear pants and a plain blouse, no floral prints. I'll see what can be done." Jun had followed his instructions and went to her room to change. When she returned to the hall, her father came up from behind and put a boy's hat over her head. "Keep walking," he whispered to her, pulling her into the group of men and boys parading down the hallway to the gate, right under her grandma's eyes, to visit the family plot.

Now, approaching the dock, Jun's memory of that happy occasion gave way to the reality of her grandma's departure. She almost wished that her father would come up with more of his quick wit and magic to whisk her back to the Garden along with her grandma. But instead, helplessly, she watched as her grandma stepped out of the sedan chair, held onto her arm and, as she set foot on the gangway, let go of it with an encouraging squeeze.

"Let's go home, Miss." Third Sister, the family cook, loaded everything on board, then turned around and disembarked to tend to Jun, who was now standing alone on the dock. Her father and grandma had already disappeared inside the cabin. She looked back to her mountain home above and felt that, like it, everything seemed suspended in the air, balanced precariously over a cliff. It felt as if every gust of wind would chip off a piece of it or threaten to tumble it down the slope.

• • •

With her grandma gone, it was hard for Jun to concentrate on preparing for her high school entrance exams, even though she knew her only pathway to a life of her own was through education. For a woman in China in those days, a college degree almost guaranteed a teaching job in a good school.

Having postponed the exams required for all the graduates from middle school the previous year, Jun had to retake them. Only if she passed would she be able to take the high school entrance exams. The notice came, and her first set of exams would be held just as the summer monsoon season began. Given the large number of students who had relocated from Fuzhou to Nanping with their families that year, the exam monitors decided to quarantine the exam takers on an island in the middle of the Min river for the duration of the tests. It would be Jun's first ever overnight away from home. Both her mother and Downstairs Grandma fussed over her on the morning of her departure. They prayed for her, they cooked her a bowl of piping hot peace noodle (noodle soup with eggs for a smooth trip), and they packed her snacks for the trip. When they were done, the sky opened up. The steep streets below resembled rapids as the Third Sister walked Jun to the dock. When Jun finally took her bedroll from Third Sister to board the ferry, it was already soaked.

The exams turned out to be, as Jun remembered, not very hard. But the stay at the camp was a nightmare. The wet quilt never dried in the damp room. Jun slept with other girls on a long communal bed, shivering all night on the thin mattress, which was just a layer of straw. On the day she was supposed to return home, the river swelled, suspending all ferry operations. The two-day excursion on the chilly island extended to a third. By the time Jun finally stepped into the house again, she collapsed in the anteroom, shaking uncontrollably.

She had contracted malaria. It raged for days and Jun felt that she was just clinging to life. The day she finally regained her clarity, she saw a tall Western man standing by her bedside. He was a missionary doctor that her father had found after Chinese doctors had given up on her, she later learned. "She will be all right now," Jun heard the doctor say reassuringly. Then she heard her two mothers, who had apparently been hovering around her for days, let out a soft "Amen!"

When, finally, after several relapses, Jun had recovered, she learned that she had passed the middle school exams but had missed the high school entrance exams. A year and a half's work had come to naught. She had been the top student in her class at the best middle school in Fuzhou, and she knew without a doubt that she had been destined for the best high school in the city. It was a small matter, perhaps, to miss an exam, given the far greater wartime suffering around her, but she was a fifteen-year-old girl and her dreams were collapsing around her. She sank back into a malarial delirium for many more days.

When she was able to get up on her own, she tried to make her way to the bathroom without help, bracing herself on the hallway wall, the door frame, the furniture; step by step, she was determined to make it. Down the hall, she could see her own mother Ah Nai sitting with Ah Niang, her father's second wife, talking in whispers with her father, and next door, she could hear her siblings and cousins whispering to each other. Was it just because they didn't want to disturb her? It didn't seem that way. Since nobody noticed her, she held on to the back of a chair in the hall and listened. And that was how Jun learned that her beloved grandmother, the family matriarch, had passed away.

Her hands started to shake, rattling the chair that she was holding on to. Her father looked up and seeing her, dashed to steady her and help her back to her room.

"Is it true?" Jun demanded, but didn't really want to hear the confirmation. Her father responded with a helpless sigh. Jun felt too weak to cry. She closed her eyes. At least, she thought to herself—striving for a silver lining—Grandma was in her own home. But with her death, Jun saw the past fade into nothingness and, almost simultaneously, the future had slipped away too. The war was like a big wave that lifted the entire family up and then smashed it to pieces on a distant shore.

• • •

My grandfather showed up in Jun's room a couple of weeks later, waving a piece of paper with almost childlike elation: "I want you to look at this!" Jun struggled to sit up and read what was on the paper. It was an advertisement from a vocational teacher-training school in Yongan, several towns southwest of Nanping, farther away from Fuzhou. It was calling for applicants for an entrance exam to be given two weeks later. But why should this unheard-of vocational school in the remote town be of interest to her? She looked at her father questioningly.

Her father sat down on her bedside next to her, pushed his eyeglasses up with his bent index finger, and asked her: "Don't you want to be a teacher?" Yes, Jun answered. Still, this was a considerable step down from the elite academic high school she'd always expected to attend. "This school will give you a leg up," her father said. "You can go there, and when you're finished, you'll take the college entrance exam, just like you would if you went to a regular high school."

Jun wanted to show enthusiasm and gratitude to her father, who was trying so hard on her behalf. But they both knew that schools like the one in Yongan, with all expenses paid by the government, were designed for students who couldn't otherwise afford post-secondary education, and after graduation they required three years of service at a survival-level income. Finances aside, she was to spend three years for a diploma from an unknown school with an unknown accreditation in an almost-unheard-of mountain town, and then waste three more years in teaching instead of trying again for an established college for a real education—and she was supposed to be happy? How far she had slid down the ladder of opportunity and expectation in just a few weeks! She asked to be left alone for a moment.

"Fortunately, she is a girl." Jun could hear the landlady in the hallway. The landlady and other neighbors sometimes visited to chat with Upstairs and Downstairs Grandmas. "She's smart and pretty. So what does it matter which school she goes to?"

"Right, so what if she doesn't go to college, or even high school? Plenty of women live a decent life without any of that . . ." It was another woman's voice. Jun sat up straight, unsure if she had just come through another nightmare. She struggled to straighten her hair and blouse, and made her way to her father's room, unsteady on her feet but firm in her conviction. With a calm smile, she greeted the ladies politely as she passed them. "Father," she said when she reached his room, "let's sign up for the exams."

On an early fall morning in 1938, when the whole house was still in deep slumber, Jun was holding the bowl of peace noodle that her mother had made for her, trying to eat as much as she could to show her appreciation. Outside the window, a morning mist was floating in the first rays of the sun, draping itself over the green of the mountains. The same bowl of noodle in hand just as that morning when she set out for that malarial island for the exams. Down below, layers of roofs were still on their eternal slide down the steep slope, until they piled on top of each other at the river's edge. She was ready for a different journey.

Jun walked alongside her father toward the bus station in the town square, the cook, Third Sister, following with the luggage. Jun's trepidation this morning was tinged with excitement. This was to be the first step on a life journey all her own, humble as it might be.

After helping her settle down in her seat, her father suddenly told the driver to wait for just one moment and rushed off the bus. He reappeared in no time, holding a short length of a sturdy rope that he proceeded to tie to the back of the seat in front of Jun. "Hold this tight when it gets bumpy," he told his daughter amid quizzical looks of the other passengers. It was the first seat belt that Jun or any of them had ever seen.

Jun's eyes followed her father as he left the bus, then through the window, his blurred shape slipping out of the corner of her tear-filled eyes.

• • •

Jun disembarked alone onto a wharf in Yongan, where boats scrambled for a spot to disgorge their people and goods. It felt darkly comical to her that these wartime refuges all had such comforting names: *Nanping* meant "southern peace"; *Yongan*, "eternal safety." As the Japanese continued to push southward at a breakneck pace, this sleepy little town upriver was rapidly expanding. The provincial government of Fujian Province and several schools had already relocated once to Nanping; now they were relocating again to Yongan. The vocational school Jun was to attend was one of those schools.

It didn't take long for Jun to develop a deep bond with her underprivileged classmates, and to admire their resolve to make the most of the opportunity they had been given, even though it was far inferior to what she had experienced in her own life. She threw herself into all kinds of activities, initiated and organized clubs and was elected a class leader. But reality came when a bomb struck one night, turning the Confucius temple, which had been used as the main classroom building, into a crater. Luckily, nobody had been inside the temple when the bomb fell, but the incident was still a lesson in the capricious hazards of war. The Japanese had taken the better part of China's eastern seaboard, and because they were running short of foot soldiers, were relying on bombs to make their presence felt, especially in the more forested inland areas. The intended target was the nearby building that housed the relocated government, but instead, the bomb had put the teachers school out of business, and though the administration swore they would find a new site for the following year, none of the students could be certain of their educational prospects there anymore.

Jun's father was thrilled with her unexpected early return, but he worried out loud to Jun about the desperate plight of China. Japan had taken Hankou and Canton, as well as Bias Bay on the coast close to Hong Kong, asserting control of all of China's main ports and railroads, all the major cities in North China, the Shandong Peninsula, the lower Yangtze Valley, and the southern coast. And this tightening grip on China was part of the momentum being gained by the Axis Powers. In Europe, Germany was challenging the Western powers, having annexed Austria and made its demand for the Sudetenland, the Czechoslovakian territory on the German border. As a last effort to avoid war, the four big European powers—Britain, France, Italy, and Germany—met at the end of September in Munich, where they gave Hitler everything he wanted in exchange for what British Prime Minister Neville Chamberlain famously called "peace for our time." On October 1, the German army marched into the Sudetenland. The Western powers had to prepare for their own conflict. China was even more on its own.

Two weeks after Jun's return home, her brother Cang was supposed to arrive by boat from Fuzhou where he was attending college. But instead of Cang, the family found a panic-stricken Third Sister, the manservant with a mismatched gendered nickname for reasons that Jun never understood, rushing in from the torrential rain. A boat had capsized in the river, and he had been unable to find Cang among the arriving passengers. Grandfather rushed out in the downpour with Third Sister, and they did not reappear until almost midnight—happily with Cang in tow, minus his luggage. His boat was indeed the one that had capsized, but he'd managed to swim ashore in the icy water.

Jun was dreading a subdued and depressing Spring Festival, but the family was grateful to be back together again, and her brother's survival from his near-drowning was a reason for celebration. The family by now had expanded: Jun had two more half-sisters, born of her Ah Niang. Along with the three older ones by her Ah Nai (including herself) and the three cousins, the constant ruckus of children of all ages seemed to keep the doom and gloom outside of the house, for the time being.

• • •

School resumed for Jun in Yongan after the Spring Festival break, with only some minor delays. She picked up her role as class president, a job made easier for her by her having been the big sister in a house full of children. The new classrooms there were seven kilometers away from the students' dorm, in a village called *Dahu*, meaning "big lake," which was actually in the fold of a valley near a small pond. The village and its surrounding area were very sparsely populated. When the time came for the school's students to begin practice teaching, the villages nearby did not have enough children to provide a class for each teacher-in-training. As a result, the seniors had to travel from village to village, and sometimes invited illiterate parents to join the classes. To accommodate the busy days of these parents, and to avoid the bombings, which were aimed at buildings, classes would be held in a family's yard under a big tree, or by a shaded creek, or among haystacks. One time, an overripe pomegranate dropped on top of a boy's head and exploded, and a flock of birds immediately descended on the mess, picking and chirping with excitement. Another time, a hen flew into a group of students, clucking triumphantly. Only Jun was startled. The children took it all in stride, explaining that the hen had just laid an egg, and that was how she announced her achievement.

The long walks every day turned Jun from a delicate city girl into an athlete, and the unusual disruptions made her more grounded. They were part of real life, and enjoyable, even, so much so that Jun even entertained the idea of becoming a village teacher, at least for the upcoming three years of mandatory work after graduation. But when a job opportunity opened up in a school near her family in Nanping—a boarding school catering primarily to students from rural areas—it seemed like a perfect fit. Jun easily got the job at Liufang School, and for the first time in her life, enjoyed the benefits that came with it: her own dorm room on campus. She was assigned to co-lead the lower school and excited about teaching a wide range of courses. The one course that she took the most pleasure in was physical education, where she could flex her newly acquired muscles.

Liufang School's lower-class graduation, 1945, Nanping. Jun is in the front row, fifth from the left.

Jun's dorm room at Liufang became the base for her new and independent life. She was just past her nineteenth birthday, and was her students' trusted big sister. They stopped by for personal advice or just to hang out. More precious to her, however, was the constant presence of her own sister, Zhen. Since she was two years younger than Jun, Zhen had mostly avoided the disruptions of family relocation. There was no postponement of her entrance exams. She passed them easily and entered the very Yinghua High School that Jun had yearned to enter a few years before. Zhen spent most of her after school time with Jun, taking pride in her sister's stature and enjoying the relative freedom from home, where Ah Niang's babies and toddlers had made the house a much busier place. Zhen particularly enjoyed occasionally being mistaken by her sister's students for "Teacher Chen," given their similar figures, short hair, and the *qipaos* that they shared.

A while into her teaching, another visitor started to frequent the groups in Jun's dorm room on weekends. His name was Cai Longbang, and he was another popular teacher at the school. Soon, Cai became Jun's ardent suitor. On one weekday in December 1941, the sisters were just settling down to do their day's work when Cai showed up and breathlessly announced some news: Japan had attacked America at a place called Pearl Harbor, which had led America to declare war on Japan!

"Well, this changes things, doesn't it?" Jun said.

"Yes, Japan has gotten itself a powerful new enemy." Cai responded.

The impact of the news on Jun was immediate. Her college dream, put away, but never buried, was starting to tug at her heart again. She went home to seek her father's advice about what she should do. "America's participation will help," he began. It would divert much of Japanese attention and their forces from the Chinese front. "But keep in mind that the American priority will always be Europe." His tone started to shift, "Moreover, even if we are finished with Japan, the Nationalists will have to deal with the Communists, who have emerged as a powerful adversary. China's troubles aren't going to be over soon."

My grandfather was right, as subsequent events would prove. Jun did her internship for three years while the war ground on. But since there was very little fighting in the immediate area, life for Jun took on a kind of normalcy. By 1944, Jun's three-year mandatory service was up, and she opted for signing a short-term, year-to-year contract with the school. Zhen was entering her senior year at the high school, and although she was offered guaranteed early admission to Xiamen University, the best in Fujian Province, she decided to prepare for the entrance exams for medical school instead. Medical schools in China have always taken students directly out of high school, though with far more stringent admission criteria than other colleges or universities. To leave Zhen more time to concentrate, Jun often took walks with Cai.

On one of those walks, Cai proposed. This was certainly not entirely unexpected, but Jun didn't know how to respond. She wasn't in love with Cai. She knew that. But what, she asked herself, did marriage exactly mean anyway? She'd had no occasion to give the question much serious thought, but now that it was a real possibility, it began to seem to her like something that would be entirely hers, her own; something different from the busy house of her parents—full, hectic, and noisy, a syncopation of the rhythm in the Garden that she knew. Maybe marriage would give her a new start, now that she was aging out of college. One day, the war would be over, and Zhen would be going to college, and Jun herself would be married . . . but what kind of a new start would it be with the gaping hole left by her unfulfilled college dream?

Then, an idea occurred to her. Why shouldn't she apply to college also, old as she was compared to the new high school graduates? She responded to Cai's proposal with one of her own. Apply to college together! Let's start a life in a new place! Cai could hardly refuse. The two of them joined Zhen in college preparation.

Nanping was sweltering that summer of 1945, with the mountains trapping the hot air in the valley. The Liufang School was emptying out as students trickled home after their college entrance exams, though there was tension in the air. Everybody around Jun was waiting nervously to learn the exam results—whether and where they would be accepted for the next stage of their lives. Many students stopped by at Jun's room to say goodbye to her and to Cai, her constant companion. Zhen and her boyfriend, Hu Xizhong, who had both taken the medical school exam, were among them.

It was late on one of these sultry days that the two couples, having finally gotten their exam results, converged again in Jun's room, and the news was good, or mostly good. Both Zhen and Hu Xizhong were going to Fujian Medical College, the province's best, and Jun, too, was at last going to the college of her dreams, Fujian Normal University. Cai alone did not pass.

But Jun took her dejected fiancé's hands in her own. "We're going to sign the papers before I leave for Fuzhou," she announced, 'the papers' being the marriage certificate. Cai was visibly shaken. So were the others in the room. "Cai will try again next year and we'll meet up back in Fuzhou," Jun said calmly.

The summer ended for them with the glorious news of the victory over Japan on August 15. There was a kind of stunned silence in Jun's dorm room that day, a muted acknowledgment of the long years of fear and despair, a moment of hesitation in the face of a new hope.

Eight years of war was, for Jun, eight years of detour from her direct path to college. In this collective internal exile, the entire nation had been devastated, cities reduced to rubble, and millions dead and displaced. And yet now, Jun and Zhen both held in their hands admission slips for a bright future. Or so it should have been. But Jun, the older sister and the one whose life had been more disrupted, was less optimistic about what the future would hold. The twists and turns of the eight years of war and occupation made her cautious about rushing to embrace anything that might turn out to be just another false hope. At the age of twenty-two, she should have been celebrating her graduation from college, but here she was, celebrating her acceptance to college instead.

Perhaps it was these thoughts that led Jun to go ahead and marry Cai. Perhaps signing the marriage certificate didn't seem to her so much a new beginning as an end to a painful past. Or maybe she was simply clinging to one of the few things that had seemed safe and dependable to her during the years of exile, this man who had come to stand reliably by her side. Did she marry out of sympathy for him? It's hard for anyone to say, and not a subject that Jun wished to discuss with me. Maybe she hoped that, with this partner

in life, she might finally achieve some stability in an unpredictable world.

Meanwhile, millions of people dislocated by the war were
returning to homes abandoned years before. The schools and
government offices that had moved to Nanping and Yongan
during the war were returning to Fuzhou. The Chen family's return home was to take place in two waves. Grandfather
would first take Ah Niang and her five children back, while
Ah Nai would stay behind to keep Jun company as she finished her work at the Liufang School. But Ah Niang's oldest
daughter, Xiang—my mother—had grown very attached to
Jun and pleaded to stay behind with her, so Jun was more
than happy to keep a bubbly admirer by her side.

College admission was finally in hand. The Chen clan
would be going back to their hilltop Garden in Fuzhou. The
world would return to normal, and life resume its course,
despite the long detour.

• • •

But Jun's father didn't show up on the day of his scheduled
return to Nanping. He was supposed to fetch the rest of the
family and bring them back to the Flower Fragrant Garden.
This was very unusual for him, Jun thought; he was, after all,
a military man. War and chaos were not excuses for him; they
were the very reasons to be punctual. But he didn't arrive
that day, or the day after. He showed up two days after his
scheduled time. Jun threw herself into his arms. He tenderly
stroked her hair and let out a sort of deep sigh. In Jun's experience, a sigh like that always prefigured something that he
didn't want to tell her.

"What's the matter?"

Jun's father looked through the window into the distance,

one arm still wrapped around Jun's shoulder. Finally, he spoke, slowly:

"The Garden has been sold," he said.

Some trinkets Jun had been holding dropped from her hands and fell heavily onto the floor. Something with a sharp edge landed on her bare foot. The pain didn't register.

Jun tried but failed to remain stoical when her father could not give her a full explanation. Third Uncle had signed the papers that turned over the family's treasured home to somebody else. That was all he knew, at least at this point. Their family was temporarily staying at Seventh Uncle's new house—he too had had to move out of the Garden. Third Uncle, who had kept an apartment for himself and his family on the grounds, was the only one still in the Garden. As for the rest of them, Jun's father was in the process of renting a farmhouse in the middle of the fields at the foot of the Cangqian Hill, and that would be their home for a while, it seemed.

PART II

Leaving

IT WAS A SUMMER AFTERNOON in 1949 in the city of Xiamen on China's southeast coast. Jun was boarding a ferry on her way to the island of Jinmen. She looked elegant, a simple sleeveless *qipao* covering her slim figure, a small suitcase in one hand. She walked straight to the bow, lifted her face to the wind, and allowed something that she'd not had much of to wash over her, a feeling of happiness, a sense of a true new beginning to her life.

That very morning, Jun had learned that she'd been selected for a much sought-after position teaching history at a prestigious private secondary school near Xiamen. And not only had she gotten a job for herself, but her best friend from college, Qingxi Fu, had been hired as well, though Qingxi didn't even know of her own good fortune yet. But, knowing that Jun would be coming to Xiamen for the job interview, Qingxi had invited her to spend a few weeks of vacation at her family's grand house on Jinmen, a small island a mile off the coast of Fujian province. Now, with the two appointment letters in hand, Jun was on her way there.

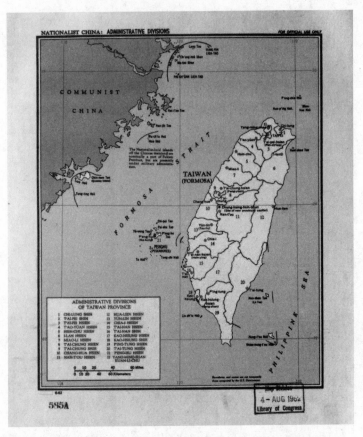

Taiwan and the Taiwan Strait. (COURTESY OF LIBRARY OF CONGRESS GEOGRAPHY AND MAP DIVISION)

She could hardly contain the thrill of breaking the news to her friend.

Just a few weeks earlier, things had seemed utterly hopeless, her life a sore and weary burden. She had even worried that she had grown prematurely old at the age of twenty-six, unable to feel the ebb and flow of youthful optimism. Her college had been a safe harbor for her for most of her four years there, even though Cai had failed the entry exam a second

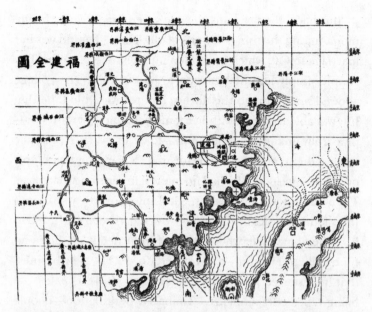

The island of Jinmen (Quemoy; now still under the Nationalist control) is shown connected to the island of Xiamen (now still under Communist control) in the shape of an "H" in lower center. They are actually separate islands, but so close (a mile or so apart) that they were mistakenly presented as one island on this 1832 map. (COURTESY OF BROWN LIBRARY, ROCK CHINESE COLLECTION)

time and never came to join her. But in recent months, the reality of China outside the institution's gate—the civil war's climactic battles, the collapse of the Nationalist government, and the raging inflation that had turned everyday life into a scramble to cover the necessities of life—had started to show up on campus. The usual free meals had been reduced from two dishes to one, from a couple of slices of meat to none, from vegetables to pickles, and from rice to a soupy gruel. As graduation day approached, the college announced that the commencement ceremony would be canceled because there was no money to print the diplomas. Like many of her classmates, Jun had looked into the future and seen only a void.

Jun had other reasons to want to embrace a new beginning. Among the things she was gladly leaving behind was her
marriage to Cai, which had fallen into a kind of atrophy. The
couple simply had no occasion to be together: The college
allowed no visitors to the dorms, and for the little time that
Jun was able to spend with her family, she did not want Cai—
practically unknown to the family—to be an awkward presence
among them; and for Jun, returning to Nanping was simply
out of the question. She had no interest in revisiting that place.
Then there was her family's spiral into poverty and illness.
Jun's father's hotel in Nanping—which had been entrusted to
his general manager when the family returned from their wartime exile to Fuzhou—had burned down. The new business
that he'd started in Fuzhou, the Taijiang Movie Theater, was
being repeatedly vandalized. China's hyperinflation—people
going shopping with almost useless cash in wheelbarrows—
was threatening everything her father still possessed. Every
time she visited home during those last days of college, she
felt that the domestic gloom had deepened. Her father, usually a commanding figure, seemed to have shrunk. He spent
more and more of his time playing mahjong and had started
to drink and to smoke, things he had never done before.

And then, a miracle happened. Jun and Qingxi Fu were
the only two women to receive notices summoning them to
job interviews at the Jimei School near Xiamen. All through
their college years, the two women took pleasure in reciting
poetry and prose together; they worked on student publica-
tions and organized debates, competitions, and parties, and
now they were given licenses to dream about living and teaching together. More important for Jun, this was her chance, if
the upcoming interview actually led to an offer of a teaching
post, to find a new start for herself and for her family.

Jun's (Chen Wenjun) college photo.

And so, on her last day of college, she left the campus, going home as a fresh college graduate and with a summons to her interview. She followed the dirt road that turned at the Garden's gate. She passed the tree in which she and her father had once lost a kite, the little bridge that was once a coffin plank from the nearby graveyard, and she walked by the residential school for the blind where her favorite childhood friend lived. She paused to say a last goodbye to the Garden, where her college dream was born. Then the path hitched back to the road. A passing car kicked up clouds of dust, obscuring everything on the trail.

The farmhouse where the Chen family lived after they returned from Nanping had always seemed lonely to Jun,

isolated amid a vast stretch of fields. But the family nonetheless continued to grow. Jun now had a total of six half-siblings—all children of her father's second wife, my Downstairs
Grandmother. Zhen was starting her internship in the city's
Union Hospital, founded in 1928 by Christian missionaries
and the best in the city; her brother Cang had married, and
was also living in Fuzhou.

Stepping into the house, Jun saw her father's face light up
at her appearance. "Wenjun is back!"—using her full name—
he announced to the empty front hall that opened to different parts of the house. Soon, children of different ages
rushed in, trailed by their caretakers with the littler ones in
hand. Jun heard the measured footsteps of her mother, Ah
Nai, from upstairs. "What's the commotion down there?" she
feigned puzzlement as she descended the stairs, graceful with
her usual neat chignon.

Jun's report on the upcoming interview near Xiamen and
on the trip she would then take to the island of Jinmen for a
short vacation brought a smile to her father's pale face. "I like
your friend Qingxi very much," her mother said. Jun planned
to take the train to Xiamen for the interview, then catch the
ferry to Jinmen, but to her surprise, the next day her father
left the house, and he returned with an airplane ticket in his
hand. His face was animated, and his color restored. "Here's
a plane ticket to Xiamen," he said. "It's my graduation gift for
you. I've hired a car to go to the airport tomorrow."

Morning came, and it was time to say goodbye. Jun's baby
half-brother, Guang, sensing the excitement, crawled to her
feet just as she stepped out of the door. Jun bent to pick him
up and gave him a good squeeze. He giggled, then screamed
in protest when the nanny peeled him away. Her two youngest half-sisters, Xiang (my mother) and Yu, scrambled into
the car, insisting on accompanying her to the airport.

On the way there, her father explained why he had gotten her an airplane ticket rather than allowing her to go to Xiamen by train. Over the previous months, the Communist People's Liberation Army (PLA) had swept into China's southern provinces, crossing the Yangzi River, winning victory after victory over the armies of the Nationalist government. It seemed only a matter of time before the Communists would declare complete victory, and until then, it was safer to fly than to go anywhere overland. As their car inched forward in Fuzhou's congested streets, Jun's sisters glued their faces to the windows and reported what they saw: a street contortionist, a blind musician, a beggar, a dirty naked child.

Artillery boomed in the distance. Yu, the younger girl, clutched Jun's arm. Jun looked into her face. Jun hadn't known fear when she was Yu's age. Their father had been able to shelter the family and provide for it in a way he was no longer able to do. The traces of mending on Yu's plain cotton hand-me-down shirt looked like her mother's handiwork, her superb skill of embroidery on silk. How different from her last trip through this city center on New Year's Day in 1937, a dozen years before, where people in their new festive clothes set off firecrackers to chase away the evil spirits of yesteryear and to bring in good fortune. Now the sounds were of a different sort, and Jun had to wonder, what would these distant explosions bring?

The hour-long flight from Fuzhou to Xiamen was Jun's first ever airplane ride. She looked with disbelieving wide-open eyes as the ground sank beneath her. The crowds shrank—that last waving man had to be her father. The buildings diminished, the fields turned into a patchwork quilt, and finally the entire city became a collage of gray and green. Then whiffs of white clouds airbrushed the image in the window frame, the whole world vanished, and Jun felt enveloped in loneliness.

The Jimei School was right on the beach, an idyllic oasis away from the clamor of Xiamen, a port city once known to foreigners as Amoy. Jun did her interview and since she was the last candidate, she spent a couple of nights in the very pleasant school guesthouse waiting for the results. And then, life finally smiled at her: She received a formal offer of a job teaching at the Jimei School, an offer she saw as her long-postponed license to the independent life of her dreams. Her hands were unsteady with excitement when she dashed off a letter telling her parents of her triumph. Then she headed straight to the dock.

There, she was instantly sucked into the commotion. The entire ruling elite of the Nationalist government and army were now pooling along the southeast coast of China, anxious to be ferried to nearby islands in their desperate effort to escape capture. Jun pushed her way through the milling crowd, managed to check into the waiting room of the ferry terminal, and once she was inside, paused to take in the hustle and bustle outside: Horse carts and rickshaws tangled with mule carts and bicycles. Anxious families elbowed their way through the throng. Malnourished porters, weighed down by their loads, trailed their well-dressed clients, much bigger and stronger than they were. Farmers and peddlers struggled to move forward as they carried heavy loads on bamboo balancing poles. And then there were the beggars scouring for a bit of sympathy, and the listless migrants with no money and no tickets waiting for some miracle. All these went on in the midst of a huge cacophony—peddlers hawked their wares, children screamed their discomfort, and shoppers bargained. Occasionally, a car would drive up to the quay, honking incessantly, pushing through the crowd, discharging passengers rich and privileged enough to command motorized transport.

The bell in the dock house rang, the iron gate shrieked to a grinding close. The boat rocked under the last boarding passengers jockeying for a seat, it swayed one last time, and then pushed off. Jun held on to the guardrail at the bow. She could make out Jinmen Island on the horizon, the closest island to Xiamen, a sister island in the same Xiamen Bay. Qingxi would be there waiting for her, Jun would tell her the good news, they would scream with joy, and together, they would make plans to take the ferry back to Xiamen City together in time for the school term to begin.

As the boat approached the island, Jun felt the first chill of the day, so she took out the white cardigan that her mother had wisely insisted on packing. She draped it over her shoulders and thought of the pride her parents would feel when they got her letter. As for Jun herself, after the initial excitement, she was feeling something deeper, calling to mind lines from her favorite Tang dynasty poet, Li Po:

> *The sun rises in its eastern nook*
> *Seems to have emerged from beneath the earth's step*
> *It courses through the heaven, and dips back into the deep*
> 日出东方隈
> 似从地里来
> 历天又如海

There was, Jun knew, a certain natural constancy in the world, and though she hadn't had much of that in her life, she hoped that a certain natural power would reassert itself and steady her course from now on.

• • •

The ferry touched the dock in Jinmen, and Jun instantly picked out Qingxi from the waiting crowd. She jumped off the boat and thrust Qingxi's job offer into her hands. How her heart leapt watching her friend read the letter with trembling hands! They squealed with so much happiness and excitement and exhilaration that she thought that she would altogether explode or disintegrate right there, along with her best friend, right on this paradise of an island.

Qingxi's family home was a strikingly modern three-story concrete-and-glass mansion on what was called Summit Castle Bluff. It was the only one of its kind in its part of the island. It still is. I went there decades later, saw the lush garden between the house's two wings, walked up the wide marble front steps, climbed the stairs to what would have been Jun's room on the second floor, and looked at the island spread out below, bounded by the ocean, on the other side of which was the low coastline of China stretching to the horizon.

Jun was happy to be on Jinmen, in her friend's dreamy house, on vacation, but things got complicated very soon. As soon as Jun settled in, she learned from Qingxi that on August 17, the night after she'd left Fuzhou, it had been occupied by the Communists' People's Liberation Army. Jun was alarmed and dashed off a letter home. There was nothing more she could do but wait anxiously for a reply. Her father's former Nationalist associations worried her, even though she never knew the exact nature of his work before his return home for good. But during her visits to her father's study, the two of them, interested in history, had talked about the settling of the accounts that always took place in China at times of dynastic change, and that did not portend well for her father or other members of her family. News continued to stream in. Days after the PLA took Fuzhou, it took Changsha to the northwest of Fuzhou, and marched toward Guangdong Province to the South.

In order to help her friend cope with her worries, Qingxi took Jun on a tour of her island home. Jinmen, in the dead center of Xiamen Bay, is shaped like a dumbbell, eighteen miles across, three miles wide at its narrowest point. It was inhabited mostly by fishermen and their families, a few merchants, and a smaller number of wealthy families like the Fus, who had made their fortune in Malaysia. But in the past couple of years, the Nationalist government had turned it into a small fortress, taking over more and more farmland for building military installations. It was rocky on the west coast, and sandy on the east. Small villages were tucked between hills among what arable land there was, and fishing villages were nestled into the nooks and crannies on the coast. The sandy soil yielded mostly peanuts and sweet potatoes, which the local people exchanged, along with fish and fresh vegetables, with the troops stationed there, who were well-supplied with rice.

Qingxi's effort to relieve Jun's anxiety helped, but then a letter arrived addressed to Qingxi that changed everything for both of them. It was from the Jimei School, and it announced that the school would be closed for the fall term because of the uncertainty brought on by the civil war. All new hires would be notified when classes would resume, the letter said.

Jun was silent as Qingxi read the letter out loud. Would her job still be there at the end of the fall semester? Would the war ever end? Jun could still feel the warm and enthusiastic reception she had had at the school just over a week before; she could almost recite the letter of appointment from memory. And now here was another letter saying,

"School delayed . . . ," "Sincere apologies." Suddenly, her dream that was at hand was once again deferred, and she couldn't know for how long.

Qingxi put the letter down on the table and dashed out the door without a word. Jun turned to go up the stairs to her room. She stared at the little suitcase that she'd brought with her for the short island stay. Next to it were the things she'd picked up on her excursion around the island—some leaves, some pebbles, some sand in a shell. She could hear the exploding of artillery shells coming across the water from the Mainland. The whole of Jinmen Island was locked in the tense uncertainty of an invisible yet palpable military grip. Jun could smell it in the sulfuric remains of live ammunition practice and in the engine exhaust of army vehicles; she could hear it in the clicking of guns, the grinding of heavy machinery, the call of bugles; and she could see it in the rooster tails of dust kicked up by endless military convoys on unpaved roads. The war rumbled in her guts. It didn't matter where she was or what she was doing, or trying to do. It was a kind of hand that lashed out at will, beyond the power of comprehension or control.

She saw Qingxi reappear under her window, running back into the house, almost out of breath. Jun stepped out of her room, bumping into her friend headed in her direction, panting. Teaching jobs at the local Jinmen School for both of them were theirs for the asking, Qingxi reported. She had just talked to the principal, who was an old acquaintance of her late father. He had told her that, even in the best of times, getting two top students from a top teachers college at the same time was an unheard-of windfall for this little school on a small island. And so, both of them would be welcome, for as short or as long a time as they wanted.

"At least we'll be able to teach together for a while as we wait for things to settle down a bit," Qingxi said. Jun was impressed by Qingxi's quick wit, and grateful for her care and thoughtfulness. But was a temporary job on Jinmen what she wanted? Jun felt a kind of deja vu. It was uncanny how things seemed to be repeating themselves. A few years before, she'd had to trade the elite Yinghua High School for a vocational school, and now, a real job had just turned into a temporary job, and a summer break was taking on an aspect of a nightmare. She should just go home, she told her friend.

An explosion somewhere close brought them back to reality. They fell silent. The military must be using dynamite to build trenches and tunnels, or it must be practicing with live ammunition. Booms came from the Mainland too. The battle had descended all around them. The ferry had stopped running. It was now September, and decisions needed to be made fast, because school was starting. Her letters home never got a reply. Jun agreed to give Qingxi's idea a try while waiting for the military clashes along the coast to calm down enough to return home.

Jun would help teach the specialty classes at the Jinmen School, English, geography, and world history, in addition to Chinese literature, her major in college. On the very first day of class, Jun noticed that a few students didn't respond when she called their names in Mandarin Chinese; the local dialect, she realized, had preserved the consonants and vowels used in the Tang dynasty of the seventh to the tenth century! So she would have her students recite China's famous Tang poems in the local dialect, while discussions of them took place strictly in standard Mandarin. The result was magical for a native Fuzhou speaker like Jun. The Tang dynasty sounds that had previously remained abstract phonetic notations on paper in her college phonology class had now come to life for the first time. These fishermen's sons and daughters chanted the poems just as the poets would have done a millennium before!

Then, on October 1, the women heard from the radio a heavily accented squeak of a pronouncement: "The Chinese people have stood up!" It was Mao Zedong—whom the Nationalists called Bandit Mao—announcing from the reviewing stand overlooking Tiananmen Square in Beijing the founding of The People's Republic of China. His high-pitched voice and heavy Hunan accent sounded grating to their ears.

At first, Jun tried to convince herself that the Communists' triumph would mean nothing for her family. "Why should it mean anything at all?" she stubbornly insisted. But when Qingxi looked at her with a skeptical expression, she backed down, and asked this monumental question: "You really think," she said haltingly, reluctantly, "my family and I are now in different COUNTRIES?" Qingxi gave her friend a gentle, quiet, compassionate look, and said softly that maybe the Communist armies would soon arrive on Jinmen, kick out the Nationalists, and Jun would get back on the ferry and return to her home on the Mainland. After all, Jinmen was a mile from the Mainland, and had always been part of Fujian Province.

Not long after they heard Mao on the radio, the women learned that on October 17, Xiamen, visible across the bay through the large windows of the Fu family home, had been taken by the PLA. The inhabitants of Jinmen now assumed that it would soon be their turn, and this gave rise to a new hope for Jun. Until now, she had worried about the consequences a Communist victory would have for her family, her father in particular. But now, it didn't matter to her who was governing China or which army was fighting for what. She just wanted to get on a ferry and go back across the narrow strip of water that separated her from what she deemed to be her life and her future.

Like most ordinary Chinese in 1949, neither Jun nor any of the ordinary people of Jinmen knew that the Nationalists, facing the certainty of defeat on the Mainland, were planning to retreat to Taiwan, ninety miles from the Fujian coastline, and to set up a rival government that they would claim for decades was the legitimate leadership of China. They did not know that the Nationalists had silenced local dissidents in a bloody suppression two years prior, and had shipped national treasures—indispensable symbols of legitimacy in China and of the mandate to govern—to the island, and that these treasures would be enshrined, in the years to come, in a new National Museum on the outskirts of Taipei, to establish it as the authentic keeper of the Chinese tradition; they did not know that Jinmen was deemed part of the frontline defense of Taiwan, and that the Nationalists would fight stubbornly to hold onto it.

Jun had no context by which she could assess her own situation. Jinmen appeared to be settling into a kind of quiet before a storm. The island's fishermen did not go out to sea; vegetable hawkers were absent from the streets and alleys; and the Nationalist troops stationed on the island seemed to have gone underground. Even the air didn't seem to stir.

On a Sunday evening, October 23, 1949, Jun and Qingxi were preparing to teach the next day, but Jun knew she would be constantly looking out of the windows for signs of the approaching troops, listening for the artillery blast that promised to signal the opening of her path home.

The first explosion came in the predawn darkness of Monday, October 24. Decades later, Jun remembered how the sound had blasted her out of her fitful sleep. She bolted upright in her bed, her heart beating wildly. She grabbed her cardigan and draped it over her shoulders. She stared into the darkness outside, and the darkness seemed to stare back at her. A candle flickered inside a neighbor's small window down below. The explosions now came in tighter intervals, accompanied by the dense rattle of small arms fire. Jun clutched her cover and ducked into its warm folds as if taking shelter.

There was a tap on her door, and Qingxi entered the room and sat down next to Jun. She wrapped her arm around her, rubbing her gently to relax her tense shoulders. "You'll be able to go home soon," she said. "I'll take over your classes, even if I won't be as good as you in geography and English. Phys-ed too." Jun had to laugh, thinking of her ladylike friend elegant in her pencil-straight *qipao* teaching PE.

Dawn broke with a heavy exchange of fire between the attacking Communists and Nationalist defenders on the island, and it lasted all day, sometimes very close to Qingxi's house. It felt to Jun like a storm closing in, intense and unrelenting, and it only ended at nightfall when an eerie kind of hush settled over the island.

The two friends felt they needed to get out to see for themselves what had happened. They cracked open the back door and heard news that had been passed from house to house. The PLA had landed in the village of Guningtou at the northwest corner of the island, and during the day's fighting, they'd managed to advance to two other towns, Huwei and Longkou. By the end of the day, however, they were beaten back to Guningtou, where they had first landed. The fighting had been intense and casualties heavy. The chances were, everybody said, that the PLA would send reinforcements, and there would be more fighting the next day.

Jun thought of the pristine white-sand beach of Guningtou where she'd toured only weeks before. She and Qingxi had stood at the water line that day, looking across Xiamen Bay at the green mountains on the Mainland. The breeze nudged the water, and it lapped languidly at their bare feet, warm and soft. Now, all she could picture was the same beach covered with the bodies of fallen PLA soldiers. Most of these young men, Jun said to Qingxi, must have joined the Communist Army as the PLA swept down the country from the North, and they had never tasted defeat in their short fighting careers. They had literally run the Nationalist Army out to sea. Here, far away from their hometowns, they were supposed to claim this little island for the motherland, and then to continue their conquest of all of China.

On Jinmen, the Communists' confidence in the inevitability of success collided with the Nationalists' desperate need for some kind of reprieve from the succession of defeats, and for a line of defense for Taiwan. Driving the PLA off the island would effectively stop the Communists at the water's edge, containing them on the Mainland. Would the Communists stop at their first attempt and leave this part of China to the Nationalists for the time being, or would they try again?

The next morning, the two women listened, helpless and anxious, as another battle raged all day. The PLA had indeed sent in reinforcements, and with their help, the Communist troops had pushed out of Guningtou to the neighboring village of Lincuo, where they fought a brave and tenacious street battle. But then Nationalist reinforcements under General Hu Lien, one of the Nationalists' more capable commanders, reached the island from the sea, prompting heavy exchanges of fire on all fronts. Outnumbered, attacked from both land and sea, and strafed by Nationalist Air Force planes, the PLA men were again pushed back to Guningtou. There they found that the tide had gone out, grounding their boats and leaving some of them in splinters. When darkness fell, the PLA on the Mainland's shore was unable to send in more reinforcements as they had depleted the local supply of boats. The remaining Communist soldiers on Guningtou Beach were no match for the superior Nationalist forces. The fierce two-day battle came to an end. Not one of the more than nine thousand PLA soldiers made it back to the Mainland. The vast majority of them died in the battle.

When morning again came, Jun and Qingxi could hear Nationalist airplanes screeching overhead as they took victory runs, and jubilant voices in the streets. Alleys and main roads everywhere, abandoned during the fighting, erupted in a spontaneous celebration. The two friends stepped out the door and moved toward the center of town. They saw people streaming in from all directions, cheering and shouting, "It's over! It's all over!" Stores reopened after days of inactivity. Nationalist soldiers fresh from the battlefield, holding aloft Twelfth Army banners, paraded down the main street, civilians respectfully parting to make way for them to pass.

Jun drifted with the current of people. She listened to their cheers. She didn't know whether they were cheering the defeat of the Communists or whether they were simply relieved that the fighting was over. She heard the warnings being passed mouth to mouth: Don't go near the beach.

Bodies were piled layers deep there. She shuddered at the description. She found no reason to cheer, only lines from "National Sorrow" in the Song of Chu, about another Chinese battle at the dawn of the civilization:

> *They left home to fight, never more to return,*
> *On the plains they lie, far, far away they remain . . .*
> 出不入兮往不反
> 平原忽兮路超远

Sixty years later, in 2008, I visited the scene of the Guningtou battle. Despite the passage of over half a century, bullet holes were everywhere, in almost every old wall of every house, those abandoned and those still in use. Abandoned tanks still stood on the edge of vegetable fields. Pillboxes, some of them swarming with children who had turned them into playhouses, looked out silently from the village playgrounds, the center of traffic circles, and from the thickets of the subtropical foliage. I visited the Guningtou beach, cordoned off with wires hung with triangular red-metal signs at regular intervals that were spray-painted with white skulls-and-bones: "Land Mines, Danger." The unused beach had reverted to nature. Tufts of grass clung to the loose sand. Sea birds took off and landed. One section of the beach had been cleared of mines and turned into a museum, where visitors could see wall-sized posters and maps recounting the Battle of Jinmen. A Nationalist military outpost occupied some high ground outside the museum's rear gate, marked off by forbidding rolls of razor wire.

I followed a few straggling visitors to the museum on a road alongside the sea, marked off by those signs warning of land mines, to a bunker at the water's edge. Signs identified each room: the machine gun room, the kitchen, and a latrine with a flush toilet that still worked.

Xiamen was visible from the lookout station, across the expanse of water separating the island from the Mainland territory. My parents at the time were living in one of the high-rises making up the city's ever more modern skyline. With a good pair of binoculars, I might have been able to find their window and my old playground, the beach where my father had taught me to swim. A breeze came by, fluttering Taiwan's national flag on a flagpole next to me. The breeze shifted the sand on the no-man's-land of a beach below, and the water lapped against the shore, making me think of a clock, history receding, memory fading with each tick and tock. Peaceful as it was, Jinmen Island was a fortress. It still is, on Taiwan's defensive front line.

Standing on that very same beach, I imagined how it must have looked to Aunt Jun sixty years before: She would have seen occasional glimmers of light in Xiamen across the bay, and thought of her parents and her family's past, as I thought of mine. All of her recent dreams, all of her life's goals had suddenly been reduced to nothing. The summer warmth would soon give way to cool autumn evenings, when she'd shiver inside the cardigan sweater that was her only warm article of clothing. She didn't want to be stranded here, unable to take up her new job when the school resumed, prevented from earning a salary to help her troubled, increasingly impoverished family. She didn't want to start her life all over again, and certainly not on this spec of an island that had suddenly become enemy territory.

But the ferry she'd taken to Jinmen was no longer in service.

The East Is Red

I T WAS THE POLICE, uniformed officers of China's Public Security Bureau (PSB). They burst uninvited through Zhen's office door one day in the early 1950s. She was the doctor on duty at Fuzhou's Union Hospital, and the police told her that there was an emergency. They needed a doctor right away to take a look at a person who happened to be in a building right across the street.

"We don't examine patients outside the hospital," Zhen said. "You need to bring the patient here."

"He's a counterrevolutionary," was the response, as if that would somehow overrule the hospital's requirements. "He's dead. Killed himself. You just have to give us a death certificate."

The campaign for Suppressing Counterrevolutionaries was in full swing in those early days after the Communist take-over, one of Chairman Mao's first stabs at purge and ideological purification. Zhen was painfully aware of her own complicated background, and that word "complicated," *fu-tza* in Chinese, was deeply problematic. What you wanted was to be simple—a worker, a peasant, a soldier, not *fu-tza*, like a capitalist or a Nationalist or a person who had studied in America. An altercation with the PSB could lead someplace where nobody wanted to go in China in those days. Zhen elected to drop the rules and comply with the policeman's request.

It was dark and damp in the small house across the street. The agents pointed her to a rickety ladder going to an attic. It seemed even darker up there, and Zhen wanted the agents to show the way, but they insisted that she go up first. Zhen was afraid to, but she had no choice. A few curious children had gathered in the house, holding their breath as she went up rung by shaky rung.

At the top, once her eyes had adjusted to the dim light that trickled in from a single porthole window, she made out two bodies lying next to each other on a board in the center of the space. A man and a woman, neither of them showing signs of life. Against a wall she saw a small shelf full of medicine bottles, the labels all smeared with mold and age. She went to the man first and checked his vital signs. The police were correct. He was dead.

Then she moved to take up the wrist of the woman next to the man's corpse to feel her pulse. The woman bolted up screaming: "What are you trying to do to me?!" Zhen stepped back, startled. Downstairs she heard the children screaming at what they thought must be a ghost.

"What's going on?" Zhen gently asked the woman, after calming her down.

"My father-in-law was persecuted to death," the woman said, or words to that effect. "He took his own life. My husband,"—the woman nodded at the dead man lying beside her—"thought he would be next. So he took some medicine from his father's cabinets, and . . ."

"Yes, I see," Zhen said. "And what about you?"

"Me?" the woman said. "When I saw that my husband was dead, I figured, what was the point of living all by myself, with all . . . with all . . ." The woman was lost for words and her last burst of energy waned. But Zhen could see that she feared shouldering alone the political weight from the suicides of her husband and father-in-law, who most likely had a bad class background. She would be guilty by association. "So I took some of the medicine too," the woman concluded.

Zhen hastened as quickly as she could down the ladder.

"The man is dead," she announced. "The woman needs to come to the hospital right away."

There, she ordered a nurse to flush the woman's stomach. Later that day, the woman was able to walk out of the hospital on her own, into the world that she had tried, and failed, to escape.

The revolution in those early days, and for years to come, meant a new beginning for China and for many Chinese, but a tragic end for thousands and millions of others. For Zhen, it was something of both. It was a wreckage for her family, but she fought, scrapped, labored, and suffered to make a life for herself out of that wreckage. This is what made her different from others. What that woman's husband and father-in-law had done was a way out perhaps for them, but to Zhen it seemed an escape without a fight. She chose a different path. Then and for the rest of her life, she opted to live a public life submitting to the Party's authority and accepting it as necessary for herself, her family, and her country. Nestled inside this public façade like a Fabergé egg was her true self that would never be allowed to come to light. She chose to survive, and survival for her demanded a strict separation of the public image and the private self.

In 1952, Zhen returned home from her hospital one day to find her father sitting alone in the front hall. He didn't look good. His face was ashen and drawn from lack of nutrition. Still, his eyes lit up seeing his daughter, who was carrying a small, precious piece of beef that she'd gotten in the market she passed on the way. It was her regular gift for him, a rare portion of good food that he looked forward to every week.

In addition to the beef, Zhen had arrived with good news: Hu Xizhong, the man she had been going out with since before they were both in medical school, had been transferred to her very hospital in Fuzhou. Pride and happiness shone on her father's pale face as he heard how Zhen's personal and professional lives were coming together in such an encouraging way. Then Zhen saw his attention stray and his eyes fix on something behind her. She turned around and to her great surprise, saw her Ninth Uncle.

Ninth Uncle was her father's youngest brother. He was also the most elusive member of the family. Before the "liberation" in 1949, he worked for the Nationalist secret police, headed by a man named Dai Li, one of the darkest and most notorious figures in Chiang Kai-shek's now defeated government, believed responsible for many deaths and disappearances. Nobody knew exactly what Ninth Uncle had done in Dai Li's shadowy world. It was best not to ask. What the family did know was that he and his family had been living in Shanghai and that he rarely came to Fuzhou, which made his sudden appearance especially surprising. Zhen sensed her father's puzzlement, even as she saw him greet his brother cordially.

Ninth Uncle paid no attention to Zhen. He may not even have known who she was. Instead, he got right to the purpose of his visit. "Do you still have the mink coats we bought in Shanghai?" he asked. Zhen vaguely knew about the New Year's gifts that her father had bought for his two wives before the war and the revolution when such luxuries were possible. But what did Ninth Uncle want with them? There was something ominous in his peremptory request.

But Grandfather didn't protest. He called out to Xiang, my mother, to fetch them, and in a minute, she was there, the two coats, heavy and luxuriant, in her arms.

Then, as suddenly as he came, Ninth Uncle was gone, taking the coats with him.

"But those are the two last valuables in the house!" Xiang cried. She was stalking toward the door, evidently to chase after her uncle, but her father called her back.

"Your uncle needs money to travel to find your big sister," he said. This effort to comfort his daughter was transparently false. Everybody in the family knew that their father had no way of knowing how Ninth Uncle would use the money he got for the minks. He hadn't said anything about Jun when he demanded them.

Zhen turned to go to the kitchen. The meat was now simmering in a fragrant broth. Ah Nai was grinding a handful of grain. "Ah Nai, don't you see there are worms in the rice?" Zhen couldn't believe her eyes as her mother continued her grinding, worms and all. "Protein," she calmly replied.

"I only get enough money for wormy rice," Xiang said. She had followed Zhen into the kitchen and related a new story of hardship. She had been given the task of pawning the family's valuables in order to buy food for its many hungry mouths.

The last time she'd been able to get a bag of rice in a farmer's market, she'd been knocked down by a flash flood while crossing a stream in a heavy downpour and the rice had been swept away. When she got home, her father scolded her for losing it. "I was almost drowned." Xiang added.

Zhen could hear her father coughing loudly, uncontrollably, in the front room, and she rushed to check on him. He seemed to have become even more afflicted, shriveled, and gray, in just the few minutes she'd been out of the room. His frame shook as he coughed into a handkerchief crumpled in his bony hand. Zhen feared tuberculosis. She would have to make arrangements for him to be checked. She thought about the mink coats. They would have come in handy if they needed to pay expensive medical costs. But if Ninth Uncle really did use them to find Jun, she told herself, that would be good also.

The outbreak of the Korean War, less than a year after Jun had left on her intended vacation to Jinmen and Fuzhou was captured, the following day, by the PLA, had resulted in the stationing of the American Seventh Fleet in the Taiwan Strait. This sealed the separation of Taiwan from the Mainland, Jun from Zhen. From then on, Zhen understood that the responsibility of taking care of her family fell to her, and it would be for the long haul. So every month, she offered to give her mother 10 *yuan*, and Ah Niang, the mother of six growing children, 30 *yuan*, which accounted for almost all of her monthly pay. She lived in the hospital dorm and ate at work as much as she could.

Ah Nai refused to take the money. Instead, she went out to work as a seamstress at an orphanage, which brought her a small income. Ah Niang also began her own clandestine operation, slipping away to a local market to sell flowers and vegetables from her garden, getting a small income in return. Fearing that it would hurt their husband's pride if it was known that his wives had to work outside of the house, Ah Nai kept the little payment for her job a secret. She said she was leaving the house to do charity work.

The work done by my two grandmothers helped, but still the family's troubles mounted.

A few days after her visit home, Zhen sifted through a pile of papers on her hospital desk and found her father's test results. He had tuberculosis, still a killer disease in those days. Zhen was not exactly surprised, but the result still hit hard. While she was still holding the test result in her hand, a nurse popped in to say that someone in the lobby wanted to see her. She took a moment to compose herself and made her way down the hall, apprehensive, gripped by a sense of foreboding, as if her father's illness was bringing more bad fortune in its wake.

Even from the opposite end of the long corridor, Zhen could see that the person waiting for her, a thin man of medium height with a shock of stiff black hair, was none other than Cai Longbang, Jun's estranged husband. He was standing there in his usual awkward manner. He had always been rather meek and deferential—at least he had been in the days when he had come to the house to see Jun—but now he locked his eyes aggressively on Zhen. A sheaf of papers was in his hand.

Zhen never understood Jun's relationship with Cai. She remembered the evening they learned of Japan's surrender, when Jun promised Cai to marry him if they both succeeded in getting into college. But Jun married him even when he failed, out of a kind of self-destructive sympathy. There hadn't even been a real wedding ceremony. By the time Cai failed the college entrance exam again the following year Jun was already thriving in her college in Fuzhou. The two never really had much contact after that. Zhen, who had never much liked Cai, didn't regret it.

But now, without warning, here he was, glowering, angry, threatening, not bothering with any pleasantries.

"Look," he said. He unfurled some of the papers he had in his hand. Zhen took a glance. It was a stack of Jinmen newspapers!

"Your sister is safe and sound behind enemy lines and writing articles for an enemy newspaper," Cai said. His tone was accusatory, aggrieved. "She is not exactly hiding. In fact, she's working as a cheerleader for the enemy. What do you want to do about this?"

Zhen didn't know whether to be frightened or astonished. Certainly, she was full of questions: How could this man be so careless as to walk into the hospital lobby holding a pile of newspapers from enemy territory? How did he get his hands on them in the first place? And what was his purpose? Zhen remembered that just before she'd left for Jinmen on her expected vacation, Jun had entrusted her with the jewelry that Cai had given her as a wedding present, telling her that if something should happen to her while she was away, the valuables were to be sold and the money used for the family. Could Cai now be waving his pile of Jinmen contraband in Zhen's face to get back the jewelry?

But no, Zhen realized. The jewelry, a gold ring and a gold necklace, wasn't worth enough for Cai to take this risk.

And anyway, he said nothing about the jewelry. Instead, he demanded Jun's address on Jinmen, for what purpose exactly Zhen didn't know.

Zhen stared into Cai's angry eyes and told him, honestly, that she was not aware that her sister was writing for a newspaper in enemy-controlled territory, and that if he was able to get her articles, surely, he would also be able to find her address. Zhen's steadfastness sent Cai walking out fuming. But the terrible implications of Cai's unexpected visit started to sink in as Zhen turned back to the hospital wards. The ongoing campaign against counterrevolutionaries singled out capitalists, especially those who had connections to the former political and economic system, for punishment, and it mobilized a mass expression of vitriol against them. Zhen's father was a natural, almost inevitable target because he had graduated from China's first military academy, been a well-to-do businessman, and also once been a Nationalist Party official in Shanghai. And now, here was her sister's husband walking around in broad daylight with contraband clutched in his hands showing that Jun had effectively defected to the "wrong" side and worked for them.

Cai, Zhen knew, had connections to the Communists. His brother had even once been treated in her very hospital. He'd been wounded while working as an underground Communist agent, and this made Zhen pretty sure that she had just brushed off a Communist operative.

Zhen knew what she had to do, and it was ruthless and unsparing. When she told me about it, she put it in such a way that it sounded as if it were a clinical conclusion, though it would alienate her from her beloved older sister forever. She burned all the letters Jun had sent her from Jinmen—as sporadic as they had been—along with Jun's address. She was the family's sole contact with her sister after the Guningtou battle, and she would be the one to make a clean break.

What choice did she have? Survival in the revolution demanded tough, unsentimental calculations. Zhen couldn't cut herself off from her father or any of the family in Fuzhou, though some people did do exactly that for self-preservation. But to sever all contact and connection with Jun would eliminate one of her family's most incriminating political associations. It was the only way, in Zhen's reasoning, that all of them, perhaps even Jun, would have a chance to survive.

The following weekend, Zhen made her usual visit to the family, stopping at the market to buy the usual piece of beef, carrying her father's grim test results. When she showed them to him, he took it in with such equanimity that it made his two wives hold back their tears. He looked up with his eyes burning in his thin face and announced his pride in his children's achievements: he had raised a doctor (Zhen), a teacher (Jun), and an accountant (Cang, the oldest boy); a chemical engineer at the province's most elite university (Hou, Downstairs Grandma's oldest boy), where he also expected that his younger daughter (Xiang, my mother) would study.

"You belong to the New China," he said to his children gathered around him, "and you already have a good start."

He delivered this homily in one coughless breath, as if it were a well-rehearsed stage act. But deep down, Zhen knew that things were going to get much rougher soon. Only nutrition and rest could help slow the progression of her father's illness, but her father had neither. Strangely, given his condition, the first members of the family to be hospitalized were

Ah Niang's two younger children: Zhen's baby half-brother, Guang, and her half-sister, Yu. They had contracted their father's disease. Fortunately, Yu recovered quickly, but Guang took a fall one day and broke a bone in his leg, which seemed to weaken him in the face of his TB. Zhen spent a lot of her time running between her little brother in the hospital and her weakening father at home.

Meanwhile, adding to her burden, the hospital was undergoing a major transformation.

The Union Hospital traced its roots to 1860, when it was founded by some Congregationalist missionaries. In 1928, the various Protestant groups—Congregationalist, Methodist, and Anglican—consolidated their several clinics into the single Foochow Christian Union Hospital on the site of the original Congregationalist hospital. The missionaries who ran the hospital appointed foreigners to all the key positions. A new main building, known as the Red Building, was completed in 1938, and it instantly became a landmark in the city, not only because it drew patients from near and far but also because it was the most modern building in Fuzhou, with the most modern facilities and practices. Signs saying "Welcome" in both English and Chinese were hung near its permanently open doors. Nurses were required to wear standard white frocks and soft-sole shoes, their hair tied up and covered with white scarves. The hospital had Fuzhou's first elevator, its most advanced sanitation, electricity, central heat and hot-and-cold water supply systems, and Western porcelain toilets throughout. The top floor, the fifth, housed the tuberculosis department and its sick wards. English was the main language among doctors. Each year, the hospital accepted only one or two of the many Chinese interns who applied to be trained as fully integrated physicians working alongside their foreign counterparts. Zhen and her boyfriend Hu Xizhong were among this cream of the crop.

When the Communist Party took control in Zhen's second year, a military officer, rather than a physician, was put in charge of the hospital. English was banned, foreign personnel were ordered to leave, and the old "Welcome" signs were replaced by revolutionary slogans written in bright red characters—"Leniency for Confession, Harsh Punishment for Resistance!" The departure of the foreigners meant that there were suddenly vacancies for China-trained doctors, and both Zhen and Hu Xizhong were promoted to full physicians ahead of the normal schedule. The hospital also waived its fees for Zhen's family members, in recognition of her good work. She was able to move her father from home to the hospital, where her half-brother had already been admitted.

But soon after, Zhen received a summons to meet with the army officer who was the hospital's new chief. What, she wondered, as she walked the corridors on her rounds, could have prompted this request? As if in answer to her questions, she spotted her brother-in-law in the lobby once again. He was asking the front desk something. Zhen turned to walk away, but Cai pushed through the scrum of patients and headed straight to her.

He had the same hostile, aggressive look in his eyes as during his earlier visit. In his hand he clutched a new stack of newspapers with articles bearing Jun's name. But now he spat out even more alarming news:

"Your sister," he said, "is keeping company with an enemy general."

Zhen struggled to remain calm and unruffled, even as she

asked herself how Cai had acquired this information, which she, Zhen, didn't know.

"Look," she finally said, "fighting for survival takes different forms for different people under different circumstances. As for my sister's personal life, I have no way of knowing anything about it, since we have no communication with each other."

Zhen turned to leave, but Cai wasn't done. He told Zhen that if she cared about the well-being of her only full sister, she would go to Jinmen to bring her back. If she agreed to do that, he said, he would guarantee safe passage for them both.

The audacity of Cai's demand was so enraging to Zhen that she was momentarily at a loss for words.

"I have my father and brother in the hospital right now," Zhen told him finally, looking straight into his eyes, "and the rest of the family back at home. I'm the only person keeping them alive. And you want me to just pick up and go?"

"Yes," Cai said. He promised that he would take care of her family. Zhen took a hard look at this man whom she had never liked or trusted, and as far as she was concerned, was never part of her family. She then took a deep breath.

"If you can guarantee safe passage, you should go yourself."

But Cai replied that only Zhen could stop her sister from drifting farther into the Nationalist camp and save everyone at home from direct connections with the wrong side.

"This is your last chance to save us all," he said. "Take it or leave it."

Zhen turned away without another word and continued straight to her father's ward to check on him. Cang, her brother, was there. She told both of them about her encounter with Cai downstairs moments before.

"If you don't want to go, I'll go." Cang jumped at the opportunity. Zhen knew that her brother had also been battling his own political investigations. But she was waiting for her father's response.

"If you are asking for my opinion," her father said, ignoring Cang's outburst, "I think you should go join your sister, and together you may find it easier to get ahead in life."

Zhen could hardly believe what she was hearing. This obviously was not her usual clear-thinking father, she thought. Although she knew that he was worried about Jun and longed for her return, she didn't consider her father's proposal for a minute. He had not served in a public office for a dozen years since the beginning of the Anti-Japanese War in 1937 and couldn't possibly appreciate the political threat from his past Nationalist affiliation or the way Jun's presence on Taiwan intensified the danger. Besides, she had made her political choice, which precluded any thought of doing what her father was suggesting. But it would be futile to explain everything to him.

To the young, idealistic, confident Zhen, her clear-headed, sharp-thinking father, the protector of the family, was simply no longer himself. His mind had atrophied with his body.

Within a week, my grandfather's entire body went numb. The tuberculosis had spread to his brain where meningitis had set in. There was nothing more the hospital could do for him, and so, with Hu Xizhong's help, Zhen took him home. For the next two days, he went in and out of a coma. On the third day, he gestured for Zhen to sit at his bedside. Zhen dropped her conversation with her mothers and walked over to him. She propped him up and realized that tears were trickling down his emaciated cheeks. He wanted to write something but he couldn't.

"Are you worried about the family?" Zhen asked him,

talking into his ear. He nodded his head with difficulty, as tears continued to roll down his cheeks. "Don't worry, Father," she said, turning for a moment to look at the family gathered around them. "If I have a mouthful to eat, each and everyone in the family will, too."

Grandfather struggled to keep his eyes open. "Also," Zhen said, "I promise to find Jun. I'm sure she'll come back once she knows that you are ill."

Grandfather closed his eyes for the last time.

The following day was chilly and cloudy. Zhen rushed home after work. The family couldn't figure out whether Grandfather was still sleeping or had slipped into another coma.

"It's time to get ready," Zhen told Cang. They set out to survey the family's burial ground and to locate their father's plot.

Zhen went straight to her father's room upon their return. In the eerie stillness of the space, she saw that her baby brother, Guang, had crawled on his own into the room, and was struggling to stand up by holding on to the bedpost. Her mothers must have left the room momentarily to tend to some family chores, as maids had long ago been dismissed. Zhen hurried over to help him, and as she did so, she saw that her father had passed away. She recalled what the fortune-teller had said after her father had fallen ill—that only one of his many children would be present at his deathbed. And it happened to be the one who was too young to be aware of the loss that he was witnessing.

The day of the funeral was cold and drizzly, and Zhen was delayed by an emergency at the hospital. When she got home, the first thing she saw in the front hall was the coffin.

Women were sobbing. Only little Guang was standing, holding onto a chair. Looking around him, he seemed both confused and scared, wide-eyed and quiet. The coffin was the crudest one Zhen had ever seen: made of four thin planks of wood. The grains of the wood zigzagged under the thin and uneven paint. Strangely, it was that sight, the shabbiness of the coffin, that let loose Zhen's tears. Her father deserved more than this flimsy vessel to the other world. He had served his country and his family. He was in the first generation of modernizing Chinese, an early graduate of the country's first modern military academy, an officer in what was then the national army, an official in what was the national government, a patriot who strove to advance the cause of his country. And to all his children, he had tried his best to be a good father. He had survived the battlefield. He had succeeded in the difficult jobs he had undertaken. Life's exhaustion had taken him: The declining fortunes of the family had consumed him, and the missing daughter whom he had sent on her first airplane ride gnawed at him. He was fifty-nine, lying emaciated in a humiliatingly inadequate box.

Zhen picked up Guang in her arms. The boy himself embodied the family's difficulties. At the age of four, he was still unable to walk on his own. He felt pathetically light and small. Someone handed him a weeping stick, which, according to tradition, should be held high by the youngest son at his father's funeral procession. Grandfather's two brothers arrived, one after the other, carrying umbrellas against the heavy rain outside. Seventh Uncle dropped his at the door and threw himself over the coffin and started to weep. Third Uncle paused and went over to Ah Niang, six months pregnant and weeping bitterly, her swelling belly shaking. Ninth Uncle wasn't there.

"Don't cry, sister," Third Uncle said to Ah Niang. "It'll

disturb the baby. Brother has had his share of good times in his life."

"His share of good times in his life"—Zhen took the words as an insult, coming as they did from the Third Uncle who had sold the Garden built and designed by her own father.

A loud bang startled her. They were putting the nails in the coffin's cover. The weeping and wailing rose to a crescendo. The group went out in the rain, walking up the trail winding around the hill and toward the family burial ground behind the Garden. The mourners huddled under oilpaper umbrellas, shivering in the wind-driven freezing rain. Occasionally a sharp wailing pierced the leaden cold of this late autumn storm.

Later, much later, Zhen would think of the things her father's early death had spared him. He died without knowing that his youngest son would be crippled for the rest of his life because of the bacteria he had given him, and that his Ninth Brother who took his last mink coats did go to see Jun, but then vanished after taking money that Jun had given him to take to the family. Her father left without having to know, also, how long a shadow he would cast on every member of his family through the revolutions yet to come, in the even more tumultuous years ahead in modern China's history.

Only weeks after his death, streptomycin became available. It was the first antibiotic effective against tuberculosis. It was late by a few weeks for Grandfather, but streptomycin stopped the progression of Guang's infection. By the time the New Year came, he was able to start walking, though because of the prolonged damage and malnutrition, his tibia and fibula never developed fully. As a result, his left leg ended up being a few inches shorter than the right one.

Decades later, when I asked Uncle Guang if he

remembered anything about his father, he took a moment, and then said haltingly: "Yes, maybe, the way he held me in his arms . . . and the loud bang on what I later realized was his coffin."

• • •

The military representative got straight to the point: Was Zhen the president of the Nationalist Women's Youth League when she was at medical school? Her pre-1949 history was a page that Zhen was eager to flip over. She graduated from medical school that year, and she liked to emphasize the fact that she walked into the New China right out of medical school, just in time to serve the people. Now her leader wanted to open that very page. She remained calm because it happened to be an easy question for her to answer in the negative, but she had to wonder where the question had come from and where it was headed, particularly in the current mood of paranoia and suspicion that pervaded the new Communist government. She understood that the mood was propelled by the outbreak of the Korean War just a year after the People's Republic was proclaimed. She saw how quickly the Communists expelled Western nationals. And in the name of national unity to defend the New China, Chairman Mao and the Chinese Communist Party (CCP) moved to consolidate the power of the new government by mobilizing a nationwide ideological and social cleansing: Anyone with connections, even the most seemingly innocuous connections, to the former Nationalist government—the party, the army, its youth organizations, or anything else—was suspected of being a "counterrevolutionary." Millions of people suspected of such connections were put under investigation or punished for harboring pro-Nationalist sentiments.

The military representative, sitting at his desk, the portrait of Chairman Mao behind him a symbol of his authority, asked the question again.

"I was president of the Nationalist Women's Youth League in high school, yes," Zhen replied. She had been elected to head the League as a mark of recognition from her classmates. "But in medical school, no."

The military representative sat with his chin on interlocked fingers and waited for further explanation:

"The medical school," Zhen began, "planned to establish a Youth League, and there was talk that they would like me to be its leader. But there weren't enough women students, so the organization was never formed."

She stopped. She had nothing more to explain. She could have said something like, "But as a patriotic person who opposed American imperialism and its running dog, Chiang Kai-shek, and who wholeheartedly supported the proletarian revolution, I would have immediately rejected any such proposal." But she didn't say that. She waited for the military representative's verdict.

"What you did in high school doesn't matter," he said at last. "But a membership in the League at the college level—and we have been told that you were to be the leader—would be a conscious political choice made by an adult."

But Zhen was telling the truth. There had been no Women's Youth League and therefore she had never made a conscious political choice. She suggested, politely, that perhaps the Comrade Military Representative could verify her account with the medical school records?

"Unfortunately," came the reply, with what Zhen detected a touch of regret, "the school lost many of its records when it moved during the war. But every college had a Women's

Youth League, so finding no record of one in the case of Fujian Medical School didn't necessarily mean that there wasn't one there."

"Well, there wasn't," Zhen reaffirmed. "Could I ask who told you that there was and that I was its leader?"

"Do you remember Zhang Cuijiao?" the representative asked. "She was your friend."

Zhen did remember.

"She has told us that there was a woman's branch of the League and that since you were always a leader, you must have been its president."

Zhen was stunned. How could her old friend have told this untruth? And how to prove that it was untrue? It would be her word against Cuijiao's, and while there wouldn't be a scrap of evidence to support either side, Zhen knew that Cuijiao also knew her family's Nationalist connections, which could easily be corroborated by the government records now in Communists' possession. And not only that; Zhen also knew, thanks to Cai, that the Communists were likely aware of her sister Jun's articles in a newspaper on Jinmen. Could Cai, she wondered, have already turned them over, or, if he hadn't, would he? Providing the evidence of Jun's treason would accomplish the double purpose of avenging himself on the Chen family and currying favor with the country's new holders of power.

But even as Zhen entertained these dark thoughts, the military representative provided some relief.

"I am putting you on probation," he announced, not without a hint of sympathy in his tone. "You will attend regular thought reform and self-criticism sessions while you work full time at the hospital." He gestured to Zhen that that meeting was at an end.

The hospital, having expelled its foreigners, was in dire need of skilled physicians, and Zhen was the star among the young Chinese doctors there. She walked out of the meeting feeling that she'd gained a reprieve of a sort that others in her position wouldn't have gotten. She decided right away to take the chance being offered to recreate herself. She wanted to believe in the goodness of the new leadership and the new society, and she knew that to be part of that new world she would need to have a clean start. Immediately, she volunteered to do double shifts. She went to the weekly self-criticism sessions, which she took seriously as an opportunity to forge a correct political narrative. After each session, she would write a report on her progress in thought reform, embellishing her texts with the approved political terms: the teachings of Chairman Mao, the dictatorship of the proletariat leadership, and class enemies, and many other new expressions.

And she made each self-criticism a building block in her overall argument. First, she had to stay clear of her *fu-tza*, complicated, family past. And then, as she documented and highlighted her progress in raising her political awareness, she was careful not to provide anything that might even suggest that she herself was ever on the wrong side of the Communist Party.

In her self-criticisms, she pointed out that her family's background wasn't chosen by her, but she knew that she had been infected by feudal and reactionary thoughts. She would work to rebel against the old traditions as a condition for transforming herself into a good citizen in the new Communist society. She was grateful to be given the chance to reflect on her own past, she wrote, a chance to sort things out in order to establish a revolutionary identity. After repeated soul-searching and examining of her own conduct, she hadn't found any specific personal wrongdoing, and therefore, she shouldn't make declarations of her innocence. That would make it look as if her purpose was to defend herself, when the whole point of these sessions was to gain a deeper understanding of the new ideology and to acquire a correct attitude toward ideological reform. So she said that her self-criticisms had truly prepared her well to serve the people.

Deep down, Zhen never really believed that she deserved to be treated as a suspected class enemy, or that she really needed to remold her thinking. But she thought of the good that the Party could do for China, and she therefore would do what was expected of her: the ritual of self-examination, confessions of her faults, and expressions of her gratitude and loyalty to the Party. It was a price she was willing to pay. From this moment on, Zhen would adopt this line of truthtelling to redeem herself time and time again.

In the eyes of the Party, her sister Jun had committed a wrongdoing simply by living in enemy territory, and Zhen felt she had to address that issue preemptively. She reported, honestly, that before her departure to her vacation in Jinmen, Jun had written a letter to the family expressing her excitement at landing a job to teach the children of the New China. That letter, which Zhen presented as evidence, proved that her sister was trapped on enemy territory against her will. Zhen vowed to stand vigilant against enemy infiltration and to redouble her vigilance against subversion on the home front, and to stand firm with the Communist Party without being soft or swayed by bourgeois attachments. To show her resolution, she announced, she and her family had cut all ties to Jun, in the event that Jun switched her allegiance to the Nationalists under duress in order to survive on enemy territory.

Starting from these early days, Zhen tried to stay in lock-step with the Party, and she never wavered. Through relentless political study sessions reading Chairman Mao's "highest directives," she became a master of an entirely new language, with its own revolutionary vocabulary and slogans. She likened her mastery of this language to political armor. Forged in these early years of revolution, it would be retooled and refitted in every subsequent wave of political upheaval.

"I have learned a lot through these sessions," she began, capping her many weekly reports addressing every potentially incriminating issue she could think of. "After months of study and examination of my past conduct, I now truly understand what revolution is, and I think I'm now ready to better serve the people and to help build and defend our motherland."

The military representative nodded as he listened, and Zhen could see that for the moment at least, she had succeeded with her self-criticism in heading off political complications. Making a new beginning was possible, she was starting to believe. Even Jun's husband Cai Longbang, who had seemed such a threat only a few months before, appeared to have faded from the scene. She was determined to keep him away from the Chen family as long as Jun was not home, this likely Communist agent with a license to threaten from within.

Zhen's successful completion of her first thought reform earned her a seat at one of the Party representative's banquets held in the hospital. After years of propping up her father's large starving family with almost all her salary, she was dazzled by the spread in front of her, reviving her long-lost sense for the bounty of the verdant coastal city of Fuzhou, once everyday fare for her family in the Garden: the freshest seafood and meats, and the vegetables glistening with their generous coats of oil. She never knew what the banquet was exactly for, but she indulged herself in the elaborate array of dishes—a treat to the palate that also intensified the pain within. In securing her own new beginning, she'd managed to keep her ties to her family in Fuzhou, but she'd had to cast off her older sister.

• • •

Meanwhile she was barely keeping the family from starvation. After her father's death, many mouths were to be fed with only one salary, her own. There was nothing left of any value to bring to the pawnshop, and Ah Niang was about to give birth to a fatherless baby. In addition, Hou, her oldest half-brother by Ah Niang who was studying at Xiamen University, needed some money, and Zhen vowed to send him five *yuan* (Chinese dollar; worth about twelve U.S. cents) a month to cover his expenses.

Then, just as Zhen's anxieties became overwhelming, Hu Xizhong proposed to her. He made his case more on practical than romantic grounds, but practicality was suitable to this moment in her life. He would take care of their needs, he said, so Zhen could give all her salary to her family.

Xizhong's proposal made Zhen realize how much she had relied on him in the past year. Through it all—her political investigation, the family's poverty, the illnesses, her father's death—she would never have made it without his calm, his humor, and his understanding; in short, his love. He had been by her side, her rock and her comfort. What more could a person ask for in a partner? Zhen said yes.

The wedding took place at the hospital on January 11, 1953. It was a Sunday. The date 1/11 was chosen for the combination of three "ones" indicating a new beginning. The

couple wore matching male and female versions of Mao suits
in a sort of dark bluish gray, specially made for the occasion.
They each sported newly cut hair—the no-fuss short, straight
hairstyles popular at the time—and were completely without
adornment. Streamers and flowers in the grand hall in the
Union Hospital, perhaps the only heated room in the city,
distracted people's attention from the cracks and dust on the
walls. The lights were turned bright, and the stage was set.
Rounds of revolutionary songs were sung, and then amid the
squealing of children and the cheering of adults, the couple
was ushered to the stage. The military representative took the
microphone and the ruckus came to a halt, replaced by the
rustling of candy wrappers.

"The first new couple in the New China's oldest hospital
in the province!" he declared. Instead of a cheer, the crowd
remained quiet and expectant. Needless to say, the military
representative provided some political inspiration. "Comrades," he said, "these are two of China's very own doctors
in this hospital founded by American missionaries a century
ago. Think of that. They both graduated with distinction
from Fujian's own medical school. They replaced foreign
experts. As Chairman Mao said: 'The Chinese people have
stood up!' Today we are all masters of this new country, and
we have Chinese doctors treating fellow countrymen. This is
a glorious revolutionary union . . ."

The representative's speech ended and the mandatory
shouting—"Long live the New China!" ensued. The leader
of the Workers' Union took his turn to wish the couple happiness under the Communist Party's leadership. Xizhong's
father, a former Methodist priest, peppered his toast with
newly acquired revolutionary boilerplate. Even Zhen's
mother, wearing her first pair of pants and making her revolutionary debut as a modern woman representing her family,

gave her blessings to the newlyweds: "The New China has given us new opportunities, and I'm very happy to see you work hard as you always have, and serve in the revolutionary cause. I wish you happiness even when your hair is white as mine."

That night, happy as she was, Zhen felt the absence of her father, the head of the family that she had been fighting so hard to care for and sustain. He would've been proud and happy tonight. He was an eloquent man and would've made a speech to remember. But she also understood, in the aftermath of her revolutionary wedding, that his absence had given her some distance from her family's political liabilities, and that his passing had in its way cleared a path on which she could lead the family forward in the New China.

Not long afterward, Zhen became pregnant. She was profoundly grateful. As it happened, there had been two other new lives in her family—Ah Niang had given birth to a son and her brother Cang's first child had been born. The loudspeakers and newspapers and meetings all declared that the country was on the threshold of a great national renewal, and Zhen reveled in the conviction that all this new life was a part of her country's new beginning.

• • •

On a beautiful spring day, Zhen headed home with Hu Xizhong, bringing her monthly pay with them. Against her husband's advice, Zhen had insisted on walking the whole way to save the bus fare. She and Xizhong were on their way to announce their good news. As they approached the house, children ran out to greet them, expecting candies, and they were not disappointed. Then Zhen hurried into the house, greeted both Ah Nai and Ah Niang, and before announcing her own news, eagerly asked to see Ah Niang's baby, her new half-brother.

The women's faces froze. Zhen dashed into the room where she last saw the baby. The cradle was still there, but the baby was not.

"Where is he? What has happened?" Zhen was unable to keep the panic from her voice.

"The baby was crying non-stop from hunger, day and night," Ah Niang said. Zhen saw the hollowness in her eyes. "He wasn't growing. He was burning up the little fat he had. What could I do?"

Zhen stared at her Ah Niang. "What DID you do?"

"I couldn't just watch as he starved to death," Ah Niang said.

Zhen waited.

"I handed him over to a PLA couple," Ah Niang finally admitted, herself seemingly struck lifeless by grief.

Zhen felt as if a brick had dropped on her head. She was a doctor. Why had her mother not sent for her? Why hadn't she brought the boy to the hospital? She wanted to charge out of the house, to snatch the baby back.

"To whom exactly? Where is he?"

Ah Niang didn't know. The handover of the baby was arranged through an acquaintance. It wasn't even an adoption, but a mere exchange: the Chen family's youngest baby boy for a small sack of rice. The baby had gone to a childless couple. The husband was a high-ranking military officer on his way to fight in Korea. The wife planned to have the baby to keep her company while her husband performed his duties at the front.

"Has their unit left the city?" But Zhen knew that civilians wouldn't know about the army's movements.

"I think the baby's in good hands," Ah Niang murmured. She looked down.

"Good hands!" The words struck Zhen where they hurt the most. The hands of the baby's own mother were not good enough! The hands of his big sister who wanted to help raise him were not good enough! All the many hands in the family were not good enough! The child who would never see his own father in the "good hands" of strangers! Zhen looked at the empty cradle, tucked into the corner of the dark bedroom, a section of hollowed-out log set on two upward bending pieces of wood. A rocking cradle that rocked no more.

Zhen looked at her hands and realized she was holding some baby clothes, intended for her half-brother.

"I guess Cang's baby could use these," she mumbled.

She saw Ah Nai and Ah Niang exchange a worried look.

"Is it wrong to do that?" Zhen asked. She wondered if there was something in the tradition that she was violating, clothes intended for a child no longer there given to one who was.

"It's not that, Zhen. It's not that." This time, it was the voice of her mother, Ah Nai, that quavered. She came closer, taking Zhen's hands into hers. "It's that . . . there's no need . . ."

"What do you mean?"

"Cang has been classified as a counterrevolutionary. He's been dismissed from work. His pay has been stopped."

Cang was an accountant, nothing wrong with that, except from time to time there was gossip about his dabbling in various other businesses and mixing up with shady social or political groups through his drinking and card-playing buddies.

She and he had both been investigated, and while things had gone well for her, they hadn't for him.

Zhen clutched the baby clothes in her hand, red, blue, and blazing yellow, realizing what must have happened, but at the same time it all stopped making sense to her. Not both babies. It can't be. They had squirmed lazily in her hands when she'd met them only a couple of weeks before.

"He also sold his baby to a PLA officer," Ah Nai finally said.

For many years after that day, Zhen told me decades later, she would scrutinize every boy she saw in a military family who looked about her brother's and nephew's age, hoping that she might find them and get them back. She kept alive the hope, the fantasy, that one day a boy or a man with the Chen features on his face would pass her on the street, and she would take him home, making her family complete again.

• • •

It was 1953. The Korean War ended in an armistice. Zhen and Hu Xizhong's first daughter was born at the end of the year. They gave her the simplest name: *Hu Yi*, or Hu the First, Hu Number One. The name was a kind of metaphor for a chance to start again, like their choice of a wedding on the eleventh day of the first month. Zhen always remembered her first look at her daughter, her face wrinkled yet placid like an old sage. A loud cry came out of her tiny mouth; she kicked as if she was ready for a fight, giving her parents and the other people in the room a good laugh. Zhen discreetly wiped away the tears welling in the corner of her eye, and Xizhong gently reached for the baby to look for himself.

When Zhen woke up the next morning, she asked for her baby. The nurse gently laid her, neatly swaddled, in the cradle of Zhen's curved arm, and turned to pull open the curtain.

Morning sunlight poured through the window. From the far end of the hospital campus, a loudspeaker crackled to life.

The east is red, the sun rises, and from China rises a Mao Zedong. He works to bring happiness to the people. He is our great savior.

Zhen wanted to believe that the old world—her father's world, Jun's world before her departure, and especially the world in which babies were abandoned—had come to an end, just as this sparkling morning had replaced the dark of the night before. As she saw it, her team had just gotten bigger. Moreover, she and Xizhong had been promoted, promised higher salaries to ease their financial burden. The economy of the New China was improving. The country had stood up to the American imperialists in Korea. Despite the poverty, there was a palpable mood of optimism, and Zhen was ready to be swept up in it. Hu the First would be the first person in her generation to live a better life than anyone in her parents' generation—so they hoped, and for that her parents were ready to give all they had.

Adrift

J UN RETURNED HOME one day from teaching, and found
a young man waiting for her in the front hall. Polite
and courteous, he didn't so much alarm Jun by his presence
as make her curious. The local bureau of one of Taiwan's
newspapers had sent him, the young man explained. After
the now famed Guningtou battle, Jinmen had become a hot
news spot. When his office sought help at the local school,
hoping to find someone to share the burden of filing articles in the heavier-than-normal news cycles, Jun's name
came up repeatedly, he said, and when the school showed
the bureau some of Jun's writings, they knew that they had
the perfect person. Would she be willing to consider writing
for them?

Before Jun could muster any kind of response, the young
man added excitedly that Madame Chiang, the First Lady
of the Republic of China, as the Nationalists now called Taiwan and the surrounding islands under their control, was
planning to visit the island. The assignment of covering the
visit would be Jun's if she would agree to be their special

reporter—in a temporary arrangement to start with, in addition to her teaching.

Under different circumstances, this would have been an offer too good to refuse. But would she want to start a new job by reporting on the First Lady of Taiwan, on her first trip to the front line of the Nationalist defense against the Communist controlled Mainland? She needed time to think about it, she told the young man.

Jun's mind was a jumble of thoughts: Words could kill, and they could kill in some unexpected ways. Writers tripped on political taboos; dynasties changed and the men in power changed with them. Jun was a history teacher. She had studied the transition of one dynasty to another, and though never before had she thought that the lessons she learned would apply to herself in this modern era, she now knew that they did. From the Mainland perspective, she was already behind enemy lines. How much worse would it be if she were to become a journalist there, writing favorably about the wife of the leader of the Enemy? It would have to be favorably, of course. The First Lady's visit to the frontline would be the biggest honor that the island had ever had.

Foremost in her mind was the likelihood that her name in a Taiwan newspaper would draw unwelcome attention to her father and his former Nationalist connections, and from her father to the rest of her family. Jun went back and forth—should she, or shouldn't she take up the offer? She was caught between her own chance for independence and her father's and her family's well-being. Neither side of the argument could easily prevail.

She remembered those photographs of carnage that she'd seen when she was a girl in her father's study—scenes of the destruction of Shanghai, then the stories of the Nanjing massacre that she learned that night in Nanping. The power of images and facts. Being a journalist would give her the opportunity to capture and convey such moments of history, the kind of power that once shook her to her core. Moreover, there weren't other opportunities on this small island. The Battle of Guningtou had cut off Jinmen's line of supply and communication to Xiamen, which had always been a kind of umbilical cord between the Jinmen and the outside world, a relay station for goods and remittances. Many merchants and fishermen spent long months away on business in Southeast Asia, sent remittances via Xiamen to support their families back home on Jinmen. But these remittances had now stopped, as Xiamen, an old port city on the nearest island, was under Communist control, forcing some of the students in Jun's school to skip classes in order to help out at home.

And the island as a whole had been transformed as well. Jun had just recently made a trip with Qingxi to check on the tenant farmers living on some land that her family owned in Lincuo, which had been a battlefield just weeks before. Approaching the village, the two women were puzzled by the sight of men who seemed to be hunting, rather than working in the fields. Not until they met a student did they learn that the men were actually catching field mice. The student explained: After the victory in the Battle of Guningtou, general Hu Lien, a northerner who prized wheat products, asked the cooks to prepare white flour noodles and buns for a big celebration. But the majority of the troops were new recruits from the Guangdong area, the last stop in their retreat on the Mainland where they replenished the ranks. For these southerners, a real treat would be the snakes that they saw in the mountains. So they soon were given the permission to fan out to hunt snakes. Only weeks after the feast, the farmers found that their maturing sweet potatoes were being raided by large armies of field mice, since their main predator, the snakes, had been eaten by the soldiers. Field mice were also delicacies, those same soldiers told General Hu, who was more than happy to both indulge the soldiers and appease the farmers by letting the soldiers hunt for them too.

But the military's reach went far beyond that. The island of some thirty thousand inhabitants now quartered a large national military force, large enough to threaten to deplete the island's modest natural resources and infrastructure. Water shortages were made worse, narrow unpaved roads were jammed by roaring military vehicles, and with the demand for wood skyrocketing, the limited supply of mature trees had been quickly exhausted. There were complaints that soldiers were taking away door planks from civilian houses for their timber. Just about anything usable for military purpose, some said, was either bought or taken from the civilians in order to defend their homeland from further Communist invasion. On this highly militarized and politicized speck of land, Jun needed to explore ways to restart her own life. Living off her friend Qingxi's kindness was only a temporary measure.

• • •

And so, a week after the young emissary's visit, on a blustery day in December, there she was, notebook and pen in hand, observing the rows of soldiers at the Jinmen landing strip waiting for the First Lady's arrival. The wind was whipping up sand on the beach and pelting it on everyone's faces. Then, the plane swooped down the runway with a huge roar, the ladder unfolded, the brass band struck up, and the luminous lady appeared atop the ladder, waving to the sea of uniforms standing at attention.

The ceremony at the airport was followed by a banquet in Madame Chiang's honor, where she gave a toast of gratitude and encouragement. Jun was impressed by the verve she showed in the impromptu part of her speech: She was struck by the barren landscape of the island, she said, and she wanted to make sure that the government sent in tree seedlings to reforest the island, making it a home for all those who had already sacrificed so much of their comfort to safeguard the Republic. The First Lady's observation and compassion deeply impressed Jun, and she joined the applause that reverberated through the great mess hall, a cavernous space festooned with long, red banners hanging from the ceiling while painted scenes of the battlefield lined the walls and fresh flowers flown in for the occasion decorated every table. Jun saw some young men discretely dab their eyes.

The party of officers and the guest of honor then moved to the officers' dining room, where the brass started arriving. Stiff in their uniforms, the party reminded Jun of her father as pictured in the yearbook of the Baoding Military Academy: wearing the same kind of uniform, and with a sword by his side. Madame Chiang appeared at the door, followed by General Hu. The men in uniform all saluted, and Jun involuntarily made a slight curtsy, the way she'd been taught to do when honored guests came to the Flower Fragrant Garden. The curtsy seemed to catch the attention of General Hu who, learning that Jun was a newspaper reporter covering the event, introduced her to the First Lady. And when Madame Chiang talked about her plans to organize women to help support the military efforts on the front, she turned to Jun and smiled as if to recruit her to that program. Jun politely returned the smile, but her heart skipped a beat as she thought of the way she was being pulled across a line that she knew she wasn't ready to cross.

When it came time to write her article, it took her some effort to cast her own feelings aside and to craft a neutral, factual headline: "Madame Chiang Commends Soldiers' Bravery, Urges Reforestation of Island."

A signed picture of Madame Chiang Kai-shek, 1951.

• • • ,

The footsteps of spring came drip, drip, drip, daintily land-ing under the eaves of the house and on the banana leaves outside, filling the air with a translucent mist. Jun's report on Madame Chiang's visit to Jinmen launched her career as a journalist. She gradually shifted from teaching to writing more for the paper, but she tried her best to steer clear of politics. She saw her writing as a way for her to connect with people on a personal level.

The Qingming Festival arrived, and Qingxi's family went out to sweep their parents' tombs in the hills. Jun decided to take a walk on her own to clear her mind. She had been home-sick and racked with guilt for being unable to fulfill her respon-sibilities as the oldest girl in the family. Jun wanted at least to send home some of the money she earned from her job as a teacher, meager as the income may have been, but that was dif-ficult with the whole island now sealed off by the military. One night, Jun put together all the money that she had saved and planned to mail it to a distant relative in Hong Kong, hoping that it would be redirected home. But before she was able to do that, she got a note from Taipei, in which her Ninth Uncle informed her that he was making a brief stop in Jinmen on an official trip to Hong Kong. This uncle who had worked in the Nationalist secret police was planning to settle in that city. Jun was overjoyed to see her uncle and entrusted all she had accumulated to her uncle to be sent home from Hong Kong.

Now, clouds smudged the misty green hills in the dis-tance. Clusters of people dotted the mountainside trails with colorful miniature paper houses and furniture on swinging bamboo shoulder poles, and food that the ancestors could consume in the netherworld. Jun thought of some lines from the Tang poetry, by Du Mu and Wang Wei:

The misty rain of Qingming drifts
Leaving the traveler's soul bereft
清明时节雨纷纷
路上行人欲断魂

Alone in a strange land, I'm a stranger alone
The holiday returns, doubling the thoughts of one's own
From afar I can see
My brothers hike to some place high
Each donning a dogwood sprig, missing me
独在异乡为异客
每逢佳节倍思亲
遥知兄弟登高处
独插茱萸少一人

By the time she finished reciting the poem, an idea came to her: She would write a column about ancient poetry for her paper. Soldiers toiling in faraway garrisons and women longing for their return had always been a theme in classical Chinese poetry. If the current separation from home was hard for herself, Jun thought, it must have been just as hard for the soldiers stationed on Jinmen. The thought made her feel a big-sisterly tenderness toward them. Her idea was readily accepted.

She was finishing dinner a few weeks after she'd begun her column when she saw a young soldier getting out of a jeep in front of her house. He was a messenger with a startling invitation. General Shen Min, the commander of civilian affairs of the Jinmen garrison, wanted to talk to her, the soldier said, adding by way of explanation that both the general and himself liked her column.

"When?" Jun asked.

"Well, right now, if that would be convenient for you," the soldier said.

It was already dark when the jeep pulled up to a brightly lit military compound on top of Jinmen's tallest mountain, Taiwu. Jun saw three men through a wide-open door, drinking tea around a small makeshift low table, two in uniform, and one in a white shirt who stood up and walked to the car.

Jun noticed at once that he was a handsome man, nearly six feet tall, with round, dark eyes shining from under two equally dark, thick eyebrows. He wore his white shirt with the collar opened and the sleeves rolled up, and he extended his right hand: "I'm Shen Min," he said. "Thank you for coming."

Min introduced Jun to the other officers and then got right to the point. They had been discussing setting up a branch of the Anti-Communist and Resist Russia Union on Jinmen, he said. Jun knew of this organization, founded by Madame Chiang to build grassroots support for the military. It would have various activities, Min said, including organizing free movie nights for the public and visits to schools by officers and soldiers. Jun must have known right away that the general was not explaining this to her to make idle conversation, and that he was luring her into yet another step with political implications. But she did not balk when he asked if she'd be willing to be the organization's civilian representative, helping to coordinate its activities with the army. The two officers would support her work, he told her, and the military would pay her a salary, rent her a place of her own choice, and offer her all the privileges of an army officer, a major to be exact, a title commensurate with her college degree.

What an offer! But when Min got to the point about a military rank, Jun's brain screeched to a halt. "No! No! I don't want to be a major. I don't want a military rank!" she thought to herself. Yet at the same time, she could sense a strange power that would come with a rank, a power that she had never thought would have any connection to her life. And at the very heart of the offer, she saw the independence that she had craved. All civilians on the island were now forbidden to leave, as the government tried to retain a civilian base for military support—for food, service, and to maintain a viable local economy. Her only chance of eventually leaving the island lay in some kind of affiliation with the stationing army. The army had the ultimate authority to call the shots on the island, for it had the direct line to the central government in Taipei.

"Please take some time to think about it, Miss Chen," General Shen said, detecting the uncertainty on Jun's face, and bringing the meeting to a close. That night, Jun tossed and turned in bed. The proposal seemed so outlandish in its way, for a young woman who only a year before expected to live her life as a schoolteacher in the new Communist China to be offered a position as a major in the Nationalist Army. But she was trapped on this island with no other prospects in sight, and she liked Min, his deep voice, his easy manner, his genuine smile. His handshake never seemed to loosen its grip.

• • •

"What a name!" Qingxi said when she asked about Jun's excursion the night before. The "Anti-Communist and Resist Russia Union!" She repeated the name, so blatant, a parody of itself. But the actual activities of this Union—movie nights, classroom visits, planting trees—seemed pretty innocuous, and, anyway, the two friends knew that there was a certain harsh fact in Jun's situation that had to be faced. Even when the ban on leaving the island was lifted, which it surely would be eventually, Qingxi had an extended family in Malaysia to rejoin, but where would Jun go? Not to the Mainland. That would remain forbidden. And so, there she was, stuck on Jinmen with what seemed like an awfully good opportunity placed in her lap but one with profound, life-altering implications.

"It's worth it," Qingxi said, holding Jun's hand, knowing that her friend must be thinking about her family, so close and yet so far away. "And even if you decide to rent a place, remember, this house will always be your home, as long as I'm here."

Jun's pass. Issued on July 16th, 1951, for attending the conference celebrating the first anniversary of the founding of the Anti-Communist Resist-Russia Women's Union.

And so, almost two years after she first set foot on Jinmen, Jun moved into her own apartment near the military base at the foothills of Taiwu Mountain and threw herself into work. She was given an office across the hallway from Min's, and they shared the same orderly, Little Yang. Among her other duties—making connections in villages, visiting schools, helping Min clear up the backlog in his correspondence—she wrote the speeches that some of the officers gave to audiences around the island. One morning, she showed Min a speech she'd just finished that was to be delivered by an officer named Wang. It was intended for a battalion of foot soldiers assigned to plant trees on the island.

"Oh dear," Min said, having finished the speech. Jun was momentarily alarmed at what seemed a cloudy look on her boss's face. Was the speech that bad? She thought it was pretty good. Maybe she shouldn't be writing speeches at all.

"I'd forgotten that Officer Wang was supposed to give this speech today," Min said finally. "The problem is he's sick and can't do it."

For a minute, Min seemed uncharacteristically indecisive, but just for a minute. "I have an idea," he said, his smile returning. "You make this speech in Officer Wang's place, and I'll come with you to introduce you."

Jun felt she was struck by a thunderbolt. While she was relieved that the problem wasn't the speech itself, she'd never imagined herself standing in front of a group of soldiers and delivering an address to them.

"You wrote the speech, didn't you?" Min said, sensing her hesitation. "Just change it the way you need to make it your speech, and we'll get going." He called out to Little Yang to be ready to leave in half an hour. Jun went back to the speech right away. The idea of the day's event, scheduled on the anniversary of Madame Chiang's visit, was to plant saplings that she had sent to reforest the island. That didn't seem very complicated, and yet, Jun was frozen, seized by writer's block. By the time she got in the jeep with Min, she was on the verge of tears. But Min seemed oblivious. He told Little Yang to lower the jeep canopy, so as they cruised along the dirt path hugging the shoreline, they were pelted by the sand in the salty breeze rushing at them from the sea. Jun looked at the foamy chop, felt the wind tangling her short hair, sand mixed in it.

"Remember," Min said, "it was blustery like this when Madame Chiang arrived?" He looked at Jun. "Remember that cold wind? Remember the sand and the pebbles blowing into our eyes?" Jun nodded, still not getting the point. "Well," Min continued, "you go out there and tell those young soldiers to use their own hands to stop this wind by planting trees, to help make this island a friendlier place. Think of them as your brothers, or your students, restless for a good cause, and in your own words, capture their enthusiasm, unleash their youthful energy. That's all there is to it."

A few minutes later, Jun's calm was restored. She could feel the power of words inside her as she looked out from the stage at an entire battalion of soldiers. All of them so young, like her little brothers at home, like the students at her school. Min introduced her, and she plunged ahead, beginning with an act of blatant plagiarism.

"Remember that blustery day when Madame Chiang arrived on her visit to our island?" she said. "Remember the cold wind? Remember the sand and the pebbles that flew with the wind that day?" From there it was easy. They had the power to stop the wind, she told them. They could restore the natural environment that had been damaged in the war.

They were the ones who had brought peace to the island, and while they were keeping that peace, they could bring beauty and comfort as well. And when they grew old like the old farmers they saw on the island, when they counted the wrinkles on their hands, they would be proud to recall the good deeds their once youthful hands had done. In the end, their mission was not just to restore and keep peace but to help bring about a better life and a better world.

Jun thought she'd done pretty well for a first timer, but she was still startled by the thunderous applause that greeted her peroration. She froze for a moment behind the lectern, until Min stepped up to finish the ceremony. Many years later, from time to time they joked about Jun's debut as a public speaker, and Min would often tease her, "I should've known how good you'd be at plagiarism!"

In 1952, with the Korean War raging and the U.S. Seventh Fleet patrolling the Taiwan Strait, the Nationalists got some precious breathing room to consolidate their hold on the Penghu Archipelago. The chain, in which Jinmen was the largest link, was ten times closer to the Mainland than to Taiwan, and it had always been under the jurisdiction of Fujian Province. Now it was a special administrative zone and the most important defensive Nationalist outpost. Min's civilian operations were effecting a major transformation: new permanent structures were starting to obscure sleepy fishermen's homes; new roads were replacing old ones and extending further; defense systems continued to be perfected; reservoirs built; pieces of pristine beaches and land cordoned off, mined, and its shallows packed with sunken defensive obstacles to block any potential amphibious assault.

Jun became increasingly immersed in her work. She made more inspirational speeches, organized festivals and entertainment programs, took student performances to military bases, and introduced army officers when they spoke at schools. She loved it. She'd never felt so genuinely happy before.

But the situation with the Mainland was tense and intermittently dangerous. All during the 1950s, the Mainland from time to time carried out campaigns of artillery bombardment of Jinmen, Mazu, and the other offshore islands, all of it a mostly failed effort to force the Nationalists to abandon these outposts. At times, the shelling created a daily, terrifying part of life on Jinmen, and it made Jun's journey to the other islands especially hazardous, since the small boats in which she traveled had to venture within firing range of the Mainland's artillery. On one trip just before Christmas, Jun was on board with a few civilian and military officials as they motored from island to island making speeches and delivering mail and gifts. As they approached Mazu Island, artillery shells started exploding around their little boat. The civilians began loudly demanding that the party turn back, while the military men snickered at the sight of the civilians cringing and ducking for cover. The motorboat driver wouldn't retreat without a proper order, and so the boat continued to shoot forward. But when a shell landed right by the stern, it rocked the boat so violently that it almost dumped them all into the water, and the military officer in charge finally relented and ordered the boat to turn back. In an instant, the firing ceased. Nobody spoke. It was a lesson in the precarious reality of holding on to islands so close to the enemy's guns.

• • •

A large bouquet of flowers was on Jun's desk when she arrived at work one morning. "What's this?" she asked Little Yang.

"It's Officer Shen's birthday," he replied.

"That doesn't explain why there are flowers on MY desk."

"Mrs. Hu sent them to him, but he said he has no use for flowers so he asked me to put them on your desk instead." He was referring to the island's military commander General Hu Lien's wife.

At the end of the day, Jun was at the door to Min's office. The door opened before she had a chance to knock. "Oh," Jun said, a bit taken off guard. "Officer Shen!"

"Oh, please don't keep calling me 'Officer Shen,' now that we are old colleagues," Min said, inviting her to sit down and have some tea.

"You've turned me into a 'tea devil,'" Jun said, as tea lovers were known.

"We Chaozhou people were born 'tea devils,'" Min said, putting new tea leaves into a small earthenware teapot that he cradled in his hand. He put the little pot in his desk, poured in boiling water, and in a moment, handed Jun a porcelain cup of *kungfu* tea. It was a tea like no other, orangy, intense, a touch bitter with a lasting sweet aftertaste, and was taken in little sips. "In my hometown," he went on, "women cook and men make tea. But my wife used to make darn good tea."

"Your wife?" Jun didn't quite expect her own surprise.

"Yes." Min told her that he married a child bride when he himself was still very young. He and his wife had two boys together before he joined Huang Wei's army. In his last visit home, just before the troops left the Mainland for Taiwan, he had secured a divorce certificate, citing their lack of common ground, his wife being an illiterate country woman. He opened his wallet and showed a picture of a very handsome boy's face looking out from behind a transparent piece of plastic. "Yes, he's a good-looking devil. He's just fifteen," Min

said, and plunged deeper into his story. He was still a teen-
ager when he joined Huang Wei's army and quickly worked
his way up to become his chief adviser, later taking charge of
his military court. General Huang was captured at Xubang
when his tank became disabled. But Min had been lucky.
His tank, which had been following the general's, was able
to keep going, and he ended up among the small number of
officers who escaped that total defeat. After the battle, General Hu Lien was given the task of rebuilding the Twelfth
Army. He took over what remained of Huang Wei's men, and
kept Min by his side.

"And what do you think of the current situation?" Jun
asked, eager to know the situation at hand. "What's going to
happen here in Jinmen?"

Min took a long sigh. He clearly had mulled this over.
"The situation as it stands—keep it between you and me—the
standoff between the two sides is irreconcilable in every way,
ideologically and politically."

"But the Communists have such overwhelming manpower,
so much land, so many people, and we're so close to them.
Couldn't they easily overwhelm a little island like this?"

"Now, now," Min said, "and I don't mean to sound conde-
scending, but a military campaign is not exactly a numbers
game." Min was warming to the topic. He said that to understand the Communists' spectacular failure in the battle of
Guningtou you had to compare it to the D-Day operations on
the coast of France.

"The early morning of June 6, 1944."

"You know the exact date!"

"That's my birthday in the lunar calendar."

"Ah, we'll have to make up for not having your birthday
celebration for you then."

"Actually," he quickly corrected himself, "Guningtou should be compared to a lesser known operation, the Dieppe Raid, also called Operation Jubilee, that preceded Operation Overlord at Normandy." Almost every strategic aspect of that operation, he pointed out—the lack of a clear plan, the lack of a clear goal, the lack of decent preparation, and the lack of reinforcements—brought about disastrous outcomes. "The Communist attack on Guningtou suffered from all of those flaws. Even the way they lost the element of surprise was identical. In the Dieppe Raid, some of the Allied landing craft blundered into a small German convoy; in Jinmen, the PLA landing crafts were spotted by a Nationalist officer who was walking to the outhouse in the morning darkness. So both operations started in the face of murderous fire from the defending army. The Dieppe casualties were about two-thirds of the total attack force, and the PLA's loss here in Jinmen was even worse, more than twice the number of about 4,100 casualties at Dieppe."

"You've probably never even heard about the Dieppe Raid," Min continued. "It's because the British government was so embarrassed at their failure there that they kept it all quiet."

"Do you think Guningtou will go down in history as a D-Day or a Dieppe?"

"It depends on which side is telling the story. For the Mainlanders, Guningtou will most likely be like Dieppe, forgotten as quickly as possible, but for us, we'll make it our D-Day."

Min poured more tea, apologizing for getting into such detail about military matters, and Jun quickly remembered that she was there to wish him a happy birthday.

"No, no, no, enough of the birthday thing, let's talk about the here and now." Looking into Jun's eyes, Min said emphatically: "You and me."

Jun's cup seemed to suspend itself in midair. Min took the cup from her hand, put it on the desk, and came around it to sit down next to her. Min told her how much her presence had transformed things for him, starting from the very first time he met her, how her charm, her ability to brighten everything had touched his life and work in more ways than he could count. He turned in his chair so he was directly facing Jun.

"Will you marry me?" he said.

Jun's heart leapt. A torrent of emotions swept away all the protections that she had painstakingly constructed over the past months, protections against feeling too much or hoping at all, not after all of the disappointments that littered the trail leading to this moment. She came to the office every day eager to hear Min's voice, see him smile at her when he strode by, sit down for an occasional game of chess over *kungfu* tea. She couldn't count how many times he'd appeared in her dreams. And now, like a hurricane wind, his question and the expression on his face knocked down the emotional rampart she'd been guarding, and she couldn't answer him in words but only held up her hand in a futile effort to cover her sobs. Min reached out his hands and wrapped them around hers, the hold as kind and firm as that first handshake that Jun had never forgotten.

Jun could feel her heart shatter as she willed herself to utter the truth: "I'm married also," she said, "and I'm not divorced." She unburdened herself of the story of her marriage to Cai and how it had been a mistake, and when she was finished, she got up to leave, but Min's hands didn't release their hold on hers.

"Don't you see, my silly girl, don't you see that that marriage ceased to exist years ago, just like mine, and don't you see, there's no way back to the Mainland, for you or for me? Don't you see that we can build a life together, even on this barren island in the middle of nowhere? Don't you see that if we have each other we could do so much more and be so much happier?

"Stand up with me," Min said, reaching out for her. "Tell me we'll do it together, together for the rest of our lives. Stand by me."

Beyond the Hospital Walls

THE NEW HOSPITAL that Zhen helped found was the direct opposite of the prestigious missionary-founded Union Hospital where she started her medical career. Its couple of dilapidated buildings were hemmed in by old neighborhoods where muddy narrow streets and sticky alleyways were hidden under slices of tile roofs. Zhen opened the window, and in rushed the street hawkers' competing calls, neighborhood buzz and brawls, and impatient honks of cars trying to make their way through.

"You think you have many patients to see in the hospital? The majority of your patients are outside these walls." Xia Meiqiong, the attending physician, was talking to the doctors gathered around her, Zhen among them. Her words, cutting through the noise of this city center, were a revelation for Zhen. They remained a kind of mantra for the rest of her career.

It was 1954, and Zhen had just joined the brand-new Fujian Women and Children's Hospital to lead its gynecology department. For Zhen, the hospital, an expansion of a small local clinic, was one of the good things the Communists were bringing to China. She had been thrilled by the promulgation of a new marriage law, which prohibited concubinage, child betrothal, and interference in the remarriage of widows. The new law also guaranteed the free choice of partners, monogamy, equal rights for both sexes, and it called for respect for the old, and care of the young. Zhen believed that neither of her mothers had ever been truly happy in their marriages to her father, and she blamed that on the conditions of Old China, which, she felt, had been done away with by the Revolution. Now, the mother of a little girl, she felt a powerful inspiration to make sure that the New China would fulfill its promise.

Still, as her husband reminded her, Zhen's move from the prestigious Union Hospital to this new, much smaller place, which had none of the glamour or prestige of the Union Hospital, was completely different from what she'd always said she wanted to do. He reminded Zhen of her medical school admissions interview soon after VJ-Day in 1945. The school was still in the mountain town of Nanping, where major institutions were taking shelter from the Japanese bombardments. The two of them had gone in for their interviews on that same day, and when they met up again afterward, Zhen had told him how she had repudiated the idea of studying gynecology and obstetrics. "The chief interviewer was the president of the medical school," Zhen retold it to me decades later, "and he'd assigned me a specialization before I even showed up for my interview." Zhen told him she wanted to study internal medicine, but the interviewer said that would not be an option for a woman. And with that, he stood up and headed for the door.

Zhen stood up too and started speaking before the

interviewer had left the room. She demanded a better reason than her sex for his decision about what she would specialize in, and she made her case for internal medicine: Her grandmother was taken by a common cold; her older sister, Jun, almost died of malaria; her other siblings also had brushes with death because of perfectly treatable diseases or accidents when they lived in Nanping during the war. Had it not been for the foreign doctor whom her father had befriended, her family would not have been the same. In her entire life, Zhen told him, not one single occasion called for a gynecologist or obstetrician, so why should she concentrate on just that?

"Young lady," the interviewer had turned around to listen. "You're clearly very bright and very determined, but how will you convince your patients to trust a woman doctor?"

"With all due respect," Zhen responded, "how can anyone know how much peoples' attitudes will have changed in four or five years' time when we graduate? Moreover, if you think that female patients would trust a male ob-gyn doctor, why wouldn't they trust a woman internist as well? Even if men don't want to be treated by a woman doctor, there will always be plenty of women who will."

The interviewer looked into Zhen's eyes and said: "I hope you'll always stand by your convictions. Maybe you'll be right in four years' time. Give it a try then."

Zhen had fought for the right to study internal medicine. But now something other than personal preference was pushing her toward the gynecology and obstetrics, though this had nothing to do with what her medical school interviewer had told her. In the past year, with Dr. Xia's encouragement, she'd spent time in different departments, and it was in ob-gyn that she came face to face with social inequality. The delivery rooms were mostly filled by fee-paying cadres and educated social elites, but the gynecology ward was filled with underprivileged women, primarily from rural areas, often victims of neglect, mistreatment, and botched deliveries, if they were lucky enough to have survived them. She could do a lot to help poor women like these to gain an equal place in what was supposed to be a brand-new world, she believed.

Zhen, in embracing the specialization she had once rejected, took up Dr. Xia's challenge to look outside of the hospital walls for knowledge and inspiration. The new "Patriotic Health Campaign" was sweeping across the country then, and she learned from a survey conducted by the Fujian provincial government that two illnesses, gynecological fistula and uterine prolapse, were rampant, especially in China's rural areas, significantly reducing women's participation in building the new socialist country. She could do something practical and meaningful about that and make it her contribution to the government's new campaign. She organized a small medical team and set out to the county that was most heavily hit by these two diseases, Nan'an, about two hundred kilometers south of Fuzhou.

Gynecologic fistula was a rupture of the birth canal caused by a prolonged obstructed labor. It wasn't usually a life-threatening condition, but once the rupture occurred, it became impossible for the patient to keep herself clean. There were bad smells, which led to virtual ostracism. Arriving in Nan'an, Zhen met with a group of local Party activists eager to help, and she asked if they knew anybody who suffered from this condition.

Everyone did. These women were outcasts, they told Zhen. Nobody wanted to be near them because of their smell. Within hours, patients started to arrive. A steady trickle soon turned into a flood that spilled over to the school's auditorium. The medical team enlisted locals to help set up makeshift beds, sometimes with the door planks set on stools. Women volunteers held flashlights to make up for the lack of lighting. The operation to repair the damage involved sewing up the openings in the birth canal, and most cases were straightforward, not difficult to cure, though there were more severe cases involving additional surgery. As the head of the team, Zhen handled these more complicated cases and made decisions on which ones needed to be sent to Fuzhou's main hospital for further treatment. Soon, she began training local medical workers. The program was extended to two weeks.

One day, a young woman was brought to Zhen's attention. She was small and delicately built. She had a rather severe case of fistula, but her muscle tone was poor, and the doctor handling her case worried that her muscles could not sustain the extensive surgery that she needed. Zhen was discussing the case with the doctor when the husband of the patient came up to her, carrying a coffin on his back. "Doctor," he said, "she needs treatment, and you are our best hope. Please don't hesitate; do what you need to do."

The man poured out his heart: The couple had prayed to every god in every shrine they could find to be given a child, and when they found out that the woman was pregnant, they thought that their prayers had been answered. "Who would've known that our nine months of happiness was just a setup!" the man said, clearly believing that the gods were tricking him. The child, a boy, died at birth. "And now," the man said, "my wife is worse than a useless person: My family thinks she is bad luck, her family has disowned her, and meanwhile the house smells like a pigsty. I have neither time nor money to find treatment for her, and I'm exhausted to the bones, so you are our god of gods, and I beg you to save our lives." Saying that, the man laid down the coffin by his side and dropped to his knees, sobbing. Zhen hurriedly helped him up and in her measured tone, laid bare the truth: his wife needed extensive treatment, and she couldn't be confident of her full recovery.

"Do it, I beg you, operate the best you can. If anything happens, it's not your responsibility. I'll take it, we'll take it! I've come with the coffin. If anything happens to her, I'll take her home on my back!" Both he and his wife were sobbing by now. Zhen had nothing more to say. She took a deep breath trying to hold back her own emotions and turned to prepare the suture. She would do her best to fix her for now, she promised, and asked the couple to seek help in her hospital for follow-up treatments. This turned out to be one of the first of many cases that required many visits and sometimes years for Zhen and her team to treat and cure.

Every case of fistula was a heartbreaking story. After surviving a difficult delivery, the birthing mother would often have to mourn the baby that she had carried to full term yet never got to see alive, and adding to that tragedy, she herself would end up incontinent and rejected. Without anyone or anywhere to turn to, many women sought to end their lives to escape the humiliation. Some struggled to eke out a living as castaways in wayside huts just so that they could occasionally have a glimpse of their growing children, those that survived, passing by. And all of this because of an ailment that was usually completely treatable.

These tragedies had deep roots in the tradition of bias against women and girls, as Zhen quickly learned, a tradition that she had never known in what she understood more and more to be her own privileged urban life. When food was scarce in the countryside, the last mouthfuls would go to the man of the house and then the sons. The tradition of child brides led many girls to start having children before their bodies, often malnourished, were strong enough or mature enough to do so safely. And in the countryside where birthing was traditionally done at home, and where roads and transportation were primitive at best, any complications during childbirth—hemorrhage being the most common— could easily become fatal. In the case of fistula, the damage was lasting.

While fistula patients tended to be younger women, many of them first-time mothers, uterine prolapse patients were more often middle-aged women who'd had multiple births. In these cases, the woman's pelvic floor muscles and ligaments were weakened or overstretched, providing inadequate support for the uterus, which descended from its normal position, sometimes in more serious cases ending up outside of the body. This usually happened when a woman started to do strenuous physical work too soon after childbirth, before their bodies were fully healed. In many more serious cases, a woman might develop prolapse of other pelvic organs, including the bladder and rectum. These prolapses were almost always painful, and they could cause many related problems, from pain during intercourse to difficulty in urination and bowel movements to infections. The best way to ease the problem was to stop doing strenuous work like lifting and carrying heavy things, but this was a luxury many women in the villages could not afford. The medical intervention was to surgically tighten the muscles or to put in an artificial mesh for support.

One prolapse patient that Zhen treated on her first Nan'an trip was a robust middle-aged woman, with high cheekbones and dark, leathery skin. She entered the triage center, announcing in a loud voice that if she was cured, she would return home accompanied by a musical band. Of course no one really took this seriously. But when the surgery was pronounced successful, the woman put on a bright red skirt that she'd made for the occasion. "For more than ten years," she shouted, "I have never worn a skirt. From now on, I'll wear one on every warm day!" Then, as she thanked every- one on the medical team, a band materialized just as she'd promised, and struck up a riotous tune. The woman practi- cally danced her way out in a cheerful cacophony of cymbals, gongs, drums, and flutes. Exploding firecrackers trailing the band sent clouds of blue smoke into the air and rained a layer of shredded red paper on the ground.

Nan'an, the place where Zhen had her first treatment cen- ter, had a special place in my life also. It was my father's hometown, and therefore, according to the Chinese tradi- tion, my ancestral village. Aunt Zhen's trip there preceded my birth by almost a decade, but what she encountered in 1954 had not changed much by the late 1960s, when I first arrived there as a five-year-old. It was the height of the Cultural Revolution, and my parents, young college professors, were sent to different far-flung villages to be re-educated, as were many of their educated peers. Unable to care for me, they deposited me in my paternal grand- mother's home in Nan'an, before they set out on their separate exiles to their respective remote villages. Grand- mother was a compact but strong woman with bound feet. When she learned from the kindergarten teachers that I knew all the words that they were teaching, she kept me at home to do chores, like collecting animal droppings for fertilizer and gleaning the fields for sweet potatoes and peanuts after the harvest. That year, I was always hungry. I would stare at the few pieces of meat we had when there was any, but rarely got permission to eat any of them. My mother was brokenhearted when she was able to return to Nan'an at the end of the year and saw me, shrunken and with a distended belly, and she swore that she would never allow me to set foot in that place again.

My mother took the emaciated me straight from Nan'an to her sister Zhen for her advice, which was simply to give me plenty of love and healthy food. My stunted look must have brought back Zhen's memories of her time in that same village. Zhen had been trained to fix problems of the body, and at the end of that first trip, she realized that she held even more than people's health on her hands. For every case she treated, she was curing a woman of a terrible, life-destroying, yet curable affliction, and at the same time she was also repairing a hole in a social web, enabling women to remain in the family fold, to return to their moorings and to have normal lives again. But she also saw that her own power and skill only went so far. When her patients would learn of Zhen's own smooth birth and her healthy girl, some would marvel at her good fortune and see hope for themselves, but others would resign themselves to the fact that they and Zhen lived in different worlds that had not intersected since time immemorial. Zhen believed that changing their lot required something beyond the will of any individual or family. It would take the determination of the new government to put an end to feudal ways and reverse the tides of history. Zhen saw herself through the eyes of her patients: the leader of the first medical team tending exclusively to women's bodies and their problems, and, along with the new marriage law, giving them the hope that they could live their lives with real choices and good prospects.

• • •

After Nan'an, Zhen went routinely on trips to the countryside, setting up temporary makeshift clinics where there had never been one, treating what she called the "two ailments," gynecologic fistula and uterine prolapse. In 1955, she took time off for the birth of her second daughter, Hu Wen. Now a mother of two baby girls, she saw campaigning for women's health as a matter of personal urgency. During Zhen's first tour of villages, her team treated more than one hundred cases in a single month, and not one single *yuan* changed hands. When healed, these women were able to work on land that, thanks to the government's extensive rural reform, most poor peasants owned for the first time. "You gave me a second life," her patients would say to her on her return visit, and Zhen understood that being a doctor for them—helping them regain their ability to contribute to their family's income and thus reclaim their status and voice in their families—had been her destiny after all. Treating these women also gave perspective on and meaning to her own life, and it was, in her view, a great achievement of the Communist Party.

Zhen documented the progress and inspirations of these early social changes in her 2015 memoir, written in celebration of her ninetieth birthday with family, colleagues, and friends. In her slim 135-page book, packed with intricacies and technicalities of her achievements in medical practice, there was no hint of the nationwide tragedy unfolding throughout her countryside tours.

In order to bring about the land reform in the early 1950s, landowners across the country had been stripped of their property, their livelihoods, and for many, their lives. The poor peasants were mobilized to denounce their former "exploiters," rejoicing in the ownership of the land that they tilled, without having to pay a share of what they produced to their landlords. In practice, this often meant the violent, ideologically-driven persecution of people who were sometimes only slightly better off than the rest. It was an enactment of Mao's theories of class struggle. Zhen bore witness to the rural poor's chance to make their livelihoods, but she did not seem to see or recognize the traumas or the tragedies experienced by modest property owners across the country, stripped of ancestral possessions and the fruit of considerable hard labor. Zhen focused as she always had on her work. She had formed a habit of knowing only what she deemed necessary for her to know, and telling just as much (or as little). Did she close her eyes to the "struggle sessions" aimed at class enemies, which resulted in the deaths of an untold number of the landlord class—estimated between one and five million people over four years, between 1949 and 1953? We may never know; Zhen showed no intention of reliving any of that.

Zhen, like the majority of the urban elite, remained oblivious to the systemic causes of suffering in the faraway villages. The New China was then starting its First Five Year Plan, an economic model copied from the Soviet Union setting agricultural and industrial production quotas. As part of the plan, peasants who had gotten ownership of land in the early days of the revolution were soon forced to contribute it to vast nationalized farms in the collectivization of agriculture. And from these collectivized farms, the government would extract the agricultural surpluses at artificially depressed prices to fuel the ambitious visions of industrialization in the cities. Within a few short years, this would bring about utter calamity in the countryside, including the worst man-made famine in twentieth-century history.

What city dwellers like Zhen witnessed between 1953 and 1957 was one of the most ambitious technology transfers in modern time. In an economic plan transplanted from Stalin's Soviet Union to Mao's China, Zhen saw the Communist Party fulfilling its promise to the urban proletariat. The plan called for China to build 694 large- and medium-sized industrial projects in five years, 156 of them to be funded with Russian aid. Accompanying this collaboration was a vast personnel exchange: 38,000 Chinese were sent to the Soviet Union for training and study, 28,000 of them as technicians for key industries; and 11,000 Soviet scientists and technicians were dispatched to China.

For Zhen and many other urbanites, this meant a rapid improvement in their material lives. Food became cheap and plentiful and opportunities expanded as a workforce was trained to participate in a more industrialized and advanced society than China had ever known before. The Chen family's faith in education was paying off, and the older children in particular, with better educations, were starting to benefit from these social changes.

The oldest of Zhen's half-siblings, Hou and his younger sister, Xiang (my mother) attended Fujian Province's best university, Xiamen University (Xiada), four years apart. Both studied Russian as their mandatory foreign language. When Hou graduated with a chemical engineering degree, he was chosen to undergo two years of intensive Russian-language training in Harbin, a major city near the border. The program would be followed by specialized training in the Soviet Union. Hou was chosen on merit and potential for this prestigious program, but when he finished his language training, he was barred from going to Russia for further technical study. His political background check, a rigorous process of vetting for anyone leaving the country, had revealed that he had a sister in Jinmen, which was Nationalist-controlled enemy territory.

Hou, who had always been a bookworm and had no interest in events outside his window, felt that his whole career—all that he had fought so hard to achieve in the past six long years—had been hijacked by politics at the last minute, just when his big dream was to become reality: going abroad, to Russia, and to study what he loved and what he was good at. How did his loving and caring big sister turn into an enemy who had so cruelly broken his dream? He was still in a fog of confusion at this sudden turn of events when he went to see his classmates off. He had wanted to watch the train switch tracks at the border, but he had not prepared for the sense of loss and desolation when the train pulled out and headed north without him. He stood there, all alone, until the stationmaster came to clear the platform. He remembered a deep sense of loss, and he remembered the added sadness when he realized that big sister Jun's image in his memory had already started to blur.

Many agonizing weeks of political studies later, Hou's unique qualifications—his technical specialty plus his knowledge of both English and Russian—were recognized by the leadership, and he was assigned to work with Russian experts in founding China's first Institute of Metallurgy in Shanghai. Things turned out well for Hou, but the sense of the cost of his divided family stayed with him.

Zhen was nursing baby Hu Wen when she opened the mail and learned that she had gotten a coveted award, one only given to a rising star like herself—a yearlong fellowship at the Xiangya Hospital in Hunan Province. Xiangya was founded in 1914 by American missionaries associated with the Yale-China Association, and over the years it had developed a reputation for providing the most advanced training in Western medicine in all of central and southern China. But for Zhen, the fellowship offer made for a hard choice: Going to Hunan meant leaving Fujian, her young daughters, and her work on the "two ailments." What should she do?

She was contemplating this choice on one of those days when both of her girls were crying, each egging on the other, and just as Zhen was at her wits' end, she heard a knock on the door. Her husband Xizhong opened it and, to her amazement, Zhen saw a middle-aged woman with a broad smile and cheeks red from a life in the fields, march into their home and their lives. The woman put down her bedroll and an additional bundle tied up with a large scarf and plunged straight into the confusion of frantic parents and crying babies. "Here!" she said, reaching her strong arms for the screaming baby, "let me calm her down."

Soon, as peace and calm descended, Zhen and Xizhong learned the reason for the woman's surprising appearance. Amah, as the family later came to call her—it's the common way to call a family helper—was from Nan'an, where Zhen had treated her daughter for fistula. The daughter had made a full recovery. But while she waited at Zhen's triage center there, Amah had seen that Zhen was pregnant. Now, figuring that the baby must have arrived, she decided to come to help. "It took me no time to find you!" she declared proudly. That was testament to Zhen's growing fame.

Amah was a godsend. Zhen and Xizhong fought to pay her for her help, but she always refused. "You gave me back my daughter, and now you want to pay me for caring for your baby?" she would say, forcing Zhen and Xizhong to strategize putting a salary for her into a special account so that they could give it to her in a lump sum as a New Year's present. Meanwhile, the two small girls took to Amah as they never did to anyone before, even to their own parents, and Amah very soon became a celebrity in the yard of the hospital's apartment complex. She was bright and resourceful, even though she was illiterate. She could produce a great meal with the simplest ingredients. She taught Hu Yi and her playmates how to make interesting things out of sticks, pieces of rock, or broken tiles and mud. All Zhen could do in return was to read Amah's daughter's letters to her and in the process teach her the Chinese characters in them. She also enjoyed sharing Amah's delight in learning that her family back home continued to do well. Most important, Amah's appearance and the wonderful calming effect she had on Zhen's hectic life enabled her to make her decision about the fellowship in Hunan. She decided to take it.

The trip to Hunan took three days and two nights on two long-distance buses and two trains, but once Zhen was there, she threw herself into things in her usual energetic way. Staying busy also kept her homesickness at bay, though she sometimes woke up in the middle of the night having heard her girls' cries in her dreams. Being away deepened her love for Hu Xizhong, whose regular letters kept her informed of doings on the home front. She missed the poker face he managed when he made her laugh, the way he looked more serious the funnier he got. She thought a lot of his calm and gentle voice, his unhurried tone, and the good advice she got from him. She felt that she was thriving in the New China and that it was Xizhong's trust and respect for her and his abiding love that enabled her to do it.

Zhen also got letters from Xiang—now a sophomore at Xiamen University. Zhen was very happy that her half-sister would get a degree, with tuition and room and board all paid for by the state, a goal that she had set out to reach years before. Back when their father had just died and the family was on the brink of starvation, Zhen remembered how Xiang helped the family during the day and studied late into the night, often on an empty stomach. She had explained to Zhen then that if she failed to get into Xiada, she would be just another mouth to feed, maybe at best earning a pittance by doing odd jobs. But she wanted something better for herself, and for the family. Now, Xiang was finally thriving in college, Zhen was gratified to see, starting on a path to a better life.

Xiang's letters came at one of the times when the Mainland rained shells on the Nationalist-held offshore islands, of which Jinmen was the largest. Her half-sister Jun weighed on Xiang's heart when she told Zhen in the letter how she could hear the boom of the artillery and see the smoke rising from Jinmen, just a mile away across the water. There were some very tense days in 1954 and 1955 when the bombing was especially intense, and Xiang watched through binoculars from the hilltop house of a friend, writing to Zhen of how queasy she'd felt, thinking of Jun there where the shells were landing.

Zhen knew of Xiang's love for her big sister, but she also knew, given the political danger that Jun represented to the Mainland family, that no sisterly sentiment could be allowed to weaken the separation; Jun had to remain cut off. Zhen was determined that the family would thrive in the New China, and the only way for that to happen was for all of them to move on with as little baggage from the past as possible. But that didn't mean forgetting.

Zhen forgot nothing. She didn't forget her first emergency case, which she recalled to me over half a century later, a seventy-three-year-old woman with a heart rate of 115, blood pressure 155/95, temperature 37.5, and oxygen saturation 89% on 4L via nasal cannula who arrived at the hospital at 5:45 a.m. on a flatbed handcart. It was the very day that Jun left for her interview and vacation, and Zhen didn't forget that she was wearing one of the *qipaos* that they used to share in Nanping. Their mother had made it for them. It was hard not to get sentimental, but as the oldest sister for all her siblings and half-siblings on the Mainland, Zhen couldn't afford sadness or regret, because the family's ties to Jun carried a real existential threat. One slip could compromise the future for her siblings and for herself, ruin what they had achieved so far. Zhen wanted to take the family as far away as she could from their near starvation in the years following their father's death in 1952.

Arriving in Taiwan

THE SPRING MORNING in the late fall of 1953 was calm, the mist over Jinmen Island thinning in the rising sun, and the Mainland cannons that would usually have begun their daily bombardment so far silent. It was a good beginning to a big day. Jun and Shen Min were about to board a military plane for the main island of Taiwan, bringing Jun's accidental three-year-plus exile on Jinmen to an end. They were now married, their wedding presided over by General Hu Lien and his wife, and they knew there wasn't much of a future on Jinmen, where, as Min liked to put it, they would spend their days "waiting either for an enemy that would never come, or for re-enforcements that would never get there in time." After over a decade as an officer in the Nationalist Army, Min was, at the age of thirty-four, eager to do something else.

They had packed one suitcase each. There was not much they wanted to bring; they yearned for a fresh start. The engine's roar was deafening, and Jun clenched her husband's hand. Before it headed out to Taiwan Island, the plane first went west toward the Mainland, giving Jun a view of Xiamen below: an island about the same size as Jinmen but, in Jun's eyes, much more developed and populated. Clusters of grand buildings here and there glistened with green tile roofs. Its tree-lined streets resembled rivulets. On Xiamen Island was Fujian Province's best university, which her half-siblings Hou and Xiang had aspired to attend. Jun counted the years: Hou must be graduating right about this time—she had never doubted Hou's ability to get in. She wondered, too, whether her younger half-sister, Xiang, had followed him. The famed campus was now just beneath her, as the plane started to bank. Jun followed the plane's direction and cast her last look beyond the Xiamen Island toward the North—home, somewhere amid the endless stretch of velvety green, fading into a horizon of shimmering mist. The plane completed the turn, pulled away from the land and headed over the sea, stretching east.

Taiwan Island was said to resemble a leaf adrift on the edge of the Pacific vastness. That's where the new couple would make their life, like the many others who had fled from the Mainland. Nobody knew exactly how many Mainlanders there were, but at least 1.2 million soldiers and civilians, possibly a good deal more.

After a half hour or so, the plane bumped down on what seemed to be a bald spot bordered by the sea on three sides. They were picked up by a military jeep taking them to the barracks that would be their temporary quarters. Jun rolled down the window, and was instantly assaulted by noise—construction, traffic, and simple human voices merging into a sort of persistent hum, punctuated by a honk or a bang somewhere. This was already so different from the daily Communist shelling of Jinmen, each explosion shattering the usual rural quiet of the place. Turning north, they could see

Yangmingshan Mountain guarding the northern tip of the island. It felt like a buffer, something that made the city safe. And it did seem safe, with the milling, untroubled crowds on the wide streets going about their affairs. These were people who had not experienced the bombing, never known the way it dictated day-to-day life.

Jun and Min both wanted a normal, civilian life. And in 1953, Taipei was as close to normal as they could find, even though, four years after the Nationalist defeat in China's civil war, its normality was of a nervous and fraught kind. Among the flood of refugees, several hundred thousand were, like Shen Min himself, former officers and soldiers who had followed Chiang Kai-shek into this collective exile. To them, their situation was intended to be temporary. Chiang's Nationalist rallying cry was, as the slogan put it, "Recover the Mainland!"—to return home in triumph someday, defeating the Bandit Mao and restoring the Gimo, as Chiang was called, to rightful power.

For the Nationalists, the past was on the Mainland, the present was about securing their control of Taiwan, and the future about returning to the past.

Not long after arriving at their officers' quarters in Taipei, Jun and Min went to a Christmas reunion party at the Presidential Palace. Jun was invited because of her role in the Anti-Communist and Resist Russia Union on Jinmen, and Shen Min as a high-ranking military officer.

Jun was thrilled by this official affirmation of her work performance. Christmas music played by a military band in dress uniform struck Jun as somewhat odd, but it was the political implications of the honor—the reason that she was

invited—that made her a bit uneasy. The honor, she understood, would be her induction into the Nationalist establishment. But what she'd done on Jinmen was more personal
than political, she simply wanted to fight for better opportunities for herself. At each turn, she took the opportunity
to advance herself, using the skills that she had. It had never
been a conscious political choice. Unbeknownst to her, on
the Communist Mainland, her sister Zhen had adopted a sort
of mirror image of the same strategy.

Ever a history buff, Jun knew Taiwan's past; she even knew
something about the Presidential Palace where the party was
held. Its first resident was the governor-general sent by the
Empire of Japan. The Japanese had seized Taiwan from Chinese control in 1895 and governed it as Japanese territory
until the end of World War II, when it once again became
part of China.

But there was a hole in Jun's knowledge of Taiwan's recent
history. In 1947, when it had become clear to the Nationalist
leaders that the civil war on the Mainland was going badly,
they began arranging a mass migration to Taiwan. But there
was already another population there, some six million people, mostly earlier migrants from the coastal Mainland and a
smaller number of indigenous islanders. These people, who
often referred to themselves as the native Taiwanese, had
their own dialect and native languages, incomprehensible to
the arriving Mandarin speakers. They had experienced a half-
century of Japanese colonial control, often speaking Japanese
better than they spoke Mandarin, and they tended to see the
million or so arriving Nationalist loyalists and soldiers as a
new kind of foreign invasion. The newly arriving Mainlanders
were indeed brutal in the way they imposed themselves on the
population already there. In a series of incidents beginning

on February 28, 1947, Nationalist troops massacred hundreds of members of the educated local elite, political figures, businessmen, teachers, and other professionals. Even when the killing was over, the Nationalists continued to rule with an iron fist. Martial law was declared and strictly enforced for the next forty years. Military service was mandatory. Political prisoners, most of them local Taiwanese, were shipped away to a volcanic atoll called Green Island, about thirty-three kilometers from the eastern shore of Taiwan.

Jun didn't arrive on Taiwan until well after the worst of the Nationalist repression, which may be among the reasons she never questioned the legitimacy or the necessity of the Nationalists' iron-fisted rule over the island. She was part of the Mainland migration. The government's call to build a "Free China" on Taiwan resonated with her, and for the rest of her life, she would always believe that the Taiwan that she'd embraced was just that, a democratic alternative to the Communist dictatorship back home.

And so, when Jun walked the streets newly named after Mainland cities—Shanghai Road, Fuzhou Road, Nanjing Road, Xiamen Street—she shared the nostalgia for the homeland of her fellow displaced Mainlanders. In other street names, like *Renai-lu*—Benevolence and Love Road—or *Xinyi-lu*—Trust and Righteousness Road—she found her Confucian values. Even the smells that wafted through those streets—of Sichuan hot sauce or northern peppers—enhanced the feeling that she lived in temporary exile from the vast homeland across the water. And the banners hung over these renamed streets and strung from lamp posts and buildings—Recover the Mainland! Hunt down Bandit Mao!—she saw as logical features of Taiwan's identity.

Jun didn't know many people at the Christmas party,

certainly none personally, but she did get to shake the First Lady's hand. Min, by contrast, seemed to know many of the other guests, including the most powerful of them. But Jun noticed that he also seemed quite familiar with a different group in that glamorous company, a few beautiful women who had been widowed during the war and who now were at the center of Taipei's high society. There was one in a shimmering *qipao* who had been among the hottest singers in Shanghai, Min told her. There was a certain Mrs. Liao, the widow of a lieutenant general who died, like many Nationalist officers, in the last battles of the war. Mrs. Liao made herself up to dazzle, and she did: her hairpins holding her elaborate hairdo in place, her bright red dress gliding gracefully across the marble floor, her oval face framed by earrings that showed off her bejeweled neck. When she invited Jun and Min to a party at her house the following month, Jun nodded to Min with her consent. She was eager to see the life behind the glitter.

The date of the party arrived. Jun put on her best white silk *qipao*, though she was acutely aware of her lack of jewelry. The taxi dropped them in front of a white columned mansion. Inside the grand reception room were women in beautiful silk dresses and men in military dress uniforms. Mrs. Liao greeted them with outstretched arms laden with clinking bracelets.

Again Jun saw that Min was well known and popular inside this smart set. But it wasn't until the name "Lulu" was mentioned that Jun sensed a twinge of unease on Min's part. "Did Mrs. Liao tell you that Lulu might show up later tonight?" a certain Mrs. Hua asked Min, her cigarette unspooling green smoke from slim fingers tipped with red polish. "Lulu!" another once popular Shanghai singer named Yueyuan exclaimed, overhearing the question. Min, then regaining his composure, took Jun's hand, and explained things to her: Lulu and Yueyuan were among the few sought-after singers in the old Shanghai days, just as Mrs. Hua had been herself. Min, it turned out, to Jun's surprise, had written lyrics for some of their songs. They called Min their "poet general." Lulu was particularly close to Min, and the two had talked of furthering their relationship before the Nationalist final retreat. Evidently, they never met up again before Min's rushed retreat, and in the meantime, Jun had entered the picture. But Jun didn't care what Min's relationship with Lulu may have been. Lurking behind all this glitz, she was coming to see, were unexpected twists and turns not all that different from the ones her own life had taken. Oddly, it was this realization that made her suddenly feel that she fit in with this crowd, despite her complete lack of finery. She had something in common with all of these glamorous women. All of them had been separated in one way or another. She held Min's arm tightly and smiled.

As if on cue, a musician playing an *erhu*, a two-string instrument, pulled out a melody of rich tones, wafting and undulating in the air. A zither joined in a moment later, spilling a quick succession of notes. Then a loud strike of a gong cracked out of nowhere, unleashing a series of crisp clicks on a wooden box resembling quick steps moving out to the stage.

Life on earth is like spring dreams
Let's open our hearts and take in a few drinks
人生在世如春梦
奴且开怀饮数盅

Mrs. Hua began, warming up her voice with a famous aria from *Noble Concubine Drunk on Wine,* a traditional opera.

When the accompanying music subsided, a lone voice rose from the other end of the hall, pure and soft:

> *The tips of the Li Palace pierce the clouds in the azure sky*
> *Heavenly tunes riding the wind travel far and wide*
> 骊宫高处入青云
> 仙乐风飘处处闻

This must be Lulu, Jun thought. Slim and delicate, silky black hair draped over a turquoise *qipao*, she had announced her arrival with the opening lyrics of the *Palace of Eternal Youth*, among the most famous of the classic Chinese operas. It tells the tragic love story of a Tang dynasty emperor and his favorite concubine. Blamed for the fall of the capital, the concubine had to be killed in front of the emperor before the army was willing to fight to regain the empire. Jun had committed the poem to memory long ago, but she'd never heard it sung, and sung so beautifully:

> *Shaking the earth, the battle drums from Yuyang rumbled*
> *The rainbow robes scattered and gossamer gowns tumbled*
> 渔阳鼙鼓动地来
> 惊破霓裳羽衣曲

Jun watched as Lulu acknowledged the applause, noticing also that she seemed to freeze when she noticed Min, the arm she'd been waving suspended in the air. Min, who saw it too, wrapped his arm around Jun's waist and walked with her toward Lulu. He introduced Jun and the three exchanged niceties. A thin smile soon returned to Lulu's face, masking her momentary loss of composure.

Jun understood something about the Nationalist elite that

night, the sense of loss that they felt, the formerly powerful now exiled on Taiwan. In the lyrics written a century before, telling the story of a former capital city fallen to enemies, and of an emperor's forced sacrifice of his love, these singers sang of their own pains. Jun also learned a great deal about her husband, the "poet general," that night, among his glamorous widow friends at Mrs. Liao's party, with their old Shanghai gossip, their recreation of parties past, and the poignant songs that made the whole island feel like a stage set.

Taipei reeked of that sort of nostalgia. The city was full of saloons and nightclubs blasting music and songs from the old Shanghai. Parties ran around the clock, revelers and socialites dancing and drinking with the hedonism of people not sure if there would be a tomorrow. Just like the old Shanghai, Min told his wife. Jun had never been to Shanghai, but she was skeptical about the comparison. If this was Shanghai, she told Min, it was an ersatz Shanghai, a city without a soul. The façade might be similar, but these night scenes emanated anger and something close to hysteria. It was a kind of desperate effort to reproduce the imagined *dolce vita* of Old China, but it wasn't the real thing.

Mrs. Liao's party was also Jun's last encounter with Min as Shanghai poet general. The couple was soon caught up in practical tasks, the first of which was to leave their temporary military quarters and find a permanent home. In those early days of the Nationalist migration, the standard housing was what was called *kenanfang*, literally the "overcoming-difficulties-housing," which was just a step up from a refugee camp. Luckily, Jun and Shen Min had silver dollars in severance pay that enabled them to afford something a little bit better, an apartment in a cluster of simple, newly constructed buildings, sought after by people with some modest means.

The couple rented a two-room unit, a bedroom and what they decided on calling a "development room"—for an office at first, and for the children that Jun knew she wanted to have.

But before she had a chance to talk to her husband about her dream of motherhood, Shen Min showed her a letter that he had just received from a distant cousin living in Pingdong, a town on the southern tip of Taiwan. The letter informed him that his older son, Guanting, had fled from the Mainland and had arrived at his cousin's home.

Suddenly, instead of dreaming about having her own child, all Jun could think of was the teenage boy that she had never met, who would now, inevitably, become part of her life. She felt deeply clashing feelings, marital and moral responsibility on one side, envy and a touch of self-pity on the other. What kind of new family would they now have with a teenage son who was a stranger?

Shen Min wanted to hop on the train to Pingdong the next day. Jun, collecting herself, decided that she would go to meet the boy together with her husband. And so, instead of a honeymoon, which they had never planned to have anyway, the couple took the train south, down the length of the island, passing fertile farmland and thick forests. At times, the train skirted the lacy edges of the sea and flew over breathtaking gorges. Farmers, cowherds, and cattle flashed by, as did small hamlets and bursts of wildly colorful vegetation.

Now settled into their seats, Min, who had told Jun only a few basic facts about his first marriage and his sons, tried to comb through his fraught relationship with his boys and the convoluted, morally tricky events that took place in the days before the Communist takeover of the Mainland.

During his years in the Nationalist Army, Min saw his sons a grand total of three times: once when he returned to his hometown, Chaozhou, for his father's funeral, another time when one of his underlings sought to curry favor with him by bringing the whole family, mother and boys, to Shanghai, where Min was stationed. Decades later, Shen Min's younger son would recount in a memoir how his father that month installed his family at a friend's house in a Shanghai suburb and took out an ad in a local newspaper to announce his divorce, citing as the reason a lack of common interests with his unlettered spouse. At the time in China, a husband could legally divorce by simply announcing his wish to do so, a gesture called *xiuqi*, "resting the wife."

The third and last time was after his narrow escape from the Twelfth Army's defeat in what the Communists called the Huaihai Campaign—called the Xubang Campaign by the Nationalists—a major confrontation that spelled the eventual doom of the Nationalists. Min returned to his hometown, Chaozhou, where, to maintain the appearance of normal family life, he occupied the front of their house while the boys stayed with their mother in the main living quarters at the back.

It was the waning days of Nationalist rule, and Min was swept up into the raging finale of the civil war. The Nationalist Twelfth Army, led by its new leader General Hu Lien, had arrived in the area, and he recruited Min to rejoin as his chief of staff.

"I had to send for the boys at school that very day," Min now told Jun on the train. "Once I reenlisted, I was sworn to secrecy as to my whereabouts. I was sure that I would lose communication with them."

Hu Lien's Twelfth Army, Min quickly learned, was an empty shell, having been decimated in earlier battles, and Min, a seasoned leader well connected in the region, was an indispensable asset in rebuilding it. At the time, he was certainly in a good position to request that his own family, and especially his sons, be allowed to accompany the Twelfth Army as it shipped out, and, if he had done that, the boys would most likely have been able to accompany their father when he was dispatched to Jinmen.

But that's not what happened. After summoning his sons from school, Min sat them down and described the rapidly changing situation: The Communists were winning and it might only be days before he would have to leave the area with the Nationalist Army. But exactly when he would leave and where he would go, he had no idea; he would not be able to tell them even if he did.

The second thing he said was that as far as he knew, the Communists would observe their own slogan, "Work will ensure a living." They were against exploitation, Min said. Therefore, he wanted the boys to do two things: study hard and work hard to earn both a living and the new government's trust. No matter what, he said, the Communists were Chinese. They could not possibly be worse than the Japanese invaders. Both boys, he said, needed to improve their embarrassing grades. As they were now, he said, they wouldn't be able to make a living no matter who was in power.

Guanxiu, the younger boy, was almost twelve then. For him, to learn that he would be losing his father, again, was a crushing blow. Tears flowed down his cheeks. He had been so proud to be the son of the man from whom everyone sought help. Now, everything was uncertain, except, of course, that his father was about to disappear from his life, leaving him behind with his divorced mother, his bad grades, and the Communists, whom he didn't know.

"You are young," Min told his sons, attempting to comfort them. "Most likely the Communists will leave you in peace, at least until you're eighteen years old. You still have the chance to work hard and recreate yourself, and be worthy of the Shen family."

And those were his last words to his children. He soon left with the Twelfth Army, ending up as the civilian commander of the Nationalist forces on Jinmen, making its successful last stand, while his sons stayed behind in Chaozhou, cut off from all contact. He told Jun on the train that something extraordinary must have taken place back home for Guanting to have risked his life to escape from the Mainland and to seek him out.

Jun examined her husband. He looked different in civilian clothes, she thought, softer and more handsome. His military uniform—a memory now—had always felt to Jun like a wall, a partition that shut off the real, feeling person from everyone around him, and now the loose civilian clothes seemed to be bringing out that real person. Min was no longer giving orders or speeches. Now he had doubts and uncertainties, and he spoke of them. She knew that it wasn't going to be easy for them or for his son, who was about to meet a father who had left him to face his fate on his own, whom he hardly knew, and who would be arriving with a new wife.

"Guanting was the more easygoing of the boys," Min said of his older son. "He wouldn't have made the decision to escape lightly." Jun squeezed her husband's hand and they lapsed into silence. Then she heard him murmur, as much to himself as to her: "I can't afford to lose him again."

• • •

Guanting was called from outside into his cousin's house when Jun and Min arrived. He ran toward them and came to an abrupt halt in front of them. Jun noticed that he stood almost as tall as Min, but his features were more delicate. He had the same penetrating round eyes on the familiar round face. The front of his thick, jet-black hair ruffled by the wind stood tangled for a moment before it softly fell back onto the wide, clear forehead. Out of breath from his dash into the house, he seemed lost for words, or stunned by disbelief, or perhaps he was just unaccustomed to saying "father."

"Guanting, you've grown." His father broke the silence, patting his son's shoulder, and smiling his warm smile. Still examining his father with his big round eyes under the shock of hair, Guanting took a breath. To Jun, he seemed composed beyond his years.

Min introduced Jun. "You'll have plenty of chances to get to know each other," he said, "But first, why don't you and I go for a walk, just the two of us."

When they returned to the house, Min announced that Guanting would stay where he was for the time being. He and Jun would return to Taipei right away, and they would summon the boy once they had made arrangements for him.

"The kid has seen too much," Min said when he and Jun were settled into their seats on the return train, "and much of it is because of his connection to me." From the bits and pieces that Min had been able to coax out of his son, he put Guanting's story together as best he could.

Not long after Min left Chaozhou with Hu Lien's troops, both of the boys joined their classmates as they lined the road welcoming the People's Liberation Army. The banners that the PLA soldiers were waving said: "Liberate the whole of China! Take Chiang Kai-shek alive!" "Take Hu Lien alive!" But while they were ready to show support for the new regime, their situation soon became confusing and contradictory. In the days right after the takeover, the boys were invited to join their school team in the Communist effort to eradicate illiteracy. Guanxiu, the younger boy, was especially excited to teach poor villagers how to read and write. He even organized local shows—dramatic skits and snippets of local opera—to generate enthusiasm for learning to write.

But things soured quickly. One day when the brothers, along with their entire school, were in their auditorium learning to sing, "Without the Communist Party there would be no New China," they saw the Party leader coming in their direction. He was with one of their teachers. He pointed out Guanxiu and Guanting, who were quickly led onto the stage where the whole auditorium turned against them. The boys understood: They had been made targets to be "struggled against" for the gathering. Their closest friends, and even their cousins stood up and shouted accusations: "Your father is a Nationalist counter-revolutionary, Chiang Kai-shek's running dog, and he is right now holing up in Taiwan to fight against the people!" "You're the sons of the people's enemy!" "Mercy to the enemy is cruelty to the people!" A little girl started to say that Guanting had scolded her when she forgot a word that he was teaching her, but before she was able to finish, she started to sob. When the verbal denunciations were over, the Party leader gestured for a few strong students to come up the stage. They started to kick and hit the brothers. In a few minutes, both were bloodied. The Party leader then announced that the brothers were no longer allowed to participate in revolutionary activities.

Before they returned home, Guanting, the older of the two, told Guanxiu to clean himself up before entering the house, so that their mother wouldn't see what had happened. But Guanxiu was filled with fury and confusion—at his friends' betrayal, at his father's departure, at his rejection by everyone, all while he was trying so hard to be good. He'd done what his father had told him to do, followed the Party's instructions, shown enthusiasm in the literacy campaign. At the age of twelve, he couldn't have known that he was being used as a kind of prop, so that Maoist class struggle could take place. He didn't know that his friends and cousins had been instructed to play their roles in the struggle session until a few days later, when those same friends, trying to resume their friendship, explained it to him. But more struggle sessions took place, especially after the Korean War broke out in 1950. The revolutionary fervor whipped up to purify the ranks soon spread through the village.

Their own mother became a victim too. She had taken in some of Guanxiu and Guanting's classmates during the time of war and civil war when famine had threatened their region and fed them. Now she was accused in village-wide sessions of exploiting these same boys. Guanting knew the truth. Like him and Guanxiu, the other boys did some chores around the house, and now some of these boys were hurling false accusations against their mother! More damning than the crime of exploitation was the accusation that their mother had received money from Min, even after Communists had liberated the village. All three—mother and sons—were declared enemies of the people.

And then came the most horrible and gruesome incident, the last straw for Guanting. Before he'd left Chaozhou, Min had helped a young Communist activist being sought by the local Nationalist strongman to escape to Hong Kong. This should have been deemed a good thing, especially since the boy's father, a man named Shen Shituan, unrelated to Min's family, had donated money to local Communist Party organizations, so that for a while the family was given the glorious designation of "revolutionary family." But since Min was a Nationalist officer, his role in Shen Shituan's son's escape showed that the family had a strong bond with the enemy, which led to the accusation that its donations to the Communist Party after its victory were just an attempt to cover up past evil deeds. Soon, Shen Shituan's "revolutionary family" classification was stripped away. A public denunciation was arranged. Peasants went up to the stage to accuse Shen Shituan of connections to Shen Min. Guanting and Guanxiu were forced to be present. At the end of the meeting, they saw the new village leader put a bullet into Shen Shituan's head. His corpse was left out in the open for three days, a lesson in revolutionary justice.

At least some of this was what Guanting told his father during their walk together, but then he stopped talking, unable to continue. He was visibly distraught, and Min didn't press him for more details. Guanting finished by simply sketching his route to Pingdong: He found a bicycle in Chaozhou and rode it all the way to Hong Kong, nearly three hundred miles of unfamiliar and uneven roads. His mother had given him the names and addresses of some relatives there, and they put him on a boat to Taiwan, hoping that he would be able to reconnect with his father.

Now, on the train to Taipei, Min lapsed into silence, though clearly a storm was raging in his heart, and in Jun's as well, each of them in their way grappling with the revelations contained in Guanting's story. Both Jun and Min had been sending money home via their families' respective relatives in Hong Kong. Min had hoped that his remittances would improve the family's situation, but now he'd learned that they had been used as incriminating evidence against them. And now Jun had to suppose that her remittances might have done harm as well. Never mind that she had been pinching pennies in order to have some money to send to Fuzhou.

Guanting's story also added an entirely different dimension to Taiwan's sketchy news reports about the Mainland. They did know about the Korean War, of course, and the Land Reform campaign, but they didn't know about the full extent of the struggle sessions, the public executions, the capricious applications of the label Enemy of the People. Guanting now brought them face to face with their darkest fears. What could they do now, if it was dangerous to send money home? Return to their families? Had they wanted to return, the border was still permeable in the early 1950s, and they would have been able to enter the Mainland via Hong Kong. But obviously return was not an option for a former Nationalist Army officer and his wife. And going back would have been of no help to their families.

The best solution, they both came to see, was to cut off their respective money flows to the Mainland, and to divert the funds to Pingdong for Guanting's expenses instead. Meanwhile, they would speed up making the still bare apartment that they had just purchased in Taipei into a welcoming home for Guanting.

The train chugged toward Taipei. It passed the sprawling encampments of *kenanfang* on the outskirts of the city, smudges in the deepening dusk, except for the occasional bare light bulb dangling from a wire here and there. Then streetlights started to appear as the city came into view. Finally, the train pulled into the station. The throngs of people in the platform's dim light stirred like a jumble of shadows. "Home," Jun said to herself, though it didn't feel quite like home yet.

• • •

Min's severance pay was running out, so Jun found a job teaching at a local school for children from the *kenanfang*, and Min hunkered down to write a book on law, one that he'd had in mind for a long time. His idea was to make law appealing and interesting to the general public, using stories from classical Chinese literature to illustrate how legal codes were interpreted and applied in different periods in history. The book came out to critical acclaim, and it landed him a leadership position in the newly reshuffled Judicial Yuan, the legal arm of the government.

Months later, their first child, Yiheng, was born. Jun now wanted to bring Guanting to Taipei to complete the family. Guanting, she felt, should apply to the best, and thus the most expensive, private high school that he could get into. Such schools offered the most rigorous academic training available on Taiwan in those days, as well as foreign language courses, which Jun, like her father, believed were keys to more and better career choices. She convinced Min of her plan even though it was somewhat contrary to their conservative spending habits.

Guanting did not disappoint. He passed the entrance exam, excelled at the school, and chose his career. He wanted to be an engineer building roads and bridges, he told his parents one day—he had started to call Jun "mother"—after all, "Taiwan is a world waiting to be built," he said.

Jun had several times tried to coax Guanting into telling the full story of his life on the Mainland and his escape, and gradually he opened up and told her what had happened. After Shen Shituan's public execution in the village, his mother explained to him the extreme precariousness of the Shen family's position. Guanting, she said, came from a prominent landowning family of exactly the type that was being targeted in both the Communist land reform and the first of Mao's major ideological purges, known as the Three-Anti and Five-Anti Movements. It was hard to imagine worse prospects for a young person in China given that family background at that moment. The family land had already been taken away and the house converted into a government office. The boys' grandparents were all dead, and Guanting's father was a prominent figure in the enemy's forces. "They're not interested in an old woman like me," his mother told Guanting, her oldest son, speaking of the Communists, "but I can't protect you." She wanted him to leave, to go as far as he could. And the farthest she could think of was a relative on his father's side who lived in Hong Kong, who might have information about his father. She handed him an address.

Guanting had never left the village alone in his entire life. He could not even find Hong Kong on a map. And, Guanting asked his mother, what about Guanxiu? His younger brother was his constant companion and his best friend. Perhaps their different temperaments had drawn them closer even than most other brothers. Guanting preferred the backstage, and his little brother happily soaked up the limelight. But they shared a love for books and were both fiercely protective of their mother. Guanxiu was still a kid, she told Guanting, tears welling up in her eyes. "Maybe you can go to explore the path first." Guanting understood. His mother didn't want to risk both boys at the same time. And he thought it would be better for his brother to keep their mother company. The next day, Guanting came home with a bicycle. He had bartered for it with his copy of *The Romance of the Three Kingdoms*, a coveted book among his friends.

"Grandpa's copy?" Min asked him as he told the story to his father and Jun.

"Yes, I took it from Grandpa's library before they burned all the books," Guanting replied, as the three of them lapsed into a momentary silence. Jun cringed at the image of burning books, remembering her father's library and the happy times she'd spent in it with him.

The next day, Guanting said, his mother came home with a bump on her forehead, which she explained as a result of her own careless stumble, but Guanting was sure that someone had harmed her. She was nevertheless adamant that Guanting leave that very night. As soon as darkness fell, Guanting hid the bicycle in some bushes outside the village. He went to bed to get as much sleep as he could, and when his mother woke him up at midnight, he left. "Mother gave me a piece of paper wrapped in plastic with the address of our relatives in Hong Kong and a small package to carry on my back, and she literally pushed me out of the house."

Jun wrapped her arms around the young man.

"And the rest of the trip was OK?" Min asked.

"It was OK," Guanting said. He stopped to ask for directions at a border village, and it turned out the villagers were looking for a bicycle thief. They took him in as a suspect and seized his bicycle, but he managed to run away and, after hiding in a culvert all day, literally crept toward the border that night. When he reached there he made up a story to explain to the Hong Kong border guards his sorry-looking condition: He and his father lived in Hong Kong and had crossed the border to the Mainland to sell vegetables from their family plot. They'd been beaten up by Mainlanders and got separated. Perhaps they had seen his father? He gave the guards the Hong Kong address as if he had known it all his life, and they let him go. Guanting didn't know then that he had made up a perfect story to get through the border. Until the mid-1950s, a number of border villages had farmers crossing the border daily to work in the fields straddling the border and the local commerce was still rather loosely regulated.

As Guanting finished his story, Min stood up, turned to gaze out the window, and when he returned to his son's side, his big hands fell on his shoulders. "Son," he said, "you're braver than me, and way smarter. Consider that part of your journey over. We'll make the rest of it together."

Jun and Min's second son, Shi, was born not long after Guanting joined them in Taipei. Guanting adored the baby, and was always eager to babysit for him, but he didn't hide his disappointment. He'd wanted a baby sister. The family continued to grow, and as if in answer to Guanting's wish, the next baby, Yihui, was a girl. Guanting by then was a sophomore at the university in town. Her arrival delighted him and drew him home often. The three little children looked up to Guanting as their big brother and their hero. They never knew Guanting was not their full brother until they were almost adults.

• • •

One day in 1957, Min came home and showed Jun a letter from his cousin in Pingtung, the same cousin who had taken in Guanting. It said that Guanxiu, his younger son, had also escaped from the Mainland to Hong Kong, and was ready to get himself to Pingtung.

This was, of course, good news in a way, and yet Jun's heart sank when she heard it. How bad, she wondered, were things on the Mainland that the younger son also had to flee instead of keeping his mom company? It had been almost eight years now since Jun had left Fuzhou, and it had been increasingly difficult to conjure up an accurate picture of home in her mind, given Nationalist daily broadcasts saying that people on the Mainland were either being persecuted or were starving to death. Could these propagandistic reports, which she had always doubted, actually be true?

In fact, what no one in Taiwan knew at that point—not even many people on the Mainland knew the extent of it—was the severity of the horror unfolding there on many fronts. In the countryside, collectivization had wrestled land ownership from the farmers who'd only gotten it in the land reform a few years before, sucked up their profit and cut into their own food supply. The cities did not fare better. They went through a period of successive campaigns. In the Hundred Flowers Campaign of 1956, Mao invited intellectuals to express their honest opinions on the CCP. When criticism got out of hand, the outspoken ones were severely criticized. Hundreds of thousands were branded as Rightists, becoming the target in the subsequent Anti-Rightist Campaign. This was coupled with the drastic reorganization of the economy known as the Great Leap Forward. This combination of ideological cleansing and economic upheaval pushed the country to near collapse, the scale and horror of which would become the subject of study for years to come. Even today, there is still no agreed-upon figure for the number of deaths from starvation and persecution in those years. The estimates range from 16.5 million to 45 million and even higher.

The news of Guanxiu's impending arrival generated tremendous excitement in the Shen household among the smaller children, but it caused deep anxiety for both their parents and their big brother, Guanting. Jun, who had stopped teaching in order to devote more time to caring for the three young children, asked herself the basic logistical question: Where would a twenty-one-year-old young man fit in an apartment that was already too small? And how would Guanxiu feel when he realized that, instead of finding his father and brother, he had a whole new family to deal with, along with the entirely new world of Taiwan? But despite these worries, everyone was in agreement: Guanxiu should join them as soon as he reached Taiwan. They would deal with whatever problems came up.

They needn't have worried. To everyone's relief, Guanxiu was an instant hit among the little kids at home and in the neighborhood. He would take the kids to nearby ponds to swim, catch fish and frogs, net birds, and climb trees. Just about anything a child could imagine learning to do, Guanxiu could teach them. He charmed the children's parents also. His encyclopedic memory generated endless historical stories filled with vivid details. He was also a natural showman, who could sing a host of different roles from Chaozhou operas.

Yet, despite his instant popularity, Guanxiu fit in nowhere. At twenty-one, most of the youths his age were either in college or in the army, or were helping support their families, but Guanxiu could neither find a job nor join the army. And then there were the nightmares, punctuated by shouts and moans in the dark and in the wee hours. After a while, under Jun's gentle prodding, Guanxiu started to tell his stories.

Guanting's departure in 1953 had left the boys' mother and Guanxiu even more ostracized than before, and they had difficulty finding enough food to survive. Not wanting to be a burden to his mother, Guanxiu went to live and work in a butcher shop in a neighboring village owned by a distant relative. The relative didn't like him for some unexplained reason. To make things worse, the daily slaughter of animals that Guanxiu witnessed started to mingle in his nightmares with the political persecutions and executions taking place around him. His nocturnal shouts became more frequent, further annoying the shop owner, who increased Guanxiu's workload, giving him the dirtiest and hardest jobs even as the boy struggled to keep his growing six-foot frame functioning on the bare minimum of gruel that he was given to eat. After a while, he collapsed with a high fever, and his mother was called in to take him home. But Guanxiu refused to leave, fearing that he would become a burden to his mother. When she insisted, he finally realized: "Do they think I'm going to die in their home?" he asked. When he saw his mother break down in tears, he understood. "All right, if they think I'm going to die, I'll die in my own home." Mother and son made it back to their "home," which was a doorless, windowless, half-destroyed village shrine by the road.

The nightmares never stopped. He was particularly testy with his father whenever the topic of his talent for local Chaozhou opera performance came up, even, and perhaps particularly, when the neighbors complimented him on his martial arts performance while singing the opera. Min saw his son's talent, admired his feistiness. In fact, that was something they shared. But that trait also led them into fierce confrontations that Jun was helpless to prevent. It came down to this: Even though Min had once written songs for his singer girlfriends in Shanghai years before, he didn't believe that men should be performers, and that was exactly what Guanxiu wanted to be. Even in his lyric-writing days, knowing of his son's passion for local opera, he'd sent letters admonishing him to focus on something more befitting of a man than singing.

One day, Jun remembered more than a half century later, Min suggested that Guanxiu not perform in public.

"Are you ashamed of me?" Guanxiu asked.

"It's not that," Min said, uncharacteristically defensive. Since Guanxiu's arrival, Min had tried his best not to add to the boy's psychic wounds. He knew that Guanxiu had gone through harrowing events. But now he was facing a son who had no intention of backing down, and Min refused to back down as well: "I just don't know where you got this passion for being a show boy," he said. "I don't understand what you see in the whole business."

Min's condescension and his unwillingness to understand touched something deep in Guangxiu: "Maybe what I see is a father who was never there while I grew up. I see a mother who was bullied and abandoned and could only weep, and a little boy who grew up sharing his last mouthful of rice with her, trying to comfort her. In those plays, I hear the only music in my life and the only cannon that doesn't kill, I see the heroes that I can be and the bad guys that I can beat. And, I see a boy who can dream to have a place where people cheer for him instead of spitting on him, a place you never had to be."

Min sat stone-faced and silent. He was not one who easily apologized, much less to his own son. Even if he felt guilt and hurt within, he did not voice it. "I think you should go to college instead of hanging out all the time," he said.

"College? Who wants a twenty-one-year-old freshman? And how am I to pass the entrance exam when I never got past junior high? I have no diploma; I was kicked out of every school I enrolled in because my father was a Nationalist general. I grew up in a Communist state. I'm a misfit. I was a misfit there, and now I'm a misfit here. I've become a professional misfit. I'm even a misfit to you."

"Life has a calling for everyone . . ." Min began to say.

"A calling? Even when I yelled and screamed, no one heard me. I made it out of hell like a dog."

"Guanxiu, I know you have every reason to be bitter. It hasn't been easy for you." Min softened, the closest he came to showing actual sympathy for his son. "But we need to move on. Life has made different demands on us. I have made choices that led to neglecting other demands, and, unfortunately, you were caught between my failed marriage and the tragedies of the new Communist state. So why don't you let me share some of the burdens of memory and history and let me help you with the next stage in life, make a new life in a new place?"

Min's voice was gentle now and contrite. He wrapped his arm around his son's shoulder, and Guanxiu turned his head away as the tears flowed. He went to the window, stared for a long moment at the urban landscape that was now his home, and unburdened himself:

After Guanxiu and his mother were officially labeled an anti-revolutionary family, their ostracism was complete. No one dared to go near them, not even their relatives or the orphans whom his mother had taken in during the 1943 great famine and cared for through many years thereafter. Things came to a head when a band of local militia took Guanxiu's mother away. Guanxiu secretly followed and witnessed what happened through a crack in a wall. The militiamen wanted his mother to tell them where she had put two handguns that her husband had left behind. But there were no handguns. This was an accusation fabricated by one of the orphans. When she persisted in saying she hid no guns, the militiamen, angry and frustrated, beat her until, finally, desperate for the torture to stop, she said that they had been sold by the very person who had reported their existence.

Guanxiu thought he must have cried himself to sleep that night after he came home alone, because when he woke up, his mother was lying next to him, beaten, bruised, half dead. The following day, the militiamen were back, this time to evict mother and son from their home. From then on, they stayed in an open shrine by the roadside.

But more hell awaited them. Guanxiu's mother became a constant prop in rallies held to generate revolutionary fervor, rallies that always needed an enemy to be struggled against. Guanxiu would go to each and every one of them, so as to collect his exhausted and beaten mother when the rallies were over and to help her get home. Until one day, his mother was forced to kneel on the stage along with two other "enemies of the people." All three were sentenced to be executed on the spot. Three militiamen appeared, pointing their guns at the backs of the heads of the three condemned bad elements. Guanxiu closed his eyes and heard the loud crack of gunfire coming from the stage. He turned to run away, only to be stopped by a stir in the crowd around him. He heard someone screaming. " 'Look, two of them didn't fall!' Guanxiu opened his eyes, and saw his mother still on her knees, her eyes closed, and tears streaming down her cheeks. He heard an announcement over a loudspeaker: "The Party has decided to give two of these bad elements a second chance to become good citizens of the new society."

After the fake execution, Guanxiu's mother was assigned to collect corpses. Suicides and executions were claiming a constant stream of lives, so she was sent to rallies, to open fields, and to people's houses to pick up the remains of these ruined lives. Having settled down with a regular "job," her only hope was for Guanxiu to get out to find a better future.

A silence descended.

Jun's trembling hands were drying her tears. Her heart melted for the young man standing before them. She had come to love him, just as she loved his brother. What they had endured had brought them closer to her. Then she heard Min take a deep breath. "Son, it took a lot of courage to do what you did. If you survived all of that and still came out ahead, you can come out ahead in the next stage as well."

"You know the old saying," Min said. 'Whom Heaven calls on for great tasks, it must first . . . ' "

". . . torture his soul . . ." Guanxiu finished the quotation.

"So you know that."

"I read many forbidden classics in the home of a friend I had. Her family was classified as patriotic overseas Chinese, which meant they were able to keep many books forbidden to other people."

Jun breathed a sigh of relief at this reconciliation of father and son even though questions came to her mind, questions about moral responsibilities under conditions of duress, as well as questions about Min and what he was thinking. Her stepsons' recounting of events brought their mother into Jun's emotional landscape for the first time. Until now, Min's former wife had been a kind of abstraction. Now she had become real, a mother dignified, made heroic by her sons' love, her grit, and, above all, by her sacrifice. How did Min feel, Jun had to wonder, about this courageous woman whom he had divorced in a newspaper ad? Was he moved as she was? Did he feel guilt, contrition, regret, any shades of the emotions that she herself was feeling?

But Jun never asked. To ask risked imprisoning them all in the past. All of them were victims of events beyond their control, and while this gave them a certain commonality, it also made them irreconcilably different. Jun had her family torn away from her, Min had left his by choice, and the two boys had been pushed out of their home by their mother for a chance at a better life. Jun knew that the moral burden of that fell most heavily on Min.

All this was clear to Jun, but her decision, and Min's decision, was to observe a silence, to avoid an explicit moral accounting, since, after all, what good would that do? Instead, implicitly at least, they all chose to redeem the sadness of the past with a better future for them all.

It was 1959, a year after the Mainland's forty-six-day campaign to shell the islands along the Mainland coast under Taiwan's control, Jinmen being the major target. The high number of casualties provoked a surge of anti-Communist sentiment on Taiwan, and the government responded by establishing a special quota in schools, businesses, and government agencies for people deemed to have a "high anti-Communist awareness." Riding this new tide, Guanxiu was admitted to the National Political University where he majored in Chinese language and literature.

"Continue the Leap"

MY COUSIN JIYUE WAS BORN in 1958, the third and youngest child of Zhen and Hu Xizhong. At the time of Jiyue's birth, as historian Jonathan Spence noted, the average amount of grain available to each person in China's countryside had fallen from 205 kilos in 1957 and 201 kilos in 1958 to a disastrous 183 kilos in 1959, and a catastrophic 156 kilos in 1960 and in 1961. "The result," Spence writes, "was a famine on a gigantic scale, a famine that claimed 20 million lives or more between 1959 and 1962." By 1963, the year I was born, the median age of the people dying was 9.7, which meant: "The Great Leap Forward, launched in the name of strengthening the nation by summoning all the people's energies, had turned back on itself and ended by devouring its young."*

Zhen, like the rest of her fellow countrymen, could not have known those numbers at the time. But she did have a

---

* Jonathan Spence, *The Search for Modern China.* Norton, 1991, p. 553.

rare opportunity to see some things firsthand in many villages in Fujian.

While pregnant with Jiyue, Zhen was undergoing a second round of self-criticism and reeducation during the Anti-Rightist Campaign. This was another one of Mao's ideological purges in which hundreds of thousands of intellectuals were being shipped off to cowsheds and pigsties for reform, where thousands of them died. Zhen once again escaped that fate, but the old unresolved and unproved accusation that she had been the president of the Women's Youth League in medical school was resurrected, and once again, compounded with her bad family ties, she found herself put into a politically suspect category. Once again, she had to prove her loyalty to the Party. To make the correct political statements, she read everything made available to her and diligently wrote weekly reports on her self-improvement.

Even so, her study and reform were extended when the PLA began its most severe bombardment yet of Jinmen, ramping up the tension on the two sides of the Taiwan Strait. Slogans like "We must liberate Taiwan!" were everywhere on the Mainland, bringing Zhen's connection to her sister Jun back into focus. Even though Zhen insisted that she had no knowledge of Jun's whereabouts, a new label of "potential counterrevolutionary" was added to her file.

Zhen was in the third trimester of her pregnancy when her self-criticism was extended, but that didn't crush her. She redoubled her readings about current affairs so as to enrich her weekly reports. She learned from this reading that there was a "heightened revolutionary passion" across the country. The "broad masses," the propaganda machine said, were fired up to "liberate" Taiwan, while across the countryside, the move to higher levels of collectivization was meeting with great success. Collectivization, it was said, took full advantage of everyone's strengths—women cooked and cared for children, allowing men to till the land. Any surplus labor was diverted to building backyard blast furnaces to contribute to the country's industrialization. Some counties reported a staggering tenfold increase in grain production as a result. What Zhen did not know, like most city folks at that time, was that this encouraging story was fabricated by the Party's propaganda machine, using grossly exaggerated numbers reported by overzealous cadres. When it came time for the government to collect grain, the peasants were forced to turn over surpluses that were nonexistent in the first place.

In addition to the Party mouthpiece, *The People's Daily*, a new magazine, *Red Flag*, was founded in 1958 and tasked with "removing the capitalist white flag." Zhen read it regularly and accepted its portrayal of the CCP's vision as ambitious and inspiring. Agricultural surpluses would fuel urban industrialization, and the nation's goal of "Surpassing England and Catching up with America" seemed to Zhen both glorious and realistic.

The revolutionary hysteria was indeed infectious. Jiyue's name—"Continue the Leap"—was a product of his time of birth, coming as it did just after Mao's landmark Great Leap Forward campaign. Other popular names were *Chaoying* "Surpass England" and *Ganmei* "Catch up with America." But the truth was, instead of catching up to England, China was at the time experiencing starvation on a vast scale, its economy on the verge of collapse.

Despite the name she gave to her son, Zhen never even mentions the Great Leap Forward in the memoir she wrote in 2015 on the occasion of her ninetieth birthday. The pages are packed with medical milestones of all sorts in her long career, but hardly had any personal or political details. It did not even contain the names of her husband or children. Where was she? What was she doing at the time? Did she witness the horror? When I asked her those questions years later, she pointed to an episode in her memoir about a trip she made at the time to a village far from Fuzhou, in the mountainous hinterlands called Sanmengqiao. Her account seemed to show that, yes, she knew what was happening, but she chose not to lament it or to denounce it, even as she did what she could to mitigate the suffering of the local people. This was Zhen's approach to life: document an event that she experienced but leave out comments or reflections that might betray any political leanings or thoughts of her real self. Decades after the event in question, she stuck to that stance.

The trip came during the standard fifty-six days of maternity leave allowed all new mothers. Zhen was asked to lead a twenty-student team from the medical school to check on a report of a serious measles outbreak in Fu'an County. Zhen embarked on the expedition as a way of demonstrating her political reliability at a time when her past was once again being scrutinized.

Though Fu'an wasn't far, when the delegation arrived at the county seat, the local health commissioner dispatched them immediately to the hardest-hit area, a village called Zhouning. There was no road going there, so the team set out on foot. Zhen had always prided herself on her athleticism and had come well prepared with sports shoes. But the hike turned out to be even more arduous than she could have imagined, a two-day forced march against time over two gigantic mountains. The team arrived late at night on the second day. The only inn they could find was full. The proprietor opened up an attic space, which had probably never been used since the ramshackle inn was built. But the team was so exhausted that they piled in and fell right to sleep. When Zhen woke up, she found her eyes irritated by sand, her teeth gritty. A windstorm had swept the area the night before, but she and the other team members were so exhausted, none had noticed.

In the morning, they also learned that they were still not at the end of their journey. The worst hit village, Sanmenqiao, on the verge of being wiped out by the disease, was one more mountain away, and they hurried there as fast as they could. When they arrived at the end of the day, the blisters on their feet had been broken many times over. Even in their extreme exhaustion, they were struck by the beauty of the place. Its otherworldly serenity seemed to make a mockery of the deadly health crisis awaiting them.

Sanmenqiao was nestled between something called Buffalo Hill and a crystal-clear stream. Pools of water reflected the blue and white of the sky, and the air smelled fresh and sweet. The village was a patchwork of small huts, connected in a confusing maze: courtyard after courtyard, one family's back door led to another's side door. There was no end, no beginning, no numerical designation of any sort. Almost every family they visited had a sick child, but there was no way of labeling the location of the patients. Adding to that, the remote village had no electricity. When night fell, everything was plunged into darkness.

At a certain point, the local Party secretary showed up, oil lamp in hand, and volunteered to guide the team through the maze of houses. She was eager to get them moving, though her reasons went beyond the goal of treating the children.

The collectivization of agriculture that was taking place at the time meant that the fields had been taken out of the hands of individual farmers and put into collective use, so there was no reason for anybody to work harder than anybody else. Even meals were now shared, so families no longer depended on what they produced for themselves to eat. And this being spring planting time, having a sick child at home had become everyone's excuse not to work at all. The Party secretary worried that the year's harvest would be ruined; if she had nothing to report to higher authorities in the way of agricultural production, she would have to face the consequences.

Nearly 90 percent of the children were infected with measles. Zhen's team faced two challenges: They had only two medicines with them, vitamins and sulfonamide antibiotics. But supplies were limited and there was no way to replenish them quickly. To make the situation worse, the layout of the houses in the village made isolating the sick impossible. When Zhen examined her first patient, she knew that there was no time to waste: a two-year-old boy who had been sick for more than two weeks had been reduced to a bundle of bones wrapped in shriveled skin.

To increase efficiency, Zhen invented a way to identify her patients and record their locations. One was behind the wall that bore the slogan "People's Communes are Good!" Another's front wall said "Man will triumph over nature." Still others were next to "The More People the Stronger We Are" and "The East Wind Will Suppress the West Wind," and so it went. Proximity to political slogans were used as patient addresses.

Measles is a self-limiting disease. Its normal course runs for about nine days, three for the onset of a fever, three days of itchy skin rash, and three days during which the symptoms recede. But with the severe malnutrition in the village, the children had a much harder time recovering, and there was a much higher death rate than usual in measles epidemics. Zhen's quick solution was to give the vitamins to the less severe cases, leaving the sulfonamides for the more severe ones. To boost the children's strength, she had grains and potatoes ground to make them into easily digested gruels.

After doing what they could in Sanmenqiao, Zhen and the team went on to other villages to deal with similar outbreaks. She was away from home for a month. But if the severe malnutrition that she saw in these villages did not jibe with the effusive reports of bumper harvests that she had been reading in the newspapers, she did not record it anywhere; nor did she take note of the dissonance in retelling the story to me. And concluding her account of her experience in her memoir written half a century later, she said:

> Over a month of hard work, my gains were extraordinary. 1) I deeply understood the hardship of the working people; 2) there was a dire lack of medical care and medicine; 3) faced with challenging tasks, if we worked closely with the masses, we could overcome any disaster; and 4) In our work, we showed the Party's care for the pains and illnesses of the working masses, we helped enhance the connection between the Party and the masses, and we in turn gained a deep education.

Yet clearly, she had seen during her month-long trip that something terrible was going on in these isolated villages and that the true situation made a mockery of the cheery reports she had read in *Red Flag*. From roughly 1958 to 1962, China went through what the Party later euphemistically called the "three years of great difficulty" which was actually the worst famine of the twentieth century, with up to twenty million or even more people dying of starvation. But Zhen chose, as always, to focus on what she saw as the positive side of the Party's leadership and the inspiration she felt in serving the people.

It soon became impossible, however, to ignore the evidence that something terrible was happening and not just in the countryside. Starting in the early 1960s, Zhen's colleagues got reports of emaciated corpses appearing on city streets. Workers were being dispatched to take the corpses straight to mortuaries. Soon, emaciated people started to stagger into Zhen's Women and Children's Hospital in Fuzhou. Their symptoms were all consistent with those of starvation. The doctors were perplexed: Their own food ration had been kept steady, and every day, the government propaganda had been celebrating surplus food from the bumper harvest. How could there be starvation when the grain harvest was at its record high? Could it be that some kind of mysterious infection was sweeping through the city? But there was no pathological evidence of any sort to substantiate that theory.

Then reports started to come in from the countryside that a large number of people were suffering from swelling. Women of childbearing age often had amenorrhea, the termination of menstruation, as well as increased cases of uterine prolapse. Among children, dwarfism had become common. The majority of the afflicted were women and children. Zhen received urgent instructions from the provincial health ministry. She had been chosen to lead a preliminary investigation in Wuping County, where the mortality rate among women and children was highest. She set out immediately with two other doctors in order to make it to a meeting with the county magistrate the following Monday.

Zhen had encountered and treated many uterine prolapse cases over the years but had never seen it accompanied by so many other illnesses or health problems. She instructed her team to collect detailed health histories in addition to blood and urine samples. In just over a week, the team was able to collect information on more than 130 cases. Test results came back showing severe compromises of the entire reproductive system in every case. Congenital causes were ruled out; also absent were infections or abnormal growths.

A significant percentage of the amenorrhea cases, one colleague observed from the data, were accompanied by swelling. Zhen suspected starvation as the culprit, and she decided to actually inspect the women's homes. In house after house, the woks on the stoves had nothing more than watery gruel. The few grains of rice on the bottom were given to husbands and children. The women's bowls held basically rice water.

Those trips confirmed Zhen's worst fears: Starvation was the cause of all of these health problems. Women whose bodies were weakened from lack of nutrition were prone to amenorrhea and uterine prolapse; and their children, lacking milk, didn't grow. Zhen dealt with the situation by submitting a brief and judiciously worded report on her findings, saying that the disease was "possibly" due to malnutrition and that giving the villagers more and better food would "likely" solve the problem. She showed the report to the county magistrate, a Comrade Yuan.

"What do you mean by 'possibly'?" Yuan asked her. "Are you saying that these health problems could 'possibly' be due to insufficient food intake but that they might 'possibly' be due to something else?" No, Zhen replied, she could not identify causes other than starvation. Yuan crossed out "possibly" and put in "definitely." He looked at the report some more. "And you say here that better food would 'likely' make things better. Do you mean that better nutrition will 'likely' solve the problem or that it 'will' solve the problem?" Zhen admitted that 'will' was the correct word. Yuan crossed out "likely" and put in "will."

This was a lesson. Zhen was embarrassed to have to admit to herself that her political troubles back in Fuzhou had led her to deliberately fudge the wording of her report. She did that because she faced an unsolvable dilemma. At home, she was under investigation as a suspected right-winger and a counterrevolutionary. If she depicted the situation here in Wuping County as one of starvation, she might appear to be smearing the great socialist enterprise of collectivization, which the press was holding up as a glorious success. But if she didn't forthrightly speak of starvation, she would be neglecting her duty as a physician. Zhen normally made her diagnoses confidently and unequivocally, based on the data. But this time, feeling the political pressure, she had chosen an ambiguous middle ground. Later, in her memoir, she framed this moment of revelation in the form of a self-criticism:

> I was ashamed that being a college educated intellectual, I was lacking in revolutionary awareness compared to a cadre (of far less education), who, based on the interest of the people, dared to speak the truth and bear the responsibility. I deeply respected that.

Clearly, half a century after the fact, her fudging of a politically awkward reality still haunted her. Even so, she tried to put a positive spin on her role in the crisis, going on in her memoir to describe her solution to the malnutrition epidemic she faced in Fu'an County.

Throughout the region, she writes, people were turning to practitioners of Chinese medicine and to shamans for cures. But Zhen knew that what was needed was better food. The problem was that there was no rice to be found in this rice-producing region. All Magistrate Yuan could produce was a very limited amount of flour. "But this is also the home of sugarcane, right?" Zhen asked him. Yes, Yuan replied, he could also provide some raw sugar. Zhen and her colleagues enlisted local volunteers to convert their triage center into a food distribution station for women and children. To stretch the small amount of flour available, they had volunteers collect and grind the innermost part of the trunk of banana plants—the actual bananas having been "purchased" by the government—into a batter, and then, by folding flour, sugar, and vitamins into it, to bake a kind of cookie. Afflicted women and children were urged to take these cookies as dietary supplements each day, and, to assure that these supplements went to their intended patients and not to the men in their families, Zhen made them eat their cookies right there, before they walked out the door. For patients with serious amenorrhea, Zhen gave them the same cookies with added female hormones to boost their strength. When these various treats soon showed positive results, the county took over the operation.

Fatigue had caught up with Zhen by the time she reached home after her intense month-long trip. She was unable to produce milk for Jiyue, and her blood test came back showing that she had a case of acute hepatitis. But there was also some good news. Just as she got home, a letter of commendation from Magistrate Yuan arrived in the hospital, describing her work in Wuping County in heroic terms. She had risked her own health, the letter said, and her dedication had had an immediate and positive impact. This effectively ended Zhen's political study sessions. She was no longer an ideological suspect.

Jiyue survived those years of difficulty. This baby named Continue the Leap would eventually leap over the Pacific to become a U.S. citizen in a different era. Zhen's chapter in her memoir mentioned neither Jiyue's name nor the Great Leap Forward Movement and went on to conclude that she was rewarded with two weeks of complete rest in a private hospital ward, thanks to Magistrate Yuan's commendation letter. The article that she wrote during those two weeks was soon published in the *Fujian Journal of Medicine* that year.

PART III

Re-education

O N AN EARLY MORNING in the summer of 1969, a middle-aged woman stood at the gate of the Women and Children's Hospital in Fuzhou. She was bent over, her head down as if she were reading the Chinese characters scrawled on a placard hanging from her neck. It said: "Historical counter-revolutionary quack doctor Chen Wenzhen."

Standing at the hospital gate became Aunt Zhen's full-time job. Since the hospital was located at the center of the city, unending streams of feet passed within her restricted field of vision. Occasionally she could hear, and certainly smell, one of the open-top "night soil" tanks that passed by, bumping over the potholes near her and spilling their slimy contents at her feet. Schoolchildren would practice reading the characters on her placard or try out their revolutionary slogans on this conveniently available counterrevolutionary. Many people would tease her about her half-shaven head or pelt her with rotten fruit. Sometimes, they would just spit, and the sun would first dry the front of her body, then the back, and at the end of the day, she would be taken back to her small holding cell by Chairman Mao's Red Guards. To spare her three children the pain of passing that spot, Zhen's husband, Xizhong, transferred them to a new school.

This was at the height of The Great Proletarian Cultural Revolution, the vast ideological power purge instigated by Mao in 1966 that lasted officially for the next decade. Zhen had been relieved of her position as chief physician and head of her department. Once again, her questionable political background—her family ties to the Nationalist Party and especially her supposed role as the head of the Women's Youth League in her medical school, an untrue accusation made years earlier by a medical school classmate—had come back to haunt her.

Just a couple of weeks before she began her ordeal at the hospital gates, the Red Guards stormed into Zhen's home, and began searching for evidence of "counterrevolutionary transgressions." They found nothing until, when they were about to leave, one of the teenage ransackers picked up a small Mao bust on Zhen's desk. He found cracks on it.

"Confess!" The Red Guards snarled at her. "You took out your hatred for our great leader by smashing his image!"

Zhen tried to explain. Her house helper had accidentally knocked the bust off the desk while cleaning it one day, and she did her best to put it back together. The Red Guards didn't believe her: "You not only secretly vented your hatred for our great leader but now you want to shift the blame onto the working people that you exploit every day!" one of them screamed at her. Another Red Guard chimed in: "You think we don't know what you did? We revolutionaries have eyes everywhere. We never sleep when our enemies are sharpening their knives!"

The Red Guards, prodded by Mao to see themselves, in his

words, as "the future of the world," were mainly high school and university students, sometimes even just middle school students. Their classes had been canceled, their schools closed. "To rebel is justified," Chairman Mao told them, and they responded in kind. They could ride the trains for free so they could "make revolution" around the country, with free rein to inflict their youthful zeal on anybody they chose. Their main targets were the educated elites, denounced as relics of "the Four Olds" (Old customs, habits, culture, and thinking), and "counterrevolutionaries" like Zhen and Xizhong.

Not long after the search of her home, Zhen was dragged out of one of her daily study sessions and told to go to her office to retrieve her medical license. She arrived to see the same Red Guards who had ransacked her apartment now shouting at her secretary as she tried to stop them from rifling through the medical files. When they saw Zhen, one of them triumphantly waved the license that he had just dug up and tore it to pieces in front of her. Then they took her to the office of the hospital president, now transformed into the Red Guards' revolutionary headquarters. There she was registered, forbidden to go home, then sent to a cell on the edge of the far end of the hospital next to the mortuary, where she would be kept for three months. Every morning she would be escorted to her place of shame at the hospital gate.

A week into her daily vigil, Zhen noticed a man's pair of feet in her field of vision. They seemed just planted there. The man chain-smoked, dropping cigarette butts all around her, but stayed silent as a ghost, unmoving. The shoes and the cigarette butts were there again the following day, and after a few days' absence, they returned the following week, but this time the cigarette butts bounced on the ground with unusual force.

Finally, he said something. "Yan Ling is dead." His voice was low, confiding, forced through clenched teeth. He didn't want anybody besides Zhen to hear. "They said they could do a caesarean 'without Chen Wenzhen,'" he continued. "Well, I found a metal clamp in the ashes." He paused. "Hers and the baby's." A last cigarette butt flew across Zhen's line of sight, skidding into a pool of foul water. The man disappeared for good.

Zhen remembered Yan Ling well. She was a patient and had had a normal pregnancy. Both she and her husband were the only children in their families, unusual at the time, and they had been eagerly expecting their first baby. Now she was learning that the woman and child were both dead and had been cremated. Zhen would never learn why Yan Ling had had to undergo a caesarean, but the clamp was powerful evidence of medical incompetence. She remembered Yan Ling's face, young and dreamy, peering into life's mysteries and promises, and now what was left? A clamp in her ashes.

Zhen felt a rage rise within her, blending in with the heat and dust and noise of the busy crossroads in Fuzhou where she stood. Her anger filled her chest and throat. It pounded her head and squeezed into her eyes, until, literally, she saw stars sparkling in a black void.

One day, the guards woke her up early, pulled her from the cell, and informed her that the Party was sending her to a village called Longdi.

"Re-education by the poor and lower middle-class peasants" was Mao's way of transforming bourgeois thought into

revolutionary ideology and converting counterrevolutionaries into socialist citizens. City dwellers, educated men and
women who were professionals, would gain compassion for
the suffering poor, the Party declared, and this compassion
would raise their "class awareness," which in turn would
enable them better to serve the people. This call from Mao
purged educated elite from whole urban areas and dispatched them to China's thousands of rural towns and primitive villages.

The last time Zhen saw her husband was in a study session
for suspected counterrevolutionaries before her removal.
Xizhong was among the suspects because of his family's bourgeois background. The Red Guards, whipped into a frenzied
state of righteous indignation, recited Mao's "teachings" that
class enemies and traitors to the revolution lurked everywhere. At one point, they seized Zhen. Xizhong could only
look on helplessly as she was frog-marched out of the room.
Zhen managed to throw her husband a reassuring look. She
could handle herself, as she always did, she tried to tell him
with her eyes, and she did have reason to hope that he would
be spared the worst, even if she wasn't. He had no accusation against him on his record, and his father, a Christian
preacher, had successfully rebranded himself as a "patriotic
local leader."

Since then, her only news of her family had been a month
before, when she had learned that Xizhong and their three
children had been sent to Sanming County, over three hundred miles west of Fuzhou. She didn't know how far Longdi
was from Sanming, but having spent years traversing the province for her own work, she knew a family reunion would not
be an easy thing.

The Red Guards led Zhen from her cell to her home,

where they gave her ten minutes to pack a bag. The door of their apartment had been sealed with two strips of white paper crossed over each other, which her escorts tore away. Inside the apartment, papers were strewn everywhere, linens torn off the beds, and furniture piled on top of each other— legs broken, corners missing. The moist mildewy air stirred when the door was opened, sending the spiders scampering into their nooks and crannies.

Zhen took a deep breath. Looking across the rooms, she thought she could hear the spiders blink. Her two teenage daughters giggled no more, and her boy, Jiyue, who had turned ten a week before, no longer swaggered into the front hall like the man of the house. She leaned against the bed-post, which squeaked, stirring up sighs from the dusty furniture leaning on it. The Red Guards told her that it was time to go. Zhen salvaged a few items that had tumbled out of a trunk and the dresser and gathered them up in a simple bed-roll along with a small pot and a metal mug. She was ready.

At the station, the Red Guards told her that the train would take her from Fuzhou to Sanming Township. While there, she would be given a few days for a family reunion. But there was no road from Sanming to Longdi. She would have to rely on locally arranged guides to get there. Zhen knew that the journey would be tough and that life in Longdi would be difficult and spare, but she eagerly embraced it as a relief from daily revolutionary punishment in the city. Most of all, she yearned for the reunion with her family, short as it would be.

Zhen spotted Xizhong as her train pulled into Sanming station. It took her a while longer to notice her three children standing around him. They had all grown taller, and she saw right away something new in their eyes, something more mature, grown up. Her small pot and mug clanked on the platform as she dropped her bedroll to free her hands, but as she reached her arms out for her family, her face froze into a mask, her outreaching arms dropped. She'd noticed a man watching, and, deciding he must be a Party monitor, she repressed any show of bourgeois sentiment. She would have to show restraint. "Ma!" the children called her. Zhen allowed herself to touch their faces, as if to make sure that they were all real.

Her husband quietly looked on. Their eyes met, but they said nothing. He had such a classic scholar's elegance, Zhen thought to herself. His back straight, shoulders relaxed, his head held high, tipping slightly forward as if listening attentively. The sides of his mouth always swung up with just a hint of a smile, and his eyes gleamed with concentration and compassion behind his spectacles. Zhen thought he looked even more handsome than before in his faded cotton shirt. Her boy's broad shoulders and Hu Wen's delicate build, and Hu Yi's intelligent eyes . . . all stirred so much pride in her, but, with the Party representative bearing witness, she kept it all to herself. Her eyes came to a halt on Hu Wen's hair that had been cut very short. "I had lice," her daughter explained, noticing her mother's stare, "and Daddy cut my hair off." Zhen gave a rueful laugh. Her own once half-shaven head was now covered by an irregular growth of hair. "You've all grown in just a few months!" Zhen said to them, and a smile finally came through.

She had three nights in Sanming. Xizhong and the children were living in a stand-alone hut bordering a dumping ground. She praised them on keeping the place neat and clean. "We have organized our own agricultural commune," Xizhong said. "The girls prepare our meals. I take care of the rest. I've solved the problem of lice by learning how to cut hair, and I am now a professional house cleaner." Zhen looked at her husband, not sure anymore if she could distinguish between a joke and a simple statement of fact. "I'm not kidding," Xizhong said, smiling. "Cleaning is my job in the Sanming hospital."

Xizhong was Fuzhou's best-known cardiologist—or had been until he was removed from his position. Zhen's heart pained at the thought of his surgeon's hands picking up the detritus from other less competent doctors' operations. But she cut short the thought and proceeded to help move Jiyue to the girls' room during her stay.

The children had just been enrolled in the local schools, but they were academically so much more advanced than the rest of their classmates that they were bored. They had been unable to make friends. Their parents decided to let them stay home with Zhen for the short duration of their mother's visit. The girls were both very independent, but the older one, Yi, was strong willed while Wen was more quiet, and sweet. Their different temperaments seemed to complement each other, so even though their interests differed, they made good company for each other. Jiyue, the only boy, often looked out from his window facing the dumping ground, silently watching the boys play in garbage piles.

After her long absence from her children's lives, Zhen could find no news or story to tell them. She could not even think of any advice to give, her usual "study hard and become useful people in the society" no longer having any connection to their lives. Knowledge was condemned, skills brushed aside, or used as evidence of retrograde thinking, elitist attitudes. Only revolutionaries, particularly those born to "red families"—of peasants, workers, and soldiers—had a voice in this revolution. The Hu family, in their first reunion in months, and in this town that they never knew, kept their conversations to the mundane trivia of everyday life. Gone were the rigorous conversations and debates on a wide range of topics from history or current events, or on the conditions of the countryside that Zhen used to talk about during her earlier trips. The outside world was blacked out, and the Hu family was forced to find a new family dynamic, one that, for the children at least, didn't involve homework and grades, or the thrill of showing off newly acquired information or knowledge in a heated discussion. Together, they tried to cook dishes with local ingredients: different kinds of greens, and ferns and mushrooms that farmers had gathered from the mountains and sold for some added income.

A harvest moon hung low the night before Zhen's departure. Xizhong proposed that they go out for a walk. Zhen agreed and told the children to go to bed. Jiyue grabbed her hand and asked: "Can I put my jackknife under my pillow?" Why? Zhen wanted to know. "If the bad guys come while you're out walking, I can fight them off." He answered with such confidence that Zhen consented and assured him that his sisters could help also. Tugging the boy to bed, Zhen did not want to pursue the topic of the bad guys and who they might be in her son's mind.

The jackknife was still under Jiyue's pillow when the local Party monitor showed up the next morning. The trip to Longdi would be by ferry on the Min River, and he was there to escort Zhen to the quay. She said a simple goodbye to her husband and stepped onto the small, open-top boat. The couple operating the boat told her that the trip upstream into the mountains usually took half a day. Zhen turned to look back to the dock. Hu Xizhong still stood there. The Party monitor was gone.

The water was choppy, churned up by big rocks in the riverbed. By late morning, a cliff came into view, splitting the river into two streams. A small collection of huts crouched among bamboo groves at the foot of the cliff, whose heights pierced a thick mist. This was a village called Shahu, meaning "sand pot." The Party monitor had told Zhen to get off the ferry there and walk the final leg of the trip to Longdi, "dragon land," further inland.

Sand Pot Village, sitting amid emerald green at the fork of a mountain river, reminded Zhen of "Peach Blossom Garden," an essay her father had assigned her to memorize when she was a girl. It told of a fisherman who stumbles into a small opening at the foot of a mountain by a river. He ventures in and discovers a secret world forgotten by time whose contented inhabitants, protected from wars, famines, and the rise and fall of dynasties and emperors, plead with him not to reveal their existence to the world outside. The author Tao Yuanming wrote:

> When his visit is over, the fisherman leaves through
> the opening, finds his boat, and retraces his route,
> leaving markers to find the place again. Upon his
> arrival at the prefecture town he tells the magistrate
> what he's seen. The magistrate sends an emissary to
> follow the markers and to subject the secret world to
> the emperor's rule, but they get lost and never find
> the way.

Zhen had still lived in the Flower Fragrant Garden of her childhood when she memorized that story, but soon after, the family had gone up the Min River to Nanping for shelter against the disorders of the Japanese invasion. Now thirty years later, Zhen was once again making an upstream trip on a branch of this very same river, coming face to face with her own destiny. This time, what she left behind wasn't invasion and war, but her own family and her dreams for a better life in the New China. At this moment, all those dreams seemed like the top of the cliff in front of her, disappearing into the mist. The dream had soured, their lives upended by political fanaticism and incompetence, their careers suspended, skills and talents left to waste: doctors who could have saved lives spat on at the hospital entrance and consigned to clean toilets, patients they could have saved reduced, literally, to ashes, their children taught to hate and guard against a non-existent enemy, rather than to seek useful knowledge. She felt a deep sadness.

• • •

Disembarking in Shahu, Zhen found and reported to the Party office as instructed. The farmer assigned to lead her from Shahu to Longdi had been waiting for a while and was impatient to take off at once. Zhen bought two bowls of soupy porridge at the door of the government office, giving one to the farmer, who slurped it down in a second, and they set out on their way.

Zhen tried to gauge the guide's age. Despite his haggard look, he must be quite young, she surmised. His muscles and veins bulged under the weight of two heavy loads that he carried, evidently supplies bought in Shahu, balanced on a bamboo shoulder pole. The pole creaked rhythmically like a singing cricket as the man tackled the trail, which seemed to hang from the mist above. Parts of it had been washed away or was overgrown with brambles. For most of the afternoon, they saw no sign of other humans, no houses, no cultivated fields, not even the ruins of an abandoned shed, only this primitive trail clinging to the side of a heavily forested slope, beautiful and yet forbidding. They scaled an immensely high mountain, only to come to another on the other side of a valley. The vegetation below the low clouds was a dense, impenetrable late-summer green, the air clear and supple. Here and there were splashes of flowers. Birdsongs bounced back and forth in the valley. Bamboo swayed in the air stirred by streams and waterfalls. Zhen was sweating profusely. She felt her bedroll getting heavier with every step. So much exertion after months of inactivity made her feel weak and dizzy.

When a tapestry of terraced fields came into view on an opposite slope, it felt to her almost like a sign of salvation. The fields appeared fallow, and they were so irregular that they made the whole mountainside seem like a cracked piece of pottery, sections of different shapes and sizes zigzagging and tumbling with the terrain. By the time a village came within sight, the sun was already at eye level. Zhen's guide stopped. He gestured toward the cluster of houses at the bottom of the hill and spoke for the first time: "Longdi. Go!" He then turned to uncover the loads he had been carrying and started spreading their contents onto the field.

Zhen knew from her past trips to mountain villages that the low sun would quickly disappear and leave everything in darkness. So she thanked her guide, who responded with a barely audible grunt, and started down the remaining slope. She feared that she might never get up if she fell and wouldn't be able to make out the path once it got dark.

A dog's bark brought out the shadow of a person at the house closest to the trail. Zhen asked for the reform intellectuals' hut. The man pointed to a trail that picked up from the back of his house, and then retreated inside, closing the door behind him. Following the trail, Zhen came to a hut with unfinished mud-brick walls. Painted on one wall in large red characters was "Chairman Mao Thought May Seventh Cadre School." The Chinese character for the number "five" as in the "Fifth Month (May)" had a square in the middle that happened to frame the one small window facing the path. Inside the window, Zhen could see a small flame flickering on an oil lamp. She knocked on the door and gently pushed it open. Zhen announced her arrival, and a man's voice came from within: "Come in and take the room on your right."

Zhen felt her way along a damp, cold wall and found a door to a small, even darker room inside. The bare wooden board in one corner must be the bed, she thought. She unfurled her bedroll, and plunked down, too exhausted to be dismayed by the bleakness of the dark, spare cell.

Zhen was the last arrival of the three sent from the city to be re-educated in Longdi. The other two, both men, had taken up the other rooms. The Party authorities had named one of them, Old Deng, to be their leader. He'd been a low-level cadre in the Fujian Province propaganda department. Zhen assumed he'd made some mistake that landed him in this remote village, but it seemed to have been minor enough to enable him to retain some power even in exile. The team's task was twofold, Old Deng announced at their first formal house meeting: to have their revolutionary awareness raised via their reeducation and to help the villagers increase their yields of grain.

Zhen's re-education started with a lesson about time. On her first venture out of her mud-brick hut, she ran into a man on the trail who introduced himself as the village head.

Despite the difficulty she had understanding his local dialect, she figured that he was informing her of a village-wide meeting that evening. She asked for the time of the meeting, pointing at her watch when the village head had difficulty understanding her standard Mandarin. "After the evening meal" was the answer. Afraid of being late, she asked another villager down the road what time the meeting would begin. The answer was "after sundown." It would be weeks later that Zhen learned that only one person in the village owned a watch.

This first encounter made it clear to Zhen that learning the local dialect—distinctively different from her own Fuzhou dialect—would be essential. This thought somehow picked up her spirit. Before she'd set out for Longdi, she'd feared that her worst problem, more serious than the harsh living conditions and other deprivations she expected, would be a sort of starvation of her own mind. Three months living in a locked cell at the hospital had given her a real taste of mental deprivation. She didn't know how long she would be in Longdi, or whether she would ever regain her right to practice medicine. She had come to this remote mountain town to cleanse her past and learn to be more like these villagers, most of whom may have never read a book in their lives. Longdi had no library, no newspaper; it was timeless. Learning its largely unintelligible language would be a good start. Zhen knew from her experience a decade before that some villages had a dialect unintelligible to its neighboring villages and crossing a mountain could mean crossing a communication zone. In some regions people learned to speak several mutually unintelligible dialects in order to exchange goods.

She made it on time to the meeting that night, discovering that it was a big event. Its purpose was to announce the presence of the three new arrivals, and most of the more than fifty families of Longdi, or some over two hundred people, were there. This was the first time, the village head announced, not concealing a certain pride, that rural people like them were being called on to teach city people. He then went on to introduce the village's own two most educated men: the teacher at the elementary school, who had finished high school and had some additional vocational training, and the accountant. Zhen and her two housemates from the city struggled to understand what was going on in this gathering, but Zhen, thanks to her past experience, had a head start over her two comrades, for whom the meeting might have taken place in a foreign country.

Zhen began in her first days to talk to any local person who was willing to engage a sent-down counterrevolutionary like her in conversation. The communication was often more "show," a pantomime of gestures, a lot of pointing at objects, than "tell." But she was able to learn in these first exchanges that she had arrived in a brief space of time between the harvest of the grains and the planting of late-season yams, called "winter yams."

Longdi village was not much of a village at all, as Zhen soon found out. Small huts made of mud and straw bricks dotted the steep mountainside looking like dice tossed among the boulders and crevices. In the late afternoon when the huts were cast in shadow, only the white smoke from their chimneys signaled that they were there. A few of the houses had tile roofs, but most were covered with thatch stretched over bamboo or wooden beams. The hut that Zhen lived in with the two sent-down men had the more common thatched roof.

After the meeting, the village chief assigned jobs for the upcoming winter planting of sweet potatoes. Zhen learned that she would work with a detachment of women whose job would be putting the seedlings into the soil. It was the men's job to prepare the land and shape the beds. The experienced peasants made the work look almost easy as they walked between the furrows, bending over to push one seedling into the soil at each step. But Zhen's back muscles were not accustomed to this reaching down and standing up and reaching down again, and her tender hands soon became raw from their contact with the abrasive soil.

Still Zhen worked hard, never complaining despite her obvious discomfort, and this won her friends. One young woman named Ah Xuan was particularly warm and outgoing. She became Zhen's first friend, and she introduced her to other villagers, mostly women. Zhen soon learned something that shocked her: Every person in Longdi had the same surname, Huang, and this, Zhen understood, was a consequence of the area's terrible poverty—the village was essentially an extended family. Occasionally a pretty girl from the village would be married off to a family in a better place, like Sand Pot. But the men of Longdi found it hard to find and afford brides from outside. One result was that the village's population was stagnant. Another was that incest was not uncommon. It was hard to know what generation this or that person belonged to, or who was the aunt and who was the cousin.

After the plants were in the soil, the weeding and fertilizing that followed were a bit easier for Zhen, and before she knew it, the time for the harvest had arrived. Yams, she learned, stopped growing when the temperature cooled to around 15 degrees Celsius (or 59 degrees Fahrenheit), and they would simply rot in the soil once it dipped under 9 degrees, leaving a small window for the harvest. Digging up the yams was tricky for the three city folks who sank their hoes into the yams instead of around them, shredding rather than harvesting them. And so after just a few efforts, all three of them were banned from digging; instead they were assigned to carry the potato vines to the processing ground. The tender tips of the yam plants were for human consumption, the rest of the vine was for animals.

Zhen didn't think it looked good for the three city people to be grouped together. She wanted to learn to dig. She found Ah Xuan, her new friend, to teach her. "You start from the base of the raised bed," Ah Xuan explained, "and then you work your way in to the root of the plant." Zhen practiced diligently, gaining the approval of Ah Xuan and her cohort of women friends. She could see that they were far more forgiving of her missed digs when she tried in earnest and made visible progress.

Dealing with her housemates, however, was a different matter. Deng, who was in charge, was always agitating to prove his revolutionary zeal. He regularly called his two housemates together for study sessions. He was the only one to have brought Chairman Mao's books with him. The other man, Mo, was bland, distant, and utterly uninterested in revolutionary zeal or, as far as Zhen could see, in anything at all. He hardly acknowledged the presence of his housemates, even when they were all in their shared kitchen. They wanted to have as few dealings with one another as possible, but they each had to cook their own daily meals, and one was clumsier than the other at the task.

Their staple was thin rice gruel with either pickled or fresh vegetables. Protein was a prized commodity for everyone. Sometimes a little fresh pork or chicken and egg could be purchased from the villagers, and occasionally, some farmer would sell mountain delicacies, such as frogs or birds. A piece of preserved meat could sometimes be brought back from Shahu, and it would last a long time, thinly shaved for a treat. None of them was very good at starting or nurturing the fire in their primitive wood stove, a difficulty that prolonged their time together in the kitchen. Somehow, they managed, partly because like the villagers themselves, they really didn't have much to cook anyway.

When the yam harvest was finished, all the villagers, including the inhabitants of the May Seventh Cadre School, settled in for the winter. The yams, stacked in piles on the dirt floor, would have to last until the warm weather. Zhen added a few chunks to her soupy porridge, aiming to make her rice ration last longer and to save having to trek across the snowy mountains to buy more rice in Shahu.

On the 26th of December, Zhen celebrated her forty-third birthday, the same day as Chairman Mao's. A person can make the yam or rice supply last, Zhen thought in a moment of melancholy, but how much can one stretch one's own time? Zhen kept her birthday to herself, though she celebrated privately by adding a hard-boiled egg to her dinner gruel. That night was exceedingly cold. Zhen spread her old sweater over the bare wooden boards atop her bed for a thin extra layer of padding and warmth, and she got into bed with her clothes on. Curled up to stay warm under the quilt, she clutched the letters from her family in Sanming. Sleep eluded her. The cold penetrated the wooden platform of her bed, went through her sweater and the padded pants and jacket she wore day and night, and held her bones in an icy grip. She could hear her heart beat, her watch tick, and an occasional rustle of the letter she held close to her heart.

Forty-three this year, Zhen thought to herself, the best time of her career. And she was whiling away her life in this freezing pit, alone, saving no one, helping no one, not even herself. For her, wasting time was the biggest sin, and wasting an opportunity was the biggest crime. Ever since she could read, she'd walked to school memorizing new words, and always had things in hand to read when she had to wait for something. That last time her father returned to the Flower Fragrant Garden from Shanghai she picked up a riddle book on the table while waiting for him with Jun in the foyer. Her sister had accused her of being cold and unfeeling and refused to take a stab at any of the riddles, feeling that they should be giving their full attention, anticipation, and excitement to their father's imminent arrival. "We should be talking only about him!" Jun had cried. But for Zhen, waiting was only waiting. Besides, their father would be there momentarily. Why talk about him?

Now, everything that had shaped her, everything that she had made herself into, was gone from her life—the Flower Fragrant Garden and all the privileges that came with it: Father, Jun, the missionary schools, and medical college years. The family that had prepared her for the world and her future life had become a political liability. Her very success in medical school had caused her best friend to believe that she had led the school's Nationalist Women's Youth League, turning her from a young star into a counterrevolutionary. Her new dreams, which had been born with the new People's Republic, and reborn three times with the births of her own children, seemed to shrivel in this cold, dark, silent night.

Longdi village was high in altitude, but it stood in the perpetual shadows of the mountains that surrounded it. The cold, damp air was never warmed by the sun. Most of the people stayed indoors, but Zhen felt that she had to keep moving during the day, to keep her blood from freezing. She had no relatives to visit, and the villagers didn't know her well enough to invite her to their cramped homes. Some of the villagers would engage in some small talk with Zhen when they saw her walk by their doors, and they would gather when Old Deng, assiduous as ever, summoned the townspeople together for a Mao Zedong–thought study session. But the villagers didn't feel they would know quite what to do with these city exiles inside their houses.

On New Year's Eve, Zhen, out for her usual walk, complimented a teenage girl on the red sweater she saw sticking out of her greasy padded cotton jacket, and this turned into a brief private lesson in rural poverty. The girl told Zhen that she was the daughter of the village head, and had gone to a boarding high school in Shahu. The sweater, the first that the village ever had, was her gift to her family. "We take turns wearing it when we go outside," she said. Usually in Longdi, the youngest and strongest in each family had the fewest layers of clothing. Everybody wore a single pair of homemade shoes all year round, made out of recycled cloth or hemp or straw. When people did go outside, they carried a "fire basket" with them, a kind of hand-warmer made with loosely woven bamboo strips or cane wrapped around some hot charcoals inside a clay bowl.

Zhen knew that Deng had been doing a self-taught crash course on rice cultivation. He had been asking the peasants to bring back books and information from Shahu. He had also been urging the villagers to study Mao Zedong thought, a demand that no one could ignore. Then, when winter was finally drawing to an end, he asked the village head to call a meeting of the whole village. He had a major announcement to make, he said.

Everybody was there at the appointed time, sitting in the cold meeting hall in their threadbare padded clothes, and they listened as Deng indeed announced a major change in the way Longdi would carry out its most important task, the planting of rice. From now on, he said, they would use a new variety. It was called "Pearl Short," the "short" a reference to the shorter stock and a briefer growth cycle that would enable two crops a year instead of just one. Deng looked at the assembled villagers, whose weather-beaten faces stared back at him in mute astonishment. Doubling the crop, he explained, would double the yield. Zhen, whose progress in mastering the local dialect had been rapid, translated, and as she did so, the villagers started to talk and debate among themselves. Clearly the room was agitated, but Old Deng was able to understand none of what was being said, which, in turn, made him visibly frustrated. Zhen, who could see the gap widening between Deng and the local people, proposed that either the farmers speak one at a time, so that everybody could hear, or they try to find a consensus, and let the village chief speak for them in response to Deng's proposal.

The heated conversation resumed, until finally the village chief advanced to the head of the room. He knocked his pipe a few times on the table that had been set up as a kind of dais, cleared his throat, and started to talk. Longdi was the highest town in the area, he said, its average temperature was too cold to allow for two full rice-growing seasons in a year. Only villages with lower elevations and warmer climates could have two crops. Longdi's farmers planted one rice crop and used their remaining growing time for yams, or, sometimes, peanuts, so they would have something special to eat during their holidays. This had been their way to be self-sufficient over many decades.

Old Deng evinced no interest in the peasants' time-tested practice. The Pearl Short variety, he insisted, was a new crop, and, he said, "Chairman Mao had taught us: 'Man can surely overcome Heaven.'" This slogan of the day ended the discussion. No one dared to contradict the Chairman's dictates. The villagers understood that.

But Zhen, listening intently, understood exactly what was at stake for both parties. If two crops were planted and the yield increased, Old Deng would get the credit, and the villagers would be on the losing end. This was because rice, unlike yams, was taxed by the government, so by growing a second rice crop, rather than using the land for yams, they would have to turn over more of their crop in taxes. And with what little they had left, they would also have to buy their holiday treats with their own money or barter with their own possessions. The treats were used to perform the rites to their ancestors, rites that Zhen knew well. They had been treasured parts of Zhen's childhood in the Garden.

Zhen's thoughts were cut short when Old Deng asked the village head to hand her the ledger for the village granary. She was being assigned the duty of measuring out the amounts of seed rice from the village storeroom that would be exchanged for the new Pearl Short variety, when it arrived.

She started work on her assignment right away, but working with the storeroom keepers, she soon found discrepancies between the amounts of grain recorded and the actual amounts in the storage granary. This was going to be bad for her, she realized. Perhaps hungry villagers had pulled some strings with the storeroom keepers to get a bit of extra grain. So Zhen, wary of getting involved in the intricacies of the village relationships, gave the storage keepers an evening to sort out the problem, while she kept the discrepancy a secret from Old Deng. Given what was at stake for the villagers—being caught between the need to feed their families while staying politically correct—she was confident that the villagers would find a way to work out the problem without interference from outsiders like herself or Old Deng. And they did. The next day, Zhen ran into Old Deng on the way to the granary. He told her that the night before, the production team leaders showed him a clean ledger with all the grains accounted for, presuming Zhen had accomplished her assigned task without incident. Zhen didn't know exactly how they'd managed to do that. Most likely nobody had returned missing grain to the granary, since, presumably, it had been consumed. It didn't matter. As far as Zhen was concerned, a clean ledger was good enough.

• • •

Zhen's favorite spot in Longdi was a small covered bridge at the foot of a waterfall outside the village. In late summer and during the harvest season, the waterfall was tame and gentle, spraying cool mist onto the bridge, so villagers suffering from exhaustion went there for relief. It was in that spot that villagers started to call her "Dr. Chen."

Even Old Deng turned a deaf ear to this title. Zhen had been stripped of the right to practice medicine, her license having been torn to pieces; and Old Deng would be held accountable if word got out that Zhen nonetheless did treat sick and injured people in Longdi village. But ironically, he was the first one to benefit from Zhen's medical expertise. She treated him for the stomach ulcer that she'd diagnosed, advising him, among other things, to cut pickles from his diet. Zhen's advice worked.

Over the months, Deng had witnessed how Zhen effectively dealt with accidents and emergencies. The last time was helping the women's production team leader Ah Xuan's sister give birth near the fields where they worked. When Zhen noticed Old Deng while delivering the baby, she said: "Just extending a helping hand as everybody else is doing. Mother and the baby doing great, no worries." Old Deng never said anything about Zhen's "helping hand," but he must have understood then and there that Zhen's medical skills, when added to her language proficiency, had built a special bond with the farmers, a bond that he himself would never be able to achieve. She worked alongside the villagers in the fields, an outsider who could feel their pain and ease it. She would tell the villagers what medicines to buy on their trips to Shahu, and in return, they'd purchase and bring back supplies that she needed: a sack of rice, some groceries, occasional books and newspapers.

But Zhen was also careful not to show Old Deng up. One way was to keep some distance between them. When the new rice-planting season arrived, and the village was going, at Deng's insistence, to plant Pearl Short for the first time, Zhen proposed that she work with Ah Xuan to organize a women's team and take on a certain number of fields of their own. Old Deng liked the idea. Planting rice was far harder than yams, requiring the peasants to wade ankle-deep in icy early spring water to push each seedling into the mud. But that was what Zhen and the other members of the women's team did. Then, for the rest of the ninety days that it took Pearl Short to mature, they worked hard at fertilizing and weeding. It was, for Zhen, a full course of study in hard physical labor.

When the harvest time came around, all hands labored to bring in the rice sheaves as quickly as possible, to avoid the risk of damage from bad weather. Over the years, Long-di's farmers, like farmers all over China, had learned to stage this annual mobilization of the whole village in a race against time. Villagers simply camped in and around a makeshift shed near the bridge for days on end, without returning home. Children in the village delivered food and drink; the old and frail stayed behind to help with babysitting and cooking.

During that time, dehydration, heat stroke, cuts, and bruises were common. Villagers had long been accustomed to disregarding minor health problems until they got worse. But weeks in the fields started to take a heavy toll. When a young man fainted in the field and was carried to the bridge, Zhen insisted that all those with early symptoms of overexertion, such as overheating or dizziness, take rests, before they dropped out of the workforce altogether. But Zhen never stopped doing her turns in the field herself, laboring alongside the other women until she once again would be summoned to the bridge to deal with some medical emergency. One day, Granny Huang rushed from the village to the bridge asking for Zhen, holding a little boy bloodied from a fall. Seeing that Zhen had hurried in from the field, the grateful Granny Huang told her: "You should just stay here, Dr. Chen, your team can do your share of the work in the field." She then looked at Old Deng for approval. He paused a minute, evidently thinking it over. "Why don't you stay by the bridge the rest of the day," he said finally, "and take charge of keeping the records."

The records showed that the experiment with Pearl Short was a success. For many days after the harvest season, the village seemed hushed by a kind of collective exhaustion. Only the voices of children could be heard on the footpaths or from the mud-brick houses. Old Deng was busy writing up his report on the harvest of the Pearl Short and on his plans to repeat the success for the next season. He was determined to show the villagers that two crops were possible even in the high elevation in Longdi. "Man can certainly triumph over heaven," he chanted frequently, triumphantly. The harvest had given him bragging rights and enabled him to project the image he wanted: a man of education and dedication able to contribute to the revolutionary cause. It was not clear to Zhen, however, how the villagers felt about the harvest. Certainly no one would oppose a relatively good harvest, or the promise of repeating it in a second growing season. But apart from Old Deng's crowing, Zhen noted, everybody else seemed strangely mute. There was no celebration. Zhen suspected there was something more on the villagers' minds than the number of catties of rice in their storehouse, though she didn't exactly know what.

The instant the fields were cleared of the first harvest, they were tilled and flooded anew for the second crop. The women's team had had high yields in the first planting, and now a race was on between them and the men's team about which team would excel in the second round. Zhen had become a valued and accepted team member, bending her back over the rice stalks, planting side by side with the other women. Dark from the sun and nimble, she laughed and chatted as loudly and heartily as the other village women did. Her team achieved the highest yield per acre in the village for the year. But she paid a price: excruciating back pain, made worse by the hard wooden bed that she slept on. It was Granny Huang, a highly respected village elder, who noticed Zhen's bed one day, when she stopped by her place. Soon afterward, her son-in-law, Zhao Kai, showed up to drop off a huge bundle of rice stalks. The grateful Zhen now had a mattress. Her new mattress was soft and warm, perfumed with the earthy fragrance of the fields. At dinnertime, the house that she shared with Deng and Mo smelled of new grain. It was a fragrance that she'd never known before.

Zhen by now knew Granny Huang's large family quite well. It was a rare one that boasted a son-in-law from outside the village. Having an outsider marry into her family had burnished Granny Huang's reputation as a capable and respected village elder. In Longdi, this elicited pride and hope that the village was not completely forsaken.

• • •

The Mid-Autumn Festival was coming, and Zhen and Hu Xizhong arranged for Jiyue to be with his mother for the holiday. Zhen's excitement at that happy prospect moved Ah Xuan, her women's team leader, and she invited Zhen to take a bath in her home to ease her back pain. Zhen hadn't had a bath since her arrival, yet she was a little bit apprehensive about Ah Xuan's offer. People in Longdi bathed in their kitchens, and their kitchens were dark, drafty, and sooty earthen-floored spaces filled with all sorts of food and cookware. Zhen couldn't imagine taking off her clothes in such a space. She had grown accustomed to trying to keep clean in the privacy of her room, using a towel dipped in a basin of warm water. Still, she accepted the offer.

At the appointed time, when the sun was high in the sky, Zhen arrived at Ah Xuan's house, bringing a towel, a change of clothes and a precious piece of soap with her. Ah Xuan greeted Zhen warmly and led her to the kitchen at the back of the house. A cloud of warm steam greeted Zhen as she stepped over the threshold, Ah Xuan quickly closing the door behind them. More steam billowed from a huge pot sitting on the stove. Zhen closed her eyes and breathed deeply, letting the steam seep into her.

"My husband helped me pull out the tub this morning." Ah Xuan pointed to a long, dark shadow on the ground in front of them. Every family in the village had one, usually a family heirloom, made of a single piece of mature hardwood from the mountains, hollowed out in the middle to form a tub. A hole was drilled in the bottom to serve as a drain. It was positioned over a small ditch in the kitchen floor. "If it weren't for all this steam, you'd be able to see the beautiful grain of this polished red wood, but still you'll be able to feel how smooth and solid it is," Ah Xuan said, running her hand lovingly over the rim of the tub. "It's said that my grandfather made this himself before he married my grandmother." Zhen felt the smooth edge of the bathtub as Ah Xuan mixed two pots of water, the one boiling on the stove, the other icy cold, pouring both into a wooden pail. "You first pour some on yourself," she said, "and rub your skin vigorously. You keep repeating the action until you feel clean and rinse off. In the end, plug the bathtub, and soak yourself for as long as you want with the remaining water." As she explained, she filled a new pot with water and placed it back on the stove. "When you're done with the hot water in the basin, this pot will be ready again. Use as much as you want. Now I'll leave you alone." She then cracked open the door just a little to slip through and Zhen was alone. Zhen started to pull off her dirty clothes, one layer, then the next, and with each layer off, she felt increasingly warm, the steam moistening her skin, wrapped so tightly for so long, almost forgotten. She poured water over herself and rubbed as Ah Xuan had instructed, awakening every pore. Then she stepped into the dark recess of the hollowed-out log, slipping into the warm water. It was a kind of sensuous luxury in this crude farmer's kitchen that she would never have expected. For the first time in nearly a year, her worries and exhaustion dissolved, evaporating with the steam. In the beams of light coming in from the million cracks in the wooden wall, she felt genuinely happy.

Hu Xizhong arrived with Jiyue a few days before the Mid-Autumn Festival. He had to hurry back after a couple of days because he'd been unable to bring the two girls with him, and he couldn't leave them alone for the festival. But Jiyue would stay in Longdi for a few weeks.

Zhen, of course, was thrilled to have Jiyue there, and, she soon discovered, she wasn't the only one. Jiyue instantly connected with the villagers, who exclaimed over his city looks. So fair and delicate! Like a girl! With his easy smile and gentle sweetness, he became everyone's friend in no time. Well-read and thoughtful for a pre-teen, he could entertain both adults and children with his stories both from newspapers and the classical Chinese novels that he had read. But the deeper meaning of Jiyue's stay in Longdi for Zhen was that here he was free of the nastiness of politics that even children were subjected to back in Fuzhou and now even in a small town like Sanming. There, among the schoolchildren, Jiyue and his sisters were barred from "making revolution," which was most of what their fellow students did, ostracized because their well-educated parents were being "re-educated."

But there was none of that atmosphere in Longdi. The peasants here had always been so poor that there were no rich landlords to struggle against. It was a paradox. Zhen was supposed to be a target of re-education. The inhabitants of Longdi were supposed to embody a kind of natural class wisdom that could correct the bourgeois errors of more educated people. And in a way it was true, but not in the sense that Chairman Mao had intended.

Longdi didn't so much re-educate Zhen as it provided her, and now her son, with a shelter of sorts from the political turmoil, by treating them as welcome guests. Nobody in Longdi tried to lecture her or criticize her. Instead, Zhen actually reaffirmed her faith in education as the acquisition of real knowledge and real skills to serve real people. She also came to better understand the arbitrariness of political power and control in daily life. As a doctor, Zhen had become the villagers' healthcare provider, unlike the ideologically correct Deng, more meddlesome than helpful. But while Deng could use increased rice yields as evidence of his rehabilitation and usefulness, Zhen had nothing comparable to show. Deprived of her license to practice medicine, she was also deprived of the supplies, drugs, and equipment that would enable her truly to apply her skills. She could do some good here and there, but she had no way of bringing real modern medicine to Longdi, and she got no official rehabilitation points for what she did do.

For now, with her son by her side, Zhen was content. Nobody in Longdi called Jiyue the son of counterrevolutionary quack doctors. Here he did not have to be shielded from the humiliation of his mother. He regained his self-confidence and his sparkle. For a while, Zhen thought, life in this poor, spartan, and remote corner of China could be almost normal. It was a good feeling.

The second winter of her stay closed in on Longdi. Mountain rainstorms kept the villagers from making the trek to Shahu, and that put an end to Zhen's communication—little as there was—with the outside world. The newspaper stopped coming, and Jiyue lost his loyal following of news seekers in the village. But he managed to venture out whenever there was a break in the storms. He'd return to tell Zhen of a rainbow, or of the "walking rain," the sheets of rain that moved across the valley, or of a falling rock.

But not all was well with Jiyue. The happy little boy gradually seemed to grow despondent, until one day, he refused to eat any meat, as little as there was. Then he lost interest in eating altogether. Zhen could see her son losing weight and energy, and yet she could do nothing until, one day, Jiyue finally opened up after one more attempt by his mother to hear his thoughts. It was as if he could no longer hold them in. He told his mother that he had seen how little people had to eat in houses he'd been in. Wherever he went, parents of his friends would offer him the best food while his friends looked on greedily. He'd learned that people here saved the best for their guest. But he did not want to take their food and always claimed that he was full.

"And one day when I was leaving Granny Huang's home," Jiyue went on, a hawk swooped down from nowhere, and right in front of him, picked up a chick from the yard. The mother chicken flapped her wings in rage and panic, while the dogs and cats just watched. "They didn't care!" Jiyue was incredulous recalling the scene. His eyes glistened with tears of indignation.

Poverty and the rawness of the fight for survival had crawled into the boy's consciousness, and Zhen was both pained and amazed at this realization. Jiyue had the remarkable insight that kindness to him demanded a huge sacrifice from these poor people, and this raised terrible questions. Should people give a guest the best they had? Should the guest eat his friend's share of food? Zhen was proud of her son's awareness. He in his way was being re-educated too. But the cruelty and indifference he saw around him—the dogs' indifference to the mother chicken's tragedy—reminded him of the human world that he had to survive in. The boy had seen enough in the two months, Zhen decided. Maybe it was time for him to return to Sanming.

As it happened, when the second Spring Festival approached, Old Deng told Zhen that her good work had won her permission from the higher leadership to take a week-long holiday break. Zhen didn't know exactly what she'd done to earn this reward, but very likely it was what she was actually least proud of, keeping the records of the harvest to safeguard Deng's own achievements. But Deng, who was, after all, a veteran propagandist, would figure out a safe way to account for what she was most proud of, her medical treatment of the villagers. He could call it "cultivating good relationships with the local peasants" and "supporting the Communist Party's dictatorship," or some other boilerplate phrase. She was in Deng's good graces, and yet the irony in the situation was overpowering. The villagers of Longdi, resigned to their barren land and their poverty, focused on their brute struggle to survive.

The exiles from the city, by contrast, were using them to establish their political credentials, so that they could return home, leave the village behind them, and resume their previous lives.

Zhen and Jiyue were busy preparing their departure when Granny Huang appeared at their door. She was worried, she told Zhen. Her daughter, Huang Ying, who was due to give birth when Zhen would be away, was complaining about aches and pains. Zhen listened sympathetically, but she knew that the pregnancy had been uneventful so far, and some aches and pains were normal. She would have gone to give Huang Ying a quick checkup anyway, but a storm was moving in and Zhen could see Jiyue flying down the slope, shouting: "Ma, let's go!" Huang Ying would be in fine hands with the village midwife, who handled the births in Longdi, she told Granny Huang, and she'd be back very soon. Then she said a quick goodbye and left with Jiyue on the long, rough walk to the ferry.

• • •

Even after the months of separation, Zhen was unprepared for the sweetness of the Spring Festival. Sitting with her whole family, she was moved to tears as she enjoyed the dishes prepared by her daughters. Sanming, the county seat, was much less remote than Longdi, so Hu Xizhong had occasional clandestine visits from former students and interns, at least those brave enough to risk associating with "historical counterrevolutionaries." These students and interns would bring sausages or local delicacies from Fuzhou with them.

Everybody on this night had a full bowl of steaming white rice, which Zhen, with her newly acquired farmer's knowledge, knew from its fragrance had been freshly harvested.

Her girls had cooked it just right: fluffy, translucent, each grain glistening. Zhen melted a small spoonful of fat from the sausage over the rice, and the fragrance of it brought back a distant memory, eating rich pork dishes in the Flower Fragrant Garden. Hu Xizhong dripped some good soy sauce from Fuzhou on his bowl of rice. Jiyue sprinkled sugar over a dollop of melting lard, and the girls ate theirs plain with the sausage. Deprivation had sharpened everyone's senses.

The week sped by quickly, and when it was time for her to go, Zhen insisted that Hu Xizhong stay at home with the children. Hoisting her bag on her shoulder, she walked briskly to the dock, her backpack heavier than when she arrived from Longdi, since her daughters had insisted on sending her off with what remained from the loot from Fuzhou, and she took it even though she knew they were lying when they told her it would be easy for them to get more. As Zhen reached the dock, she saw someone she knew, Old Yao, a Shahu resident who was a relative of a Longdi family, was the boatman. This clearly was a kind of message from the people of Longdi. They wanted to make sure that she was brought back to the village safely. Zhen thanked Old Yao profusely for making this trip just for her, on a holiday, and on a cold winter day. Old Yao insisted that the honor was his, since Zhen was regarded as a saint in the village.

"A saint?" Zhen was surprised.

Old Yao told her of the gratitude felt in the Longdi village. She had cured their illnesses, delivered their babies, and advised them how to stay healthy. "You know, in villages like these, the one thing that we always dread is getting sick," Old Yao said. By now they were heading upstream toward Shahu. "We have no hospital and no real doctors, and the herbal medicine men . . . well, they don't seem to always know what they're doing. People from Longdi always make a thumbs up when they talk about you. When they come to Shahu to buy things, they say, 'This is for our doctor; make sure you top it off!' "

How different this second trip to Longdi was from the first! The year before, she had been a stranger, alone, cut off from her family, apprehensive about what awaited her, and now she had found a kind of second home. She went on to ask Old Yao if he had news of the baby that the Huang family had been expecting. The old man turned quiet and looked away. He rowed vigorously. Zhen's heart sank. She knew that people did not like to talk about inauspicious things in festive times like the New Year. But she needed to be sure:

"Did Huang Ying give birth?" she pressed Old Yao.

"Yes, she did, but we just got word that the baby has died. Poor woman, the ground there now is so frozen, she can't even bury her child!" Old Yao wiped away tears with the bottom of his palm. Zhen thought of Granny Huang's last visit just before she left and was gripped by an immense regret. She asked Old Yao to go as fast as he could. She felt an urgent need to see Huang Ying, to reassure herself that she was in no danger herself. Zhen then remembered the gift she'd packed for the new child and reached into her bag to pull it out, a few colorful items of baby clothes. They made her think of the two infants she had mourned almost two decades before, her youngest half-brother and her first nephew, both put into the "good hands" of PLA officers in transit on their way to the battlefields in North Korea. Father had just passed away; Sister Jun had gotten stranded in Jinmen; Zhen and her brother, Cang, were being questioned about their past political ties, and there had been no food in the house to support two more mouths . . .

Zhen left the baby clothes on the empty seat of the boat and asked Old Yao to put them to good use. He sighed and nodded. The oars in his old gnarled hands creaked under the stress of the current. The icy water foamed over rocks and splashed into the boat, drenching the baby clothes. Zhen shivered in the cold wind.

When she arrived in Longdi after walking over the mountain passes, Zhen headed straight to Huang Ying's home, encased in a silent gloom. Red posters put up for the expected double happiness of the holiday and the birth of the baby were pasted over with the black and white crepe of mourning, the red beneath faintly bleeding through the thin white paper.

Zhen pushed open the door and quietly called for Granny Huang. A side door creaked open, and out came a shadow of a frail old man trailed by faint sobs from inside the room behind him. Seeing that it was Zhen, Grandpa Huang beckoned her to the door that he had just opened. Zhen went into the dark room, where she could just make out the pale face of a greatly shrunken Huang Ying, who was shivering under a pile of quilts, probably all the quilts the family possessed. Huang Ying saw Zhen and began to moan, as if remonstrating with the dead baby. "Why didn't you wait? Only two more days. My precious boy, why didn't you stay, stay here with mama!" Zhen, her heart breaking, fumbled in her bag for the sausages her daughters had packed. She told Granny Huang to make them for Huang Ying. She did a quick examination and finding nothing physically wrong, promised to be back.

In the days that followed, Zhen reserved some time to begin training a few young people in the village in basic healthcare. And she put in a request through Old Deng for a supply of basic medicines from the government. Old Deng promised to try to get what he could. Then, early one morning, Zhen, awakened by a knock on her door, came out to see a woman on a flatbed pushcart shivering from the cold while flushed by fever. She didn't know how to feel. She knew that she hadn't been summoned to see the woman earlier because the villagers were hesitant to bother her in the middle of the night. Still, she told them, better to wake her up in an emergency and get timely attention than to wait.

From then on, occasional late-night emergencies and weekend patient care made Zhen's full-time work in the fields even more taxing, but she didn't want to give it up, knowing that it made her stronger. In this way, it could be said that her re-education worked. Of course, if she had a choice between this life in Longdi and a medical practice in Fuzhou, she would have opted instantly for the latter. But she didn't have that choice, and there was value in that. She was able to see her own past life in a new light, to compare her fortune to the spareness and the hardness that these farmers experienced day after day, year after year. But her time in Longdi gave her something even deeper. She saw that as poor as they were, there was a kindness and sincerity to these people. She felt that more ought to be done in towns and villages as remote as, or perhaps even more remote than Longdi to give the people consigned to live in them a helping hand.

By the second planting season, Zhen had become a proficient farmer. Standing in icy water up to her calves, she kept pace with Old Huang as the two of them planted new rice seedlings. "Dr. Chen," Old Huang struck up a conversation with Zhen, "do you know the family name of these seedlings?" Zhen wasn't sure what he meant. The old man went on to make his point: These seedlings should be strong and green, yet they were yellow—huang—the last name of the village. Only the Huang people understood the *huang* plants: There was not enough fertilizer or sun to sustain two crops to double the yield. The repeated crop would only strain the soil. The books that Old Deng consulted couldn't make him understand the case in Longdi. "But I think you can understand what I mean," Old Huang concluded. Zhen looked at the yellowish seedlings in their muddy hands, and she looked up to the dark face of the old man, burnished by the sun and chiseled by the wind, and she nodded. She now finally understood why the villagers did not celebrate the increased grain yield from the repeated plantings of the Pearl Short. Healthy soil was their livelihood, and repeated planting of a single plant, while it increased short-term yield, could damage the soil in the long run.

Zhen couldn't know what the outcome of the struggle between Deng and the village would be. What she did know, planting rice seedlings alongside Old Huang that day, was that she and her fellow urban exiles had been sent to this remote village as a political punishment and that the land she was tilling would be the key to their political redemption. But this same land had always belonged to the people who lived on it permanently. Sages and tyrants, dragons, and even sent-down intellectuals may come and go, and, while she didn't know exactly when, or whether it would be months or years or decades, but one day sooner or later, like all other visitors to this place, Zhen would leave too. And when that day came, she thought, when she would again be able to resume her practice of medicine, she would strive to see to it that these people could be cared for in the same way that they cared for their land—in the way that they, kind to her in the ways that their austere lives permitted, had helped her.

"It's Our Home"

JULY IN TAIPEI, the early summer heat relented only after the sun went down. Jun turned thirty-eight that month, now a "Mom" to five children, two of them Min's boys from his previous marriage, one in college and the other doing mandatory military service. On her birthday night, the couple went out for dinner in the city. So Jun left the three young children to the care of Uncle Huang—a neighbor and a veteran who occasionally helped take the Shen children to and from schools on his tricycle—and left for the city in a taxi, a rare luxury for this frugal couple.

After dinner, Min proposed a drive, and Jun was happy to go along, grateful that Min had thought of this rare indulgence, a quiet time for themselves. The years in Taipei since their arrival from Jinmen had hardly been easy, not only because of the arrival of Min's two traumatized sons and the births of three children in rapid succession but also because their economic conditions had been strained to the breaking point. Childcare had kept Jun at home after her brief teaching career, and Min's income from his job in the Judicial Yuan

Jun and Min and their two younger children: Shi, aka Chubby, in Jun's arms and Yiheng in front.

was insufficient. To supplement their finances, Min added some new content to a book published years before that had helped him secure the Judicial Yuan position. It used the best-known classical Chinese stories to illustrate legal codes. This new edition had generated considerable interest and brought in some additional income. His other efforts included publishing a journal and setting up a retail company with a partner. The journal failed, but the retail company, which served as a funnel for a wide variety of U.S. surplus commodities as part of the U.S. postwar economic aid to their old ally, the Nationalist government, started to turn the family's finances around.

The cab took them through the neighborhoods that Min used to tell Jun resembled old Shanghai and Nanjing. Jun recalled their early days in the city—the ceremonies and celebrations at the Presidential Palace, the mahjong players, the singsong girls, and the beautiful widows in Mrs. Hua's mansion—all but a smudged memory now, layered over by the frenzy of keeping the family together and afloat. "Any word from Yueyuan and her stage sisters?" Jun asked her husband for the first time since their first dramatic meeting. Min told her that he had since lost contact with that circle years ago. "I've turned you from a poet to a breadwinner," Jun commented ruefully. The ornate neighborhood of the elites in those early years had now started to be eclipsed by new construction rising higher than any older buildings in the city. It felt as if the new population from the Mainland had decided to drive pillars deep in this once alien soil in service of a dream that was still meant to be realized back on the Mainland. Some day.

Min instructed their taxi driver to take a turn toward a more modest neighborhood, and presently they pulled up to a Japanese-style courtyard house. Jun turned to look at her husband quizzically, unsure of what to make of this unexpected stop. "Are we visiting a friend?" she finally asked. Min smiled, helped her get out of the car, and handed her a key.

"Open the door, my dear, it's our home."

Home! Jun stood at the door of the courtyard house. She turned the key, pushed the door open, and stepped into a riot of crickets. Between the income from his book, his regular job at the Judicial Yuan, the legal arm of the government, and in particular, his retail business, he had by now made enough money to purchase a house for his large family.

The serenity of that moment didn't last long. Soon, the children were bringing friends home to play, and Jun found time to entertain too, joining Min's conversations, and sometimes debates, with his fellow retired military officers. She didn't like the tone of fatalistic resignation that these military men adopted when they talked about Taiwan's stalemate with the Mainland. She preferred to keep the dream of return alive and real, and she fought back when sometimes men dismissed that attitude as naïve. Reclaiming the Mainland may be militarily difficult, and it may take time, Jun insisted, but there had to be a way to reconnect with it, somehow.

The thought of long, seemingly endless years down the road with only children in her daily life sometimes made Jun feel impatient and agitated. She was turning forty, and for many women, that would be close to the end of their working lives. Would she have a career other than being a mother and an assistant to her husband? She had helped editing and printing the journal that Min had attempted, but the business failed because they couldn't seem to find a voice that resonated with either group characterizing the population on the island: the new arrivals from the Mainland, Jun and Min among them, many of them powerful but anxious after their defeat by the Communists, or the islanders who were now subjugated to these new arrivals' rule. Or it could simply have been bad timing for a new media venture, in those initial years when the old and the new groups of the society were still dazed from their sudden collision. If she were to do something on her own, what might it be?

One day Min, who felt Jun's restlessness, returned from work and told Jun that a friend of theirs, Ah Long, had sold his import-export company. Unlike most of Min's other friends, who tended to be gruff, chain-smoking, rough-hewn veterans, Ah Long was a dashing young man who had an engineering Ph.D. from the United States and was fluent in Chinese, English, and German. He had been managing a new branch of his family's import-export company by himself.

"Ah Long?" Jun was surprised and looked up from the vegetables that she was washing. "Where is he going?"

Min explained that Ah Long's father, who lived in Singapore, was ill and wanted his son to return there to take over their main family business. "But guess who bought his company?" Min said. Jun wondered why Min seemed so excited. Why should she care who bought Ah Long's company? But Min's eagerness was now bordering on giddiness. He reached into his briefcase and produced a string of keys. He pulled his wife's hands from the kitchen wash basin, vegetables and all, and triumphantly let the bundle of metallic pieces drop in her hands.

"There you are," he said, smiling broadly. "You bought the company. It's yours now, under your name. You're the boss."

Jun later remembered the weight of the ring of keys in her hands, and she remembered how tears rushed into her eyes once she realized what had happened. So many emotions converged at that single moment. She was grateful and excited, of course, but also daunted. Something transforming had just been placed in her hands. She heard Min reassure her that, after giving it an earnest try, if she decided that it wasn't for her, they could always sell the business, but the main thing she felt was the sense of challenge that she suddenly and unexpectedly faced, a call to action. She had forgotten how invigorating such a feeling could be. An import-export company! She would never have picked something like that even if she were given all the choices in the world! But now she would have to see what she could make of it.

On the day she was going to see the office for the first time, Jun rose at 4:30, went food shopping for the day in the neighborhood market, cooked breakfast, lunch, and dinner, packed the lunches into lunch boxes for everyone—including for herself—left dinner on top of the warm stove, and scrambled to get everyone out of the house. She dropped the children off at their schools and took the bus to the office, holding in her hand a scrap of paper on which she'd written the address.

The office was on the first floor of a modest office building in the city center. Jun pulled out the key to open the door, stepped in, and leaned it shut. The sound of the door closing reverberated in the confines of the suite, and then all fell silent. Jun stood alone. A musty smell surged from the space around her and filled her nostrils. A grandfather clock standing next to her ticked and tocked—a deep and heavy cadence, steady, persistent, and deliberate. Jun surveyed the suite. The front hall where she was standing was quite roomy. To one side was a front desk, and to the other were some armchairs and a sofa that formed a conversation circle. Two doors across the hallway opened onto private offices side by side. The calendar over the front desk was turned to July 18, which was Jun's birthday. Jun smiled at the coincidence. Was it destiny? She had to wonder.

This company imported mostly clocks from the Black Forest area of Germany, and occasionally other products from Germany and other parts of Europe such as machinery or medical instruments. Though her new business was technically an import-export company, exports of mechanical products were practically nonexistent in Taiwan at the time. Advertisements from foreign companies—in English, German, and French—covered much of the wall space and were stacked up on one desk. A typewriter sat next to a stack of letterhead stationery. It had been almost three decades since Jun had had her last English class, and she realized how rusty she'd become in the language when she tried to read the documents. It had been almost as long since she used a typewriter, her father's New Year's gift to Zhen with the stipulation that it be shared with Jun, the one on which she had learned to type. But what she did manage to figure out was enough to make her realize that she needed to write a lot of letters right away. From the stuffed mailbox, she opened letter after letter, and even with her limited understanding, she could see that all demanded some kind of response.

So she set out to buy some tools: an English dictionary, a practice book for typing, and a guide and sample book on how to write English letters. For the immediate correspondence, she would search in the guidebook and lift sentences and recompose them to convey her meaning and information. Every single step was a struggle, until, finally, she reached her signature:

Wenjun Shen Chen, President

Jun kept up the routine of that first day. She got up every morning at 4:30 to prepare all three meals for everyone before setting out to her office. At the end of her day, she'd mail all the letters she'd written, trying to make it home in time to tuck the children to bed—Yiheng, not yet nine, Shi, almost six, and the youngest, Yihui, barely four years old.

The learning curve for her work started close to home. One of the work orders piled up on the desk was a contract with a local company. The company had put in an order for advanced fiber optics from Germany. Jun found that she still needed a signature and some additional details to complete the contract. So she made an appointment with the company for an in-person meeting, thinking that it would be a good chance to get to know the customer. The receptionist left her waiting for nearly half an hour before Jun insisted on meeting the manager right away. Then a gruff man showed up, looking past Jun around the otherwise empty waiting room, and then started to load his pipe, impatiently waiting for someone. Jun went up to ask him if he was the manager, and the man asked her back: "Where's your boss?"

"I am the boss." Jun was clear and calm.

"Well then, I need to talk to your technician."

"Well, I'm sorry, you're out of luck, sir. I'm the boss, the technician, the secretary, and the receptionist all in one." Then Jun proposed to go through the contract to verify some of the details.

"Sister," the man interrupted her: "We're dealing with the latest top-of-the-line product Germany has to offer." He needed to work with someone he could trust. He then canceled the deal right there and walked out.

Jun had never been so furious. No one had ever been that rude, that utterly dismissive of her before, and the reason, clearly, was simply that she was a woman. She vowed to herself never to suffer this kind of humiliation, or to lose a deal like that, ever again.

"That chauvinistic pig!" she exclaimed to Min when he asked her how her day had gone. Min tried to comfort her, feeling responsible, reminding her that they could sell the company any time she wanted.

But Jun would have none of that. She conceded that she ought to have arrived at the meeting more prepared for the possibility of encountering just such a chauvinistic pig. The next time, she resolved, she would be ready. She'd grab the man and sit him down to look through the data, the specifications, and the numbers, to get the deal sealed right then and there. It would turn out that there would be plenty of opportunities for Jun to test her resolve to push back, and to push ahead.

In order to control and better regulate the growth of the industrial sector, the government in Taiwan set up an Import and Export Bureau, which started to designate items for bidding. This gave import-export companies a way to expand. Once a local import and export company made a successful bid for an import item, it would acquire an exclusive right to sell that item. In other words, it would have a monopoly on that particular product. But it wasn't so easy. With more and more factories and business now demanding foreign machinery and equipment, the process to win a bid soon became a bare-knuckled fight among local competitors.

Jun spent hours poring over the possibilities for her first bid. Taiwan was just embarking on an ambitious program of economic development, and she knew from the outset that clocks from the Black Forest weren't going to be much in demand. She had to move to something else. As it happened, the United States was showering aid on Taiwan in its effort to foster free-market capitalism. Modernizing both the agricultural and industrial sectors in the model of free-market economy would mean more machines from the advanced industrial nations. Taiwan was ready for the transformation. It had just completed an extremely successful land reform program that resulted in a tripling of farm incomes. The increased purchasing power that it produced, Jun implicitly understood, would push the import and export sector to the forefront of the economy. Min's purchase of Ah Long's company had been well timed.

But what item should Jun, an inexperienced, female

newcomer to the business with not much seed money and very little technical knowledge, focus on? Her company now consisted of a grand total of two people, herself and a secretary-receptionist she'd just hired. With the secretary's help, Jun was able to spend long days perusing the government's list of import items. After much thought and study and just a bit of whimsy, Jun made her choice. She would import street sweepers.

Street sweepers! Jun had never seen a street sweeper in her life, or ever imagined the need for one. But the very name of the item, street sweeper, conjured up in her mind a vivid picture, a cute little buggy with a brush somewhere under it. She liked the idea instantly, and she knew that there would be a demand as Taiwan's cities expanded. So street sweepers it would be, she decided. The government's list gave a choice between two manufacturers—Ford or Elgin. Jun picked Ford, because it sounded more familiar. She put in a bid.

Very soon, she got a notice from the bureau. The good news was, she had made it to the final round. But then the bureau asked her to provide additional written material to support her bid and distinguish it from the other's. Jun had three days.

What did she know about street sweepers really? Nothing. She had never seen one in real life. She didn't even know the actual size and dimensions of the thing in relation to all other vehicles on Taiwan's streets. All she knew now, with the help of the brochures sent to her by the bureau, was from a picture of a yellow, toy-like machine, cute and futuristic at the same time. But now she needed to explain her choice of Ford, a decision which was made without technical or rational justification. And to defend her choice, she needed to compare it to Elgin's product, which, she was told, was her competitor's choice. Of course, what was important wasn't the look or the color, the original reasons of her choice, but a persuasive argument for the government to award Jun an exclusive import license. Trying to make that argument, she felt a bit like a college student cramming for an exam on a topic she wasn't prepared for.

But one thing Jun knew very well: She did not like to be a loser. So for the three days and nights, she searched in libraries, bookstores and car dealerships for more information on vehicles in general. She talked to technicians. She spent hours flipping through dictionaries trying to read the articles and passages in brochures and English technical manuals, sometimes translating one word at a time. And on the third day, she stumbled into a small section in a catalog on the shelf of a car dealership where she had gone in search of more brochures, that enumerated the advantages of the Ford street sweeper over the Elgin model. As the deadline ticked closer, she translated furiously that little section of the catalog.

When she finished the translation after hours of exhaustive work, she took her draft to a mechanic named Ah Da, an old army buddy of Min. She read him a string of broken sentences and what seemed to her nonsensical words, and he tried to make sense of it all while Jun took notes. She went back and forth verifying the accuracy with Ah Da until she was able to rewrite the whole translation in good Chinese, complete with proper technical terms. Jun worked through the night of the third day to put the finishing touches on her argument. In addition to all the technical features she listed, the Ford model had one feature that would fit Taiwan's unique situation: It had three wheels instead of Elgin's four and therefore would be able to easily rotate 360 degrees, making it suitable for Taiwan's narrow streets and dead-end alleys. Working furiously, Jun finished her document just in time to deliver it to the Import and Export Bureau when it opened its doors. A week after she handed in her translation and additional report, she was informed that she had won the bid! She was to become the exclusive seller of Ford street sweepers.

After getting the news, Jun was elated and incredulous at the same time. She looked out of her office window at the streets, choked with vehicles and dust, strewn with garbage, and could almost see her bright-yellow sweeper coming down the road, catching everyone's eyes, leaving a perfectly clean strip of pavement behind as it glided proudly by. Onlookers would gawk; store owners would smile with gratitude; and the city would become cleaner, inch by inch, day by day, because of the cute yellow buggy that she had imported from America.

Jun's first customer for the street sweeper turned out to be the Taipei city government. That was also a stroke of luck, so much so that Jun was feeling that there must have been some kind of divine intervention involved in her street sweeper enterprise. Min's purchase of Ah Long's company had drained all their family savings and then some. They'd also had to borrow money from friends. Now, in order to finance their purchase of the machines, they would need some serious bank loans, and with the government as a client, Jun could enlist its help in securing government loans.

The next step was to find more customers. Who needed big, robotic street cleaners? The labor for sanitary work was still cheap in Taiwan in the early 1960s, so the places that needed her machines, Jun reasoned, would be those that needed constant cleaning and yet lacked the space or flexibility for a large cleaning crew to be present all the time. Also, prospective purchasers needed not only the foresight and ambition to want the machines but also the resources to pay for some advanced machinery that was not really essential for a company's production processes. With this vision in mind, Jun immersed herself in public libraries and government agency offices. She found that cane sugar had accounted for 62.37% of the total national exports of 1957. Other important exports included rice, tea, bananas, and textiles. All these industries required large processing plants that needed constant cleaning, and all of them would benefit from government subsidies. Jun decided to tour some factories.

In the sugar refinery that she toured, Jun learned that production was constantly disrupted by the need to clean the plant of the sugar powder shed by the processed cane, or everything would turn inconveniently sticky. This, Jun concluded, was an industry ready to upgrade its cleaning operation, and the increase in exports was providing it with the capital to do so. Since the government, helped by American loans, was subsidizing new investment, Jun was clever enough to see her opportunity—First street sweepers, she thought to herself, then other machinery for various industries. But this meant that Jun had much more homework to do—to learn about machines. And she would need to improve her English in order to read the technical manuals that came with them.

Not long afterward, Jun received a notification that the first three street sweepers, destined for Taipei, had arrived, and the customer wanted them right away. Jun realized that she had made no provision for delivery of the product she had sold. For the first time, she confronted the reality that she couldn't just drive them off the dock to her client. A desperate call to Min and a quick exchange later, they decided to turn to Ah Da once again, Min's old friend from the military. Between Min and Ah Da, they managed to get a military truck to deliver the sweepers.

Ah Da test-drove one of the little yellow buggies, which turned out to be not so little. It executed a 360-degree turn within the government office's courtyard just as Jun had imagined, making everything perfectly clean.

"The Big Muscle"

O<small>N A LATE SPRING DAY</small> in 1973, Jiyue, Zhen's son, was walking home from his middle school. Slung across his shoulder was his new green canvas schoolbag, a cool accessory among schoolboys at the time. His family was finally back together again, both of his parents had been recalled from their respective exiles and given back their right to practice medicine. But they had been assigned to a much smaller apartment in the Women and Children's Hospital compound than they used to have, and Jiyue decided to take a detour back to their former, grander stand-alone house, where he had his own room, just to see it.

As he entered the trellised gate, he saw a chubby boy throwing stones in the direction of a house.

"Watch out, you're gonna smash the windows!" Jiyue warned.

"Who are you?!" came an angry retort.

"That used to be my house." Jiyue told him.

"Not yours anymore, it's mine now!" and the boy picked up a stone and aimed it menacingly at Jiyue, who walked away.

When he got home, he wanted to know who was living in their old home. The new Party secretary, his mother said, but why, she asked, did he want to know?

Jiyue didn't reply. He didn't want to awaken bad memories in his mother, because he knew it was the very Party secretary who had approved her removal from her work as a physician and her exile to the countryside. Now he was living in their house!

By the time Zhen and Hu Xizhong returned to Fuzhou, the peak of the Great Proletarian Cultural Revolution had passed. Many exiled intellectuals like them were trickling back to the city. Schools, hospitals, and the like were limping back to a resumption of their normal roles. Zhen and Xizhong both returned to work, but at several ranks below where they had been before their exiles, with lower salaries to match. They were also assigned the smallest apartment for a family of five in the most dilapidated of the hospital's residential buildings. Zhen and Xizhong had one of the two bedrooms, their two girls shared the other, while Jiyue was consigned to a corner of the common room next to the tiny kitchen.

Zhen could have fought for bigger housing or better pay or a higher rank, but the underlying problem for her and her husband was political. She needed to clear her name, tarnished during the decade of political witch hunts. And she needed to do it soon, so that her children—her daughters Yi and Wen, and their son Jiyue, then ages nineteen, seventeen, and fourteen, respectively—wouldn't be burdened with their parents' political legacies as they moved into the world. And so, she petitioned the Party for a removal of the bad political labels that had long been in her dossier. She'd never been a counterrevolutionary or a Rightist, she repeatedly emphasized. She had supported the Party from Day One.

While she waited for a response, she moved to protect

her children from a fate that was inescapable for millions their age at that time. In the wake of the Cultural Revolution, the government policy stipulated that only one child in a family could live in the city with their parents; all others would be sent to the countryside "to learn from the peasants," often to very remote villages, and for an indefinite time. All her three children had surmounted enough obstacles already, Zhen believed. They already had to change schools so as not to witness their parents' public humiliation, and then to endure additional years of exile where they'd been targets of denunciation in every school they enrolled in. Returning them to the countryside and on their own, Zhen worried, would be too much for them to bear. They shouldn't have to do so just as their lives were finally starting to come together.

Yi, the oldest girl, was first in line to be one of these sent-down youths. Given her parents' counterrevolutionary labels, it was almost a certainty that Yi would get an undesirable assignment. This was the moment when Zhen decided to accept her childhood friend Xianru's offer to use her connections, what the Chinese call *zou houmen*, "going the back door" to keep Yi from being sent to some very remote, poor, forbidding place. Her friend Xianru's parents were former servants to a wealthy Fuzhou family living in the prestigious Sanfang Qixiang district in the heart of the old Fuzhou city. When the wealth and the family that they had served were dispersed in the revolutionary years, Xianru's family became the sole occupants of the house. Their impeccable working-class background kept her family intact and kept them in place. Now the old house had a new master, a local Party secretary Wu, and Xianru had taken over her parents' job working for his family. She told Zhen she would talk to Secretary Wu about Yi.

Xianru delivered. Wu arranged for Yi to be "sent down" to a village that was really a suburb of Fuzhou, so she would stay close to home.

That left two. When Wen, the second daughter, graduated from high school, she was designated the one child of the family who could stay in the city. She was assigned to work in a neighborhood factory, earning 18 *yuan* (about three American dollars) a month, "One *yuan* for each year of my life," she later joked.

Jiyue graduated from high school just a year before the sent-down youth re-education system was annulled. By then both Zhen and Xizhong had started to move back up in the ranks in their hospital. Their increased status enabled them to secure for Jiyue a nearby sent-down location also. But Jiyue didn't have to stay long in the Fuzhou suburbs. In 1977, shortly after he was sent down, the college entrance exams were reinstated. All three of the children were able to take the exams and entered college. They were all right.

Zhen was nearly forty-eight when she resumed her work in the hospital, which made her all the more anxious than ever to revive her Two Ailments Campaign. But when she broached the subject to some of her colleagues, their response was decidedly unenthusiastic. "Why rock the boat?" they said. "Given your family background, why stand out?" Or, "If something goes wrong, wouldn't it go on your dossier and give you trouble?" Despite all the caution—mostly well-intentioned, Zhen would respond: "I already know what it's like to be labeled a counterrevolutionary. How much worse can it be?"

Caution, however, was not entirely unwarranted, as times

were still uncertain. The internal political power struggle had exploded into view the year before with the sudden death of Lin Biao, Mao's designated successor. At the time nobody knew exactly what had happened. It turned out that he'd tried to take power in a coup and when it failed, died in a plane crash trying to escape. But even though nobody knew the exact circumstances, Lin Biao's death was a clear indication that the situation was unpredictable even at the highest level. Most people felt it was a time to recuperate from the years of turmoil, not to take chances or to embark on new ventures. "No thanks," was the response Zhen got from one person whose help she tried to enlist for the Two Ailments campaign. "No more sleeping where the pigs shit." "You mean to cut short my hard-earned peace and quiet?" were some of the other responses.

Meanwhile, there was excellent news. Zhen's petition to remove her bad political labels was granted, and it was final. She felt like a long bed-ridden patient leaving behind her entire troubled medical history, walking away with a clean bill of health. The Party admitted it had been a mistake to label her a suspected counterrevolutionary. Zhen was one of the first to benefit from what was to become a nationwide movement that gained speed after Mao's death in 1976. In the following years, the Party would "reverse the verdict" on literally millions of people from the educated elite who had been deemed "revisionist" or "capitalist roaders" during the Cultural Revolution, and even before, in the anti-Rightist campaigns of the late 1950s. By 1985, more than 470,000 CCP Party members had been given back their Party memberships, and more than 30,000,000 other people had wrongful convictions removed from their dossiers.

Being "rehabilitated" produced different responses. Some

celebrated their restored innocence; some unleashed their anger and resentment for the suffering they had been unjustly forced to undergo. For Zhen, it was a bit of everything—confirmation of her innocence and regret for the waste of some of the prime years of her life, but also a chance to publicly reaffirm her faith in the Party: "The Party has apologized, not only to me, but to everyone whose cases were corrected after re-examination," she would say, "and it restored my name." Years later, speaking softly but with her usual tone of certainty, she told me: "People make mistakes. So did the Party." Zhen had seen the enormous waste, death, and suffering of the Maoist years, but as always, she chose to put it behind her. She parroted the Party's euphemistic boilerplate about the "mistakes" that had been made, which was a way of declaring that she'd been on the Party's side all along. She was ready to close that book and to move on.

Xizhong's name was also cleared, his former rank restored. Both he and Zhen were once again chief physicians with commensurate salaries. A newer, better apartment was promised to them in a building under construction, though Zhen turned it down, because, by the time it was finished, she said, their children would all be out of the house and they wouldn't need anything so big. It was perhaps a genuine gesture but there could also have been a dollop of calculation in it as well. She may have wanted to accumulate some merit, to put some political capital in the bank, just in case. Where one lived at that time was a key mark of stature and prestige, but Zhen and Xizhong gave up all that, reducing their profile and their risk.

• • •

With life back to more or less normal, Zhen returned to her plan to eradicate the Two Ailments. She found a close ally in her mentor Xia Meiqiong, who had brought her along to start the Women and Children's Hospital, and who had inspired her to go outside of the hospital to find their patients in the countryside, those farmers who never had the access to modern medical care. Xia had gone to medical school in the United States, which was enough for her to be branded a traitor during the Cultural Revolution, and now, after years of exile and torture, not much different from Zhen's own, she had just been restored to her former position as hospital director. One result of all those years of "making revolution," she told Zhen, was that a whole generation of medical students had finished school without gaining the knowledge they needed to work as doctors. The solution, Xia suggested, was to train the new medical school graduates on the job.

Zhen agreed. She could build into her plan a two-way training program: She would take new med school graduates to the countryside for hands-on experience and bring back health workers currently serving in remote regions for proper training. These were what was then called "barefoot doctors," a profession that had been created during the Cultural Revolution. They were usually local people or sent-down youths with high school education, who received rudimentary medical training to serve the local population, usually in places too remote for any professionally trained doctors to go. The Women and Children's Hospital would then become the heart of a new satellite system of rural care, training local medical workers and treating severe cases too complicated for those local doctors to handle.

It was a good idea, even visionary. But Xizhong pointed out that Zhen would need "big muscles" to bring it about. "Big muscles" meant financial support from the higher-up health authorities in government. And to get the "big muscles" to back her plan, Zhen had to package the proposal in such a way that it would appear to be a collective achievement, making her work part of the Party's efforts to serve the people.

And so, Zhen went to the provincial health authorities armed with recent editorials in the *People's Daily*, a CCP mouthpiece. The newspaper reiterated the "core mission" of the Communist Party, namely to "serve the people, particularly the poor and lower middle-class farmers and workers," the core supporters who had propelled it to power. Zhen proposed starting the project in an area known as Longyan, a district at the juncture of three provinces, Fujian, Jiangxi, and Guangdong, well known as the site of a meeting in 1929 where Mao Zedong had written his famous line "the little spark can set the entire prairie aflame." It was an echo of the orthodox Marxist idea that the revolution and the seizure of power should be based on the rural poor in China's vast countryside, rather than on the urban elite. Now that the spark had indeed claimed the entire prairie, Zhen, as always trying to turn the Party's slogans to her advantage, argued that the place where it all started should lead the march toward a new era.

Her Two Ailments proposal had a lot of merit, she was told, but the health ministry didn't have the money for it. The central leaders in Beijing had just called for China to embark on what it called the Four Modernizations, modernization in the fields of science and technology, industry, agriculture, and defense. The Two Ailments, and, indeed, medicine in general, were not among the designated modernizations. As it would turn out, the launch of the Four Modernizations would be the beginning of the country's economic rise.

Zhen was undaunted. Her decades of dealing with the Communist government had made her an astute political player. She recrafted her argument. The Two Ailments would be indispensable to the Four Modernizations, she pointed out. Wiping out these endemic, curable women's diseases in the countryside would help to build a healthy workforce in the agriculture sector. The project would also have the added advantage of producing fast results, because the two ailments could be cured more quickly than most medical conditions and curing them would boost the national health index, an important measurement of a modern nation.

The argument was unassailable. Zhen's proposal was approved. "Are you ready to go on the road again?" Xizhong asked his wife. Was she? Zhen was overjoyed at the approval of her plan, but she also felt a kind of anticipatory guilt because of her impending absence from home. When she traveled to remote areas in the 1950s, she often returned home so exhausted that she would fall ill. She had been in her thirties then. Now she was fifty-one, a woman with three grown children who had been through a lifetime of arduous struggle. Did she really want to endure the discomfort of China's poor, backward countryside, the winter cold, the unrefined food, the hard beds, the mud, the smell, the absence of indoor plumbing—not to mention the distance from her husband? For most people the answer would be obvious. But Zhen's mind was deeply imprinted by what she had witnessed before: the desperation of all those women afflicted by the Two Ailments, the husband who carried a coffin with him, the woman who hired a band to celebrate her cure. She told herself that the people of Longdi had never even had a chance to be treated. If she didn't take care of them, who would? Nobody would even know of their existence. They had, since time immemorial, been too far away and too insignificant to be cared for.

"Yes," she said to her husband with a sigh. "I'm ready."

———

In the fall of 1976, months before Zhen's relaunch of her Two Ailments Campaign, Mao Zedong died. It was a momentous event for those who were born or had come of age since 1949, knowing him as their only leader, as well as for the older generation like Zhen, whose life trajectories had been dramatically shifted by this man. His death brought an era to a close, an era that had meant different things to different people, but that had been tumultuous for all. To Zhen, Mao had inflicted deep and lasting personal suffering and pain, but he had also enabled her to find her most desperate patients, giving her work a meaning that she had never known before. In the uncertain lull after the Chairman's death, Zhen made preparations to tour the countryside. At the same time, she and Xizhong made arrangements to bring their widowed parents to live with them, partly to better take care of them, and partly to give the austere apartment the feel of a home, especially when Zhen would be away.

Xizhong's father was ready to move to his son and daughter-in-law's apartment, but Zhen's mother was more hesitant. During the long years of revolutions, she and Ah Niang had become each other's constant companions, secretly sharing a Bible. And Mao's revolutionary Red Guards somehow never made it to their forgotten corner of the neighborhood. Ah Nai used the Bible in the morning, praying for Jun's return as part of her routine, and Ah Niang in the evening, including Jun as part of her prayer as well. Now facing the prospect of spending the remaining days of their lives apart in the care of their own grown children, Ah Nai would only move after Ah Niang's arrangements had been made. It seemed to be a matter of time now. Both Ah Niang's more successful children, Hou and my mother Xiang, were working in other cities, and they had pledged to help their younger siblings living in Fuzhou to find an apartment large enough to accommodate their mother.

As soon as Xizhong's father moved in to Zhen and Xizhong's apartment, the cracked bust of Chairman Mao in their living room, the one that the Red Guards had accused her of desecrating years before, was replaced—with Xizhong's father's Christian cross.

• • •

Zhen's team of new medical school graduates was making their first trip to Longyan. Many had never experienced the humid heat of the mountains, so different from the sultry warmth of the city. But for Zhen, having ten years before walked to Longdi, and even more remote villages than Longyan, the heat was nothing new. She had learned to plant rice and harvest yams there. Now, she was back at work. The mountains rolled endlessly, the slopes thick with vegetation rising, then plunging, then shooting up again. "Maybe this terrain is only for dragons," Zhen joked with her team members, noting that many place names there had the word *long*—dragon—in them: *Longdi* meant "dragon land," *Longyan* "dragon rock."

Zhen and the team paused at the top of the first peak to take in the sheer volume of the "dragon rock," Longyan. She wiped the sweat from her forehead, looked to the higher mountain ahead, and let out a deep breath.

"Should we take a break?" a student asked, hearing Zhen's deep sigh. But Zhen wasn't so much tired as thoughtful. If her work hadn't been interrupted years ago, the Two Ailments would have been eradicated by now, and a whole generation of women would have escaped pain and suffering. Anyway, here she was, taking up the fight again. "Let's keep moving," she said, eager to get to their destination, chatting with the students along the way. Most of them had been chosen for medical school from among the "red" social classes, workers, peasants, and soldiers. They were eager to learn.

Longyan was the county capital, and actually had a clinic, rudimentary as it was. There was a barefoot doctor working there, and his two assistants had been instructed by the county officials to set up simple living quarters and a reception area. Zhen and her team arrived at night to beds already set up, and they woke up to an excited clamor outside. The front yard of the clinic was already packed with patients and their families, waiting to see the big doctors from the big hospital in the provincial capital. Starting from that very first morning and for the rest of the week in Longyan, the days blurred into nights as Zhen supervised the students treating patient after patient. When darkness fell, someone would call for the first light to be lit, or additional flashlights to be brought in, so they could keep going.

Their triage center quickly turned into a gathering ground. One day, the parents of a patient pulled up a hand-cart of watermelons and gave out free slices. A mother of a patient dropped to her knees and kowtowed to Zhen. A young son of a woman allowed to return to her family after recovery from fistula told her, "Mommy is coming home! Mommy is going to tuck me in tonight!"

When women thanked Zhen for giving them a second chance in life, she told them: "You have given me a second chance too."

After Longyan, the team pushed farther inland to another mountain town called Shanghang, then in the third week, it doubled back to the coast to a fishing town called Huian. Huian had an unusually high number of young women suffering from uterine prolapse, an ailment more common among middle-aged women. Trying to understand the reason for this, Zhen asked a young mother why she'd had to do the harvesting alone soon after her son was born. The woman said that her husband had to go fishing, and the harvest couldn't wait. Women often had no choice but to keep up the farm work when the husbands were out fishing.

The woman's name was Yangyang. Zhen explained to her that she needed to rest for at least a month after her surgery, or the treatment wouldn't do her much good in the end.

"No way," Yangyang told her. "He'll divorce me. Or my in-laws will kick me out."

"But you have to heal in order to be a good worker . . ."

Zhen watched the tears trickling down Yangyang's cheeks.

"And you are still young enough to fully recover, if you'll give it time to heal."

Two days later, as Zhen was about to board a bus to her next destination, she was called back to the village to treat an emergency. When she got there, she found that it was Yangyang, and she had suffered a severe cut on her leg, so deep that she would need to stay in bed for some time. Was the wound self-inflicted? Zhen wondered, but she didn't ask. Could the husband have done this to her, furious when his wife told him she couldn't work for a month? Or was it just a freak accident? Whatever the cause, the injury's silver lining would be the same: Yangyang's recovery from the deep cut—if she recovered from it– would give her time for her uterine prolapse to heal.

After over a year of traveling, Zhen was close to having the Two Ailments under control. She was confident when she went to talk to the Fujian health minister that funding would be available for the next stage to wrap up the project, and to set up a network of clinics so that rural people could get care without the long trip to the big city.

But the minister didn't say anything about more funding. Instead, he told Zhen, "Family planning policy has now been pushed to the forefront."

Zhen understood immediately. A campaign to reduce China's high birthrate had been proposed several times before, but each time had been pushed back by Mao Zedong's call for more births, not less. "The more people we have, the more powerful we are," was his view, and prominent figures who had argued in favor of reducing the population had been mercilessly persecuted. Now, with Mao safely under glass in his mausoleum, population control had been made into a priority in the larger Four Modernizations agenda, and this was going to create a dilemma for Zhen.

"With all due respect," Zhen said to the minister on that day, "I've been trained to fix the broken." But she immediately realized that neither she nor the minister was in a position to ignore a governmental directive. And the directive was clear. A *People's Daily* editorial in late January 1979 set the target—keeping population growth to below 1% starting the following year, rather than around the 2.8% it had been until then. The article had argued that overpopulation would slow down modernization. To reduce the average five births for every child-bearing woman to one would be a drastic step, and one that would be painful to implement.

But Zhen also knew that she would have no escape from this goal. In fact, right then, the minister informed her that she would be a natural choice to lead the family planning effort in Fujian province. He made no secret of the fact that it would be a campaign like no other. Already, there were reports of what was being called a guerrilla war in the countryside in provinces where the campaign had already started. Some local officials were eager to distinguish themselves by getting outstanding results. They resorted to extreme measures, including rounding up pregnant women and forcing them to undergo abortions and requiring tubal ligations for women who had just given birth, preventing them from getting pregnant again. Resistance seemed just as determined and versatile. Large family networks helped women hide and have babies in secret, sometimes continuing to do so until they obtained the holy grail of China's countryside, a boy.

"The campaign in Fujian needs a leader like you," the health minister told Zhen, "someone with good medical skills, someone who can travel, win the trust of local people, someone who knows how to get things done."

Zhen sensed that the minister wanted Fujian to avert the "guerrilla war" that was taking place elsewhere, and if she was right about that, she should try to find a way to work with him. For the moment, she asked for time to think things over. Not that she could decline the minister's request—he was only being polite in framing it as a request; actually, it was an order.

Although Zhen had grown up in a liberal family in a city, her years taking care of rural families' most personal problems gave her a unique perspective on their enduring preference for boys over girls. A boy, in the old Chinese way, stayed in the family that had him, continuing its name, working for the welfare of his parents when they got older, and marrying to bring home a wife as an extra hand. A girl was "spilled water," wrenched away by marriage even before she was fully grown. Zhen understood that a woman's resistance in this "guerrilla war" was about far more than the number of children she could have. It was a fight for her dignity and respect;

it was the difference between happiness and rejection. Once married into her husband's family, her ticket to acceptance and appreciation was to have a boy. A son would give her a place and a voice.

These deep needs were what the government's policy now confronted, the reason the local officials eager to get credit for carrying out the policy were provoking such a powerful resistance. Zhen saw the challenge. She wanted to use her medical skills to cure people, not to harm them, but reducing the population, stopping women from having babies, would not be a matter of curing people. If anything, it would be just the opposite.

Before she gave her formal answer, Zhen brought her team of healthcare workers on another rural tour, where she directly confronted her dilemma in a concrete way, not as an abstraction but with real, living people. The first stop was Yongchun, almost a hundred miles southwest of Fuzhou. Her team there dealt not only with the Two Ailments but had also expanded into more general ob-gyn care, including delivering babies when needed. The first emergency brought to them was a woman who seemed to have had an ordinary delivery—of a girl. But she wouldn't stop bleeding. Zhen diagnosed postpartum hemorrhaging due to an inverted uterus. It was a case that Zhen would have liked to handle in the hospital, but that wasn't an option here. She ordered the team to administer anesthesia, collect blood from donors on the spot, and prepare emergency equipment. Every moment counted to save the woman's life. She then worked to push the hemorrhaging uterus to its normal position, once, twice, again and again, telling the unconscious woman to hang on, hang on. "We'll fix this, we'll return you to your daughter."

The last rays of the sun were receding from the corner of the window when the hemorrhage finally stopped. Silence, fatigue, relief. Dark blood congealed on the wooden plank that the new mother was lying on, and on the ground below it. The patient, Xiaofang, seemed to gain strength as the anesthesia wore off; and she started to stir. Somewhere from a corner of the room, the baby started crying indignantly for her mother.

Given that the effort to reduce the birthrate was already being pushed into high gear, Zhen knew that the next thing she was supposed to do would be to perform a tubal ligation on Xiaofang to prevent her from becoming pregnant again. Perhaps many other doctors would have done it, even though official family planning rules allowed women in the countryside to have second births if the first one was a girl, as long as they waited at least five years to try again for a boy. Zhen didn't do it. It was out of the question in this particular patient's case, she told Xizhong when she returned home.

"A life is not just a number," she said, unburdening herself to her husband. Given the high infant mortality rate in the countryside, there was a strong possibility that the patient could lose her baby girl, and if Zhen had done a tubal ligation, Xiaofang would have had no possibility of having another child. Given the rural traditions, that would effectively end her hope for a normal life. Zhen believed in the pursuit of modernization, but she'd also witnessed how much women were called on to sacrifice for their families and communities. Now they were being called on to sacrifice their own chances of basic dignity in life for a national goal. How much more did they have to give up for the greater good? Zhen had been able to use her skills to give women a fighting chance to have dignified lives, and now she was expected to use those very same skills to end that chance.

But what could she do? No one could go against the central government's directives, not her and not the minister of health. Moreover, Zhen did not oppose the ultimate goal of reducing the population. She just didn't believe the immediate goal of bringing down the population growth to under 1% in the following year was realistic or workable. She knew that it would be cruel. If she took up leadership of the program in Fujian to reach that official goal, she would almost certainly be in the position to be responsible for the harsh practices in Fujian's vast rural regions as they were being performed in other provinces, and she might even be expected to perform them herself. What she really wanted to do was to wrap up her Two Ailments campaign and continue on to build a rural healthcare system. If she had that option, she would not touch the family planning assignment. But she didn't have that option. Nor did she have the option of refusing to become the leader of the program.

What did she do? Even before she officially took up her leadership position, she was called back to Yongchun to deal with some urgent problems that had cropped up a few months after her initial visit there. Yongchun was where Xiaofang lived, the young woman whom Zhen had declined to sterilize. The moment Zhen returned, Xiaofang's sister showed up at her door. She told Zhen that Xiaofang had disappeared, and she worried that her sister was pregnant again and the pregnancy wasn't going well because she'd been in great pain. The sister feared that Xiaofang would hide until the baby came, and that she would try to have it on her own, in secret, without help. Zhen was alarmed.

She joined Xiaofang's sister and began to search for the young woman.

They found her curled up on one of the narrow berms that divide rice fields, her face under a straw hat. When Zhen asked her how she was doing, Xiaofang responded with an angry explosion: "Take your sterilization stuff back to the city folks and leave me alone," she cried. Zhen saw in Xiaofang's fury that, in her eyes, Zhen was no longer the good doctor who had saved her life and cured other women's diseases. She was a personification of the worst aspects of population control, just like those ruthless local officials who hunted down women like her, taking away her chance to have a boy.

But Zhen stayed calm. She asked Xiaofang how her daughter was doing. "What's the use of a daughter?" Xiaofang screamed with a vehemence that didn't seem possible for someone curled up in pain and discomfort: "What does a daughter get me but pain, humiliation, and suffering? I almost lost my life for her, and what have I got? Nothing, absolutely nothing!" The straw hat slipped, revealing Xiaoifang's face smeared with tears and mud. "Don't touch me. Go back to the city. Leave me alone. I'm having a son. I want a son!" Her cries bounced between the majestic mountains around them—a son . . . a son . . . a son.

"Xiaofang," Zhen started gently, trying again, "you want a son, and that's fair. But do you know that your husband is the one who determines if your baby is going to be a girl or a boy?"

"Really?" Xiaofang perked up. "And, according to the policy," Zhen continued, "a couple with a rural household registration can have a second child five years after the birth of their first child, if the first child is a girl. And in five years you'll still be only twenty-five, the very best age for having children."

"So you mean you're not here to sterilize me?"

"No. I'm here to help people understand how to plan the best family with healthy children. In your case, having a second child so soon after your difficult birth would be dangerous to your health, and expensive"—meaning that she would have to pay a fine for having a second child in violation of the rules.

"Expensive?" Xiaofang said. "You think my life is worth something?"

"Yes, it is worth a whole world for your beautiful baby girl who's waiting for you at home. It's worth it to me to come here to take care of you."

In the end, Zhen got Xiaofang to the clinic, where she diagnosed an ectopic pregnancy, meaning that the fetus had been conceived outside of the uterus. She had to have an abortion after all, but in order to save her life, not to stop her from having another child. Zhen assured Xiaofang that after her pregnancy was terminated and she'd had time to heal, having another child shouldn't be a problem.

Xiaofang had proven to Zhen the price that women were willing to pay in their desperate attempt to have boys. It was something buried deep in their psyches from the tradition that they were steeped in, and from whose grip they had little power to extract themselves. Now it put them into direct, irreconcilable conflict with local officials eager to meet and exceed the quotas for abortions and sterilizations. Neither Zhen nor anybody else could eradicate this rural tradition or stop the actions of local officials. But she could try to help women navigate the system, avoid the worst, try to make it work to their advantage. Xiaofang helped Zhen see that she should take the leadership of the family planning campaign and steer it as humanely as she could.

Zhen's first move was adding speaking tours to her

countryside trips to treat women for the Two Ailments. She spoke in town halls in the evenings, when the husbands had returned from the fields. Her team handed out snacks for those who did not have the chance yet to have dinner. She'd tell the local health workers beforehand to bring in couples, not just women. But the women usually stood shyly on one side, and men chain smoked on the other.

"Come on in, everyone," Zhen would call to them. "Yes, you, the men too. I'll be talking to all of you." She gave basic talks on reproduction, pointing out that men were responsible for the sex of their children. "You should know," she would say to the men, "that if you don't get a boy, it's because of you; it's not because of your wife."

She explained that the government's policy actually did take into account the wish of rural people to have boys. City families could only have one child, regardless of the sex, but rural families had two chances, spaced out over five years, if the first born was a girl. This would give the mother's body time to regain strength for a healthy second child, and for a healthy mother as well. She reminded her listeners of the sad practice from before the Communist liberation when "baby girl pagodas" served as receptacles for unwanted newborn girls. And she'd end on a high note: "We all have many things to fight for, but the main thing is to have better, healthier, and happier lives." That, she said, was exactly the reason for the population control policy. "Yes, there are punishments that come with it, but the same government also sends medical workers to your homes to take care of your health."

In her leadership position, Zhen was taking a surreptitious one-person stand against a nationwide movement—surreptitious in the sense that she did enough to appear to be following orders, but in reality, she was dragging her feet. Passions flared in other parts of the country, competing for the best performance in carrying out the government's directives, and Fujian was no exception. So when an urgent request came from Zhangpu County, over three hundred kilometers south of Fuzhou, for reinforcements for the local barefoot doctors, Zhen took a team of six doctors—as requested—to the location.

Zhen and her team arrived in the village after a three-hour train ride to find a square outside the clinic filled with more than a hundred women, presumably rounded up to undergo procedures to end their child-bearing abilities. "They sat quietly waiting for their turns," Zhen wrote in her memoir years later, describing the scene. It was already early afternoon, and the local official led her and the team through the waiting crowd into the clinic. Zhen detected a certain swagger in the movements of the leader, proud to have secured medical expertise for his village from the highest level. Zhen must also have felt the heat of the waiting women's stares. In the large room that they entered, there were five makeshift operating tables—door planks on stools, three of which were being used for operations being performed at a fever pitch; two others empty, reserved for her team. Intense activity was also taking place in a smaller room off to the side, which seemed to be an abortion room.

As Zhen's team was inspecting the clinic, a cacophony of drums and gongs broke into what seemed to be a celebratory announcement of sorts, and amid the commotion, a bus pulled up to the square, festooned with streamers, as if somebody was celebrating a holiday. Zhen watched the bus door open and wailing women spilled out from within, their noisiness an invasion of the utter silence of the women waiting in the square, women resigned to their fate. Zhen was the leader of the very efforts that had brought all these women to this place. She was the expert directing a medical campaign. But she was also very clear in her mind that like every campaign that she had come through in her life thus far, this was a Communist Party campaign, waged by the Communist leadership, and it had a lofty goal of lifting the nation to a higher ground of modernity.

The local leader looked at her expectantly, as if anticipating her team to plunge into the surgical procedures for that day. But if these leaders, knowing that Zhen's team would be there, had brought in more women than the barefoot doctors could handle, that was going to be their problem. Zhen asked the leader to take her team to their guest house, insisting that they leave the clinic from the side door. Zhen knew that the local officials wouldn't dare let the women waiting outside starve; they would have to allow them to return home for dinner, and the women determined to escape would have another chance to evade the official hunt. And the officials? They'd have to deal with the consequences of their own actions.

The team settled down in the guest house until the scheduled welcoming dinner, where Zhen's team was properly welcomed by the officials, who were probably more than happy to enjoy a feast at the Party's expense.

At the end of the next day, their first full day in the village, a total of forty tubal ligations had been performed, but Zhen's team, operating on the two makeshift beds, had performed only seven of them. Zhen called all the medical workers together to summarize the day's work. She concluded that the doctors from the big hospitals weren't used to doing these kinds of procedures in such minimal conditions, so,

she announced, she and her team would observe the barefoot doctors the following day and learn from them how to
operate in a less-than-ideal medical facility—effectively slowing them down and getting them to proceed more carefully
while teaching them the complexities and intricacies of handling the human body.

Zhen's work the following day, it turned out, was damage
control. In their rush to meet the sterilization quotas, the
barefoot doctors, who didn't have much training, were disregarding the wellbeing of their patients. Zhen put it diplomat-
ically in her memoir: "Young calves are not afraid of tigers,"
she wrote, praising the enthusiasm of these local health workers while trying to stop them from doing harm. Zhen herself
found the fallopian tubes of a patient for one barefoot doctor so that he wouldn't rupture them while poking around
in search of them. She sewed up a punctured bladder. One
woman, who appeared to be approaching menopause and
for whom sterilization seemed both risky and unnecessary,
said she had to go through with it anyway because her husband was the Party leader and she needed to set a good example. Zhen asked her to bring her husband in and convinced
him that the best way to set an example would be for him to
undergo a vasectomy right on the spot, which he did.

Another case Zhen wrote about in her memoir showed
how, despite the correct political stance she always took, she
continued to make an effort in favor of simple decency and
against blind obedience to authority. One night, there was
loud banging on Zhen's door in the government guest house.
It turned out to be some local officials who had brought in a
man and a woman, hands loosely tied, as though they were
criminals. The officials demanded that Zhen perform a tubal
ligation on the woman right away, right there, in her room.

The reason for this urgency? This was a new marriage of a widow and a widower, the officials explained, and although each of them had a child from their previous marriage, they were now trying to have a child of their own to cement their new bond. "We just wanted to have one," the woman pleaded. "We're not trying for a boy!"

"They've been in hiding while you've been here doing operations," the official said. "Tonight, they thought you'd left, so they sneaked back to their home, and we got them. If you don't take care of things right away, they might just get their wish."

Zhen's hand was forced.

Under the officials' intense stare, she performed the tubal ligation. So imagine the cry of scandal when nine months later, the woman gave birth to a baby boy! Zhen's explanation was that a fertilized egg must have already been present when she'd performed the procedure and escaped her intervention, a medical possibility. "The stubborn egg fulfilled the parents' dreams and yet added one more failure to my long career," she wrote later in her memoir. Had she faked a ligation in order to give the couple a chance for happiness? Or was she actually writing a self-criticism? Zhen would never tell me.

Despite her efforts, there were no doubt many illegal births or semi-legal ones by parents who were willing to pay the required fines. And there were certainly many forced abortions and sterilizations as local officials strove to meet the population control targets. Zhen looked the other way at these practices. She did her best to keep her old Two Ailments project going—"fixing the broken," as she put it, and trying in her talks to village people to avoid the fierce "guerrilla war" seen in other provinces.

In her memoir highlighting the major accomplishments of her long career, Zhen was clearly not proud that she was once in charge of the population control program in her province; the topic of family planning is nowhere to be found in the entire book, the little episodes just mentioned tucked away in different chapters on different topics. The peak of the campaign did pass a few years later, and the widespread practice of forced tubal ligations and abortions eased. Government statistics show that between 1986 and 1990, the campaign never met the official target of 1% population growth that had been set for the whole country. In some urban areas, particularly political centers like Beijing and Shanghai, the birthrate went down to about 1.3 per couple, but the rate in the countryside was more than double that number.

Fujian was among the regions that had higher birthrates. Compared to other provinces, like neighboring Guangdong, for example, during the time when Zhen was in charge, Fujian was a leader in eradicating the Two Ailments even as it lagged behind in family planning. Zhen was not a saint, certainly not an overt dissenter from the policy, but the statistics show that she must have been a moderating force. When the nationwide reported sex ratios at birth spiked to 100 girls per 111–112 boys in 1985–86, Fujian's overall sex ratio remained steady at 100 per 106 throughout the decade, which is within the natural ratio of about 102–106 per 100.[*]

---

[*] China Data Center: https://www-china-data-online-com.revproxy.brown .edu/member/macroyr/macroyrtshow.asp; and Zeng Yi et al., "Causes and Implications of the Recent Increase in the Reported Sex Ratio at Birth in China," Population and Development Review 19, no. 2 (1993): 283–302, https://doi.org/10.2307/2938438.

Midnight Train to Gaoxiong (Kaohsiung)

J UN HAD A SPECIAL AFFECTION for the street sweepers that began her machine importing business. They were her "chosen babies." And it was no doubt their unsentimental usefulness, she believed, that made them popular with many people on Taiwan. What a strange turn of events, Jun must have thought. She had once dreamed only of teaching history to high school students and had never been interested in machines, never even thought about them. But with the success of her street sweepers, she realized that there was a bigger business opportunity for her among the other items on the lists maintained by the Import and Export Bureau. The street sweepers were avatars of industrialization, initiating a new phase of her career.

Jun's next step was to hire Ah Da, who had helped her to get the street sweepers home and to assemble them. In becoming Jun's second employee after her secretary/receptionist, this army veteran from the battlefields of Guningtou finally had a real job. Soon, the two of them were marching briskly into Taiwan's most transformative era.

While the clock business kept the company viable, Jun started to bid for different types of machines. She delegated the mechanical work and troubleshooting to Ah Da. Meanwhile, she started to improve her English during her lunch hours, taking advantage of government-sponsored intensive English-language training courses, which were designed to help professionals do business with English-speaking countries, or further their education. Taiwan during the decade of the 1960s was in the early stages of an astonishing economic boom. In 1962, for the first time, the value of the island's industrial production exceeded that of agriculture. The following year, the economy registered its first favorable trade balance. By 1965, things had improved so much that U.S. economic aid programs were no longer deemed necessary and came to an end. Medium and light industry led the expansion of the economy in the subsequent years, with striking gains registered in electronics, household goods, and chemicals. The accumulation of wealth also prompted upgrades in other sectors, from hospitals to churches.

Over those years, Jun's company imported industrial X-ray machines for shipyards and construction companies; it imported motors of all sorts, boilers and furnaces for hospitals and factories alike, and alarm systems for stores and offices. Jun's presentations were so well-informed—from her assiduous reading of technical manuals—that people would ask her whether she was an engineer by training. She liked to answer that she had learned on the job. That answer and her general demeanor earned her a reputation for modesty, one that ironically benefited her as a woman.

The exponential expansion of the company's machine department eventually led Jun to ask Min to join the company. He readily agreed. His retail business was declining anyway, as U.S. subsidies began to dry up. So he sold his shares to his partner.

Min gave Jun's company a complete makeover. First, he gave it a new name: "The New World Company," then he added a wine importing division to the original clock department and the rapidly expanding machinery department. He took out advertisements on Taiwan Central TV, where Guanxiu and his fiancée, who was one of the station's star anchors, worked. Through the ads, he rebranded the company as an industrial and lifestyle leader, importing to Taiwan the latest products from the advanced industrial nations. This new image instantly caught on among the most successful classes of the society: the emerging industrialists, the Westernized elite, and the nouveau riche in general.

Success also bred competition, and the competition was intense on a small island where entrepreneurs jostled to gain a foothold in the rapidly expanding economy. One early direct challenger was a clock store that seemed to have materialized overnight right across the street from Jun's flagship clock store in Ximenting, Taipei's main commercial district. The competitor carried very similar products but with much lower prices. To compete, Jun transformed a common idiom into a catchy slogan, *youshi youzhong*, meaning "Start well and end well," with the final syllable sounding the same as the word "clock," turning the clock into a good luck charm. In response, the competitor began using the exact same slogan.

"They even stole my message!" Jun was still incredulous when she recounted the episode to me years later. "They claimed that it was just a traditional saying."

"Then what did you do?"

Jun leaned back in her chair and smiled. "I fought back."

And fight back she did. She first went to the Import and

Export Bureau and swept up the entire import quota for clocks, including her competitor's cheaper, inferior imports. Then realizing that the cost for shipping the grandfather clocks from Germany came mostly from their heavy casing, she made the casing locally. The change turned out to give her a competitive advantage, because the designs of the new casings appealed to local tastes, even though they no longer had the "authentic" European look. Meanwhile, she continued to import the higher quality clockworks that were now put into the locally made casings. That way, Jun was able to match the competitor's price with far superior and more popular products boasting genuine imported "guts." Cut off from their source of supply and outmatched in price, the new competitor folded in months.

Clearly, being a businesswoman sparked something not just competitive but combative, even ruthless, in this usually gentle and kind woman.

To push Min's wine department to a new height, Jun created a series of advertisements evoking a Taiwanese version of the romance associated with imported wine. With the help of Guanxiu and his wife, she found media celebrities to star in the ads, which she managed to get some of the foreign wine companies to subsidize. Instead of paying the celebrities to feature in the ads, she convinced them that these were publicity opportunities, so there they were, happy to be shown on TV sipping good wine on pristine beaches or in elegant mansions, avatars of fashion, elegance, and the art of living. These ads enhanced New World's standing among Taiwan's elite.

For her machinery business, Jun found her offensive strategy, ironically, in her first visit to a church after a decades-long hiatus. She succumbed to a neighbor's repeated urging to attend Sunday mass at a Catholic church, and there she met a certain Mr. Cheng, who was seeking the Lord's guidance as he embarked on a new job leading a shipbuilding company. Years later, Jun remembered nothing of the sermon that day, but she recalled convincing Mr. Cheng to consider purchasing a top-quality industrial X-ray machine made by Siemens, used to scan and check for leaks and structural weaknesses in a new ship—from New World, of course. Cheng was concerned about the price tag, but Jun came up with an attractive deal for financing and maintenance, a strategy that she soon found very effective in winning other customers. Her good credit and her now extensive connections enabled her to get loans, and Taiwan's still cheap labor enabled her to offer prospective customers a good maintenance plan. Years later, the place where she first devised this winning strategy made her wonder: did she gain divine intervention or did she commit a punishable sin?

Jun was typing up a long inventory of clocks one Sunday night. Out in the sitting room, Min was having a drink with some friends. Suddenly, Jun heard one of the friends ask Min good-naturedly: "How can you let your wife work so hard at her age? She's the mother of three now, and look at her, still working late into the night!"

Min replied, "I couldn't rein her in when I was her commander in the army; how can I reign her in now that I'm just her husband and employee?"

A few days later, Jun was on the midnight train from Taipei to the port city of Kaohsiung on the southern tip of Taiwan. Kaohsiung had been designated a special economic development zone, to be restored to its past glory as an export hub. Jun had been making preparations in the city to capture the government's generous incentives. For each of these trips, she followed the same punishing routine. She got up that morning at 4:30 as she usually did, shopped and cooked to get the whole family ready for the day. She'd then go to her office for her usual long hours, then go overnight to Kaohsiung, sleeping a few hours on the train, spend the day there, and then take the return night train back to Taipei in time for another day at the office.

But as she settled into her seat on this particular trip, that overheard conversation between Min and his friends came back to her, and what lingered in her mind was "the mother of three." Her twelve-year-old eldest son Yiheng's health weighed on her: Just this past morning, as she was about to take the kids to school, Yiheng complained of a splitting headache and nearly collapsed on the floor. As she looked back, she realized that Yiheng had not seemed fully himself for a long time. For almost a year, Yiheng had been knitting his eyebrows tight as if he were deep in thought, or angry. His father liked to tease him: "You look as if you are carrying the weight of the entire world on your shoulders!" His mood had been subdued, and his grades had begun to slide. Just a couple of weeks before, Jun had noticed dark mucus when he blew his nose, but still did not register any alarm. Finally, when she took him to see the doctor after his near collapse from pain, the doctor told her that the boy had a severe chronic nasal infection. "This is the result of a long and repeated infection that never had a chance to clear," the doctor said, giving Jun a look that she took to be searingly accusatory, "It's rare to see a case this severe." After the doctor's visit, Jun took Yiheng to her office where he went to sleep on a cot, the "sick bed," as she called it, since that was where Jun put any of her children when they were too sick to go to school.

The train was chugging along in the calm of the night, passing the silhouettes of track-side hamlets. Scattered dim lights flickered by here and there. Because she always took the train at night, she never really saw anything of Taiwan in between Taipei in the North and Kaohsiung in the South, and now it occurred to her that, like the invisible countryside outside her window, there was a whole stretch of her life that also seemed invisible to her. She had three children, yet she could hardly remember their growing up. When Yihui ran toward her showing off the braids that the neighbor auntie had done for her, Jun remembered feeling a pang of jealousy. She wished that she had done that for her little girl herself. She remembered another time when Yiheng's monthly allowance was extorted from him by a neighborhood bully. The poor boy, in his anger and humiliation, apologized to her. Jun's heart broke for her son, and at the same time she was proud of his having the dignity to apologize. She resolved that she wanted Yiheng to have faith in human goodness and assured him that the bully would eventually pay him back. She had intended to take care of the matter by pretending that the bully had returned the money a few days later, but her work had kept her from getting around to do it. Now on the train, thinking of Yiheng lying in the sick bed in her office, she faced up to the fact that his illness had gotten serious because of her neglect. And here she was, pursuing a business deal and neglecting him again.

Sitting across from Jun's seat was a young mother who was coaxing her two little children to sleep. Jun thought of her own father and how he'd always been there for her—when she was grieving for her grandmother, when she was striving to go to school; and when she took off into the sky, he was waving from below, the last time she'd seen him. Well, she couldn't go back, either to her father or to her children's past, but she could start finding more time for them, more ways to be a part of their lives. She could at least carve out every Sunday for family time.

Early the next morning, Jun's train pulled into the Kaohsiung station. The night's fitful naps made her feel lightheaded. The city was already starting to rumble from the massive reconstruction to revive this old port city, like a gigantic animal stirring in the last phase of its sleep. And soon, the rumble would intensify. It would shake the ground and the buildings and then, it would rattle the glass. And by the end of the day, dust would settle and hide away the city for another night.

Ah Da came to pick Jun up at the station. He had been sent ahead by Jun to prepare for a possible export distribution center in the city. Taking one look at her haggard features, he suggested that they go to get what he knew was Jun's favorite breakfast drink, a bowl of hot soy milk. Ah Da was a machine man, but with Jun, his thoughtfulness and tenderness often came through the tough guy façade. Like Min, he'd been a soldier who'd retreated with the Nationalist Army to Jinmen in 1949, and like Min too, he had left a young family behind on the Mainland, but unlike Min, he'd never remarried or showed any sign of wanting to create a new family on Taiwan.

The cab of Ah Da's truck reeked of machine oil, giving Jun a headache. In fact, she was having headaches too often these days. A couple of months before, she'd been too busy to eat lunch, prompting Min to remind her, "The company won't collapse during your meal hour, but you might." As if to prove Min right, she suffered a terrible headache that night, but found it hard to keep her promise to ease off. Each time she slowed down, or took a day off, she would be so anxious and restless. It was easier for her to just keep pushing ahead.

In Gaoxiong that day, Jun toured some small new companies that Ah Da wanted her to check out for a potential partner. But Jun, who was usually exhilarated by the start of a new project, somehow could not muster any enthusiasm. She remembered the old Chinese saying that it's easier to get on a tiger than to get off one. Striving to create a toehold in a new site, Jun reasoned, risked stretching the company too thin. Ah Da agreed that playing safe would be a better choice.

Jun was eager to get back home to check on Yiheng. In the cab of Ah Da's truck at the end of the day, still smelling of machine oil, she asked him how old his son would be now. Ah Da did not have to think. Dongdong was twenty-one and his sister was nineteen, he said. As the cab fell silent, Jun was sure that they were thinking about the same thing: their children, young adults on the verge of becoming themselves and perhaps having children of their own—grandchildren whom Ah Da might never see.

"Why didn't you ever want to start another family?" she asked. Though she'd known Ah Da for a long time now and felt comfortable with him, this was the first time she'd dared to raise that delicate question.

"Getting too old," Ad Da replied at first, but then he got to the anguished heart of the matter. "You guys—Brother and Sister Shen—have been taking good care of me. But back then on the battlefields, who cared about me? What did I fight for? What did I get for putting my life on the line, for leaving my family behind? I've done it all, and I've seen it all. I've learned to treasure what I've got, and not to create more attachments, only to have to leave them behind again."

Jun felt the root of her nose tickle, and her eyes blurred. Starting in 1966, the Cultural Revolution had swept through the Mainland; then the bamboo curtain dropped in the middle of the Taiwan Strait. No one on Taiwan had heard anything from their families on the other side of the curtain ever since. Ah Da was now well into middle age, and his family was lost to him as far as he was concerned. He didn't even know what his own children looked like much less what their fate had been as the children of a one-time Nationalist soldier living on Taiwan.

Even if they didn't talk about it much, every *waishengren*—the "outside province people" like Jun and Min and Ah Da—experienced this heartache, of having been yanked away from their roots by forces beyond their control. Every former Mainlander was haunted by the rupture of past and present, the present of those left behind having become a void, a blank screen on which they projected their guilt, their sorrow, their futile wish that somehow it could have been different. At the same time, the permanence of their situation was settling in. For the first decade after they arrived, they'd kept alive the dream of returning, but that dream was becoming ever more remote, replaced by the reluctant awareness that they would never go back.

Jun also knew that things were very different for her children. The new generation had learned at school that their homeland included the Mainland and that their history extended five thousand years into the past, yet they were growing up on this tiny island without grandparents, aunts, uncles, and cousins, all those people who made up their parents' notion of family. Sitting amid the silence and the smell of Ah Da's truck, Jun felt a powerful sense of remorse that she, as a mother, had been too absent from her own children's lives to fill that void. Between the conflicting demands of finding her own purpose on Taiwan and caring for her children, she'd always given priority to the former.

But she didn't express any of that to Ad Da, who had chosen to remain solitary in his exile. As they parted ways at the end of this long day, she gave him a sisterly pat on the shoulder. "Take care," she said. Then she boarded the train home.

• • •

Meanwhile, despite Jun's melancholy thoughts, her business was prospering and so was her family. Min's older son, Guanting, was now an engineer living out his dreams of building roads and bridges all across Taiwan. He had a family of his own in Taipei. In 1967, Min's younger boy, Guanxiu, who had once quarreled so furiously with his father, got married to a star news anchor. The event was a media sensation. Guanxiu, who now used a pen name, Shen Ye, meaning "Shen the Wild," had become a leading public intellectual, writing widely read essays and commentaries, engaging in political debates. He was handsome and eloquent, over six feet tall, possessed of a magnetic voice and natural presence. The guests of honor at his wedding included the vice president and ministers of Taiwan. The press buzzed about the likelihood that he and his wife would create a media empire parallel to his parents' import and export empire.

For the younger three, Jun did make an effort to keep her Sundays clear. She installed a basketball hoop in the yard and put out a ping pong table too. The whole family made trips to the beaches. On those beach days, Jun would tell stories to Yihui, who preferred hanging out with mom to water-fighting with her brothers. She would tell her daughter stories from her Flower Fragrant Garden days, and Yihui's eyes would scan the horizon, wearing a distant and dreamy look as if listening to fairy tales. Jun would marvel at her daughter's beautiful eyes, clear like the summer sky, untinted by life's miseries. Jun did not tell her of the heartache that accompanied the thoughts of her old garden home. When Yihui grew up, and only then, she resolved, she would tell her that love could hurt, memories could torment, but that the family would always be part of her no matter how far and how long she traveled away from them. She would also tell her that life would move on, and that in the ashes of destruction and loss, one could find a perfect baby girl, like her, and the rest of her family, a family of one's own.

Then in the summer of 1970 such beach outings faded away as Min and Jun rolled out a new advertising campaign furthering the image of lifestyle glamour that had become the mark of their company. Weekends were increasingly taken up by cocktail parties and wine-tasting events in different grand settings, events for shooting film clips to use in their advertisements. With the family's strong ties to the media, the line between news reports and advertisements blurred. Going to parties where the famous, the powerful, and the beautiful frolicked on pristine beaches became a big part of Jun's routine. On a single day, she might change into four or five different outfits as she traversed the island, making appearances at different media events.

Decades later, when Aunt Jun was in her nineties, she would open her photo albums to show me the pictures reflecting the glamour of those days. She paused at one photo showing her standing with Anna Chennault, a celebrity as widow of the renowned Flying Tiger commander Claire Chennault. Pointing to Anna Chennault, Jun said, "She too was a journalist when she met General Chennault." Both women in the photo had fashionably permed short hair. Jun wore a black and white dress that showed off her curves. She looked more than glamorous. She looked content in her role as a confident businesswoman at the apex of her career and of Taiwan's social elite.

There was no hint in that photograph of the turmoil she felt within.

• • •

On New Year's Eve in 1971, Jun felt a sudden sharp ache in her stomach. It happened during a family dinner, and Jun didn't want to ruin the occasion. But Yihui saw something was wrong and followed her mother as she abruptly left the dining table and headed straight to the bathroom. She was there in time to prop her mother up when she collapsed. Against her mother's objections, she called their neighbor who happened to be the chief of internal medicine at Taipei's elite military hospital. The doctor hurried to the Shen residence. He knew that they never asked for help lightly.

Jun curled up tightly in her bed, her five-foot-two, hundred-pound frame just a small bump under the quilt. She took some pills that Dr. Yi gave her to control the pain, and when it eased in the following weeks and months, she completely forgot Dr. Yi's advice for an immediate and thorough checkup. She would rather spend her down time at home than deal with a medical condition. The children were by now in middle school and high school, and she realized that it wouldn't be long before they would leave home as their two older brothers had years before. The children would play Beatles songs for their mother and fill her in on the big news of the day—America's war in Vietnam, Mainland

China's launch of its first satellite, and then, the biggest news of all: the end of the American trade embargo against the Mainland, the move at the United Nations to give China's seat there to the Communist government in Beijing. Finally, in what was a tremendous blow to Taiwan, in February 1972, President Richard Nixon made his historic visit to Beijing, and it was clear to Jun and to everybody else on Taiwan that tides were shifting rapidly. She could sense the feeling of anxiety mixed with a resentment and indignation at the U.S.'s betrayal of its long-time ally.

Meanwhile, Jun's stomach problem persisted even as she tried to ignore it. She lost her appetite. Clothes started to hang loose on her. Then, about two weeks after the Chinese New Year in 1972, Jun was discussing with her family Nixon's trip to the PRC and his meeting with Mao Zedong when she collapsed again during a family dinner. Yihui was adamant that this time her mother get to the ER immediately, and Jun did not have the strength to resist.

Dr. Yi, their neighbor, came to deliver the result of the tests: colon cancer. Dr. Yi recommended surgery to remove the cancer and to make sure it hadn't spread. Knowing Jun's reluctance to follow his advice, he urged her to move ahead quickly. He related how his mother-in-law, after being diagnosed with the same cancer, postponed her treatment for three months and when she finally got to it, it was too late. "But," Dr. Yi added, as if for self-consolation, "she got to realize her lifelong dream to attend her youngest son's graduation from Princeton and spent time with him."

Realizing a lifelong dream—that echoed in Jun's mind. If she could hop on a plane to fly back to Fuzhou, she might have done just as the woman had done. But it would take a while to figure out how. Jun checked into the hospital. A few days after that, she had surgery.

When she awoke from the anesthesia, Jun saw Min and Yihui sitting by her side. Yihui noticed and was ecstatic: "Mommy's awake, Mommy's awake!" Jun wanted to pull her daughter close, but everything felt so heavy, her body a dead weight, her mind a feeble engine, sputtering lazily for a moment, then stalling again. Yihui's voice seemed to mingle with somebody else's, the doctor's, who seemed to be saying something about a movie—telling Yihui that her mommy would see a "movie" before she was fully awake. A movie? She remembered promising Yihui before the operation that they would go to one soon, an American Western, cowboys riding through barren canyons . . . the barren canyons . . . the barren canyons.

It was at that moment—Jun still vividly remembered her "movie" half a century later—that a blinding shaft of light seemed to rise from behind some barren canyons, like a sudden sunrise. It thrust the whole jagged landscape into three dimensions: deeply shaded ravines, soaring cliffs, straight broken lines of sharp edges. The light ascended until it rose above the tips of the highest cliff, where it blinded her. Then, as her vision returned, she saw a Holy Cross rise in the middle of that shaft of light, smoothly and silently, as if in a Eucharistic celebration at her missionary school so long ago. Jun felt herself enveloped in this warm current of brilliance, cradled in its luminance, gentle and buoyant. The Cross, steady in its power, continued its ascent, until it receded into the sky.

"Thank you, my Lord." The words gushed out of Jun's mind. "Thank you for not abandoning me after I have abandoned you for so long! Thank you, Lord, for coming to reclaim me. I promise you I'll return, I'll return home." Bits and pieces of the Holy Bible started to come back to her. "I took you from the ends of the earth, from its farthest corners I called you. I said, 'you are my servant': I have chosen you and have not rejected you." She recalled the passages from Isaiah, "So do not fear, for I am with you; do not be dismayed, for I am your God. I will strengthen you and help you: I will uphold you with my righteous right hand." An immense peace filled her as she emerged into consciousness. Christianity had shaped her early schooling. It had even inspired both of her mothers to become devout readers of the Bible and to become baptized. In the intervening decades, however, it had been sidelined as Jun tried to survive the wars and the separation and to find her own identity. But now it had come back with a full force, a force of love that gently delivered her into a new world of awareness.

Jun squeezed the hands already in hers. "Min, Yihui," she said. "So good to have you here!" and she felt that she could even smile.

"Mommy's talking!" Yihui squealed with delight. Jun felt Min's hand tightening on hers, as if to infuse her with some of his strength. Jun had always loved his Buddha smiles. "Old pal," she heard him say, "you made it! We've been waiting here all this time. We were sure you would make it."

"Oh, Mama!" Yihui broke into tears of relief.

Yihui's cries of happiness brought the doctor back, and he asked Jun if she did see a movie.

"A movie I'll never forget," Jun replied, leaving her husband and daughter completely in the fog.

Then the doctor turned to Min and told him that the operation had gone well, but because Jun was so underweight, so over-exhausted because of the prolonged distress of the digestive system, and so on and so forth, the recuperation would take a bit longer than usual. "But all in all, this is a very good start."

"A start. A very good start. I think I'm ready for a new start," Jun said to herself.

• • •

The first thing Jun learned when her team from her company came to visit her in the hospital was that a major deal for her company—the sale of a high-end, high-price industrial X-ray machine for Taiwan Shipyard, a deal that Jun believed only awaited her signature—had fallen through. "They took what they called a better deal," Ah Da told her, his head hanging low, bearing the heaviness of delivering such a blow to a boss who had just had a brush with death. Jun closed her eyes and leaned back on her propped-up hospital bed. "Why, oh why," she said to her Lord, "Why did you bring me back only to break me again?"

And yet, she told me years later, "A sense of calm somehow miraculously took over me after I put that question to God, and a different world, one of such clarity, emerged from it." She suddenly realized that this was the same kind of deal that she had worked out with Mr. Cheng at her first church visit. At the time, she saw it as a God-given business opportunity. Now looking back on it she felt it had been a missed chance of spiritual redemption. Instead of returning to the Lord's path, she'd pushed down her own path instead.

She felt calm thinking of that, and from that calm, strangely, came the story of Sisyphus that her Methodist teacher, Ms. White, had told in her middle school in Fuzhou, and that brought her an immense sense of gratitude. Zeus had punished Sisyphus by forcing him to exert his whole being toward accomplishing nothing, but, as Jun put it, "The merciful God who has been watching over me has been generous." God had allowed her to succeed but had watched her become so intoxicated by her own success that she had viewed it as purely her own, which caused her to neglect everything else in her life—her children, her family, even her health. Now she had been given a second chance.

Her recuperation was the longest time off from work that she had ever remembered. She made her return to the office by showing up at her employees' lunch. Her company now occupied two stories of a Taipei office building with over twenty core employees and was perhaps the first in Taiwan to offer free lunch. The reception was warm but the news was harsh. Their competitors had succeeded in narrowing New World's share in almost everything: the export quotas from the Import and Export Bureau, the customer base, and the market share. Customers at her flagship store in the most upscale section of the city, Ximending, were starting to ask when they would have liquidation sales.

If she were twenty, Jun thought, or even just ten years younger and a great deal stronger, her first reaction would be to up the ante by expanding more. But the light and warmth that she experienced in her awakening in the hospital room obliterated the impulse to win. She felt that she had rediscovered a world so much richer and warmer, a world of families old and new, a world infused with love. It buoyed her so that she no longer felt weighed down by the cycle of endless fights, burdened by the singular goal of prevailing over the competition.

———

There was a lot of tumult on Taiwan that Christmas of 1972, and it didn't spare the Shen household. The family's Christmas reunion was a full house, including four grandchildren. In a household of father-son political pundits and history buffs, dinner became an occasion for an intense discussion about what was widely viewed as the "American betrayal of the Republic of China." The ROC was the real China, and the real China included the Mainland, Guanxiu said. Yet to the Americans, this real China was now expendable. In college, Shi, Jun's second son, chimed in, the rhetoric was still about exterminating the Communists and uniting the country, which elicited rueful laughter from the rest of the family. "We grow up on this little island, but we learn about our five thousand years of national history that took place someplace else," Yihui said, "We sing of the sand storms in the Taklamakan desert and horses galloping in Mongolia. We read all those poems about past glories. But where are they now? We'll never catch a glimpse of any of that in our lifetimes."

That word "lifetime" got to Jun as she listened to her children speak. Would she ever see her homeland again in her lifetime? That night at dinner, she resumed a practice that she'd long since abandoned. She said a brief grace. "Oh Lord, forgive me for being away from you for so long. Thank you for bringing my family together, thank you for all the fulfillment you've brought to my life, Amen." Her mother used to say a silent grace before every meal. Jun wondered if she still kept up that practice.

After dinner, she asked Guanxiu to take her to a new Methodist church. It sat on a small rise in the neighborhood. Jun slowly made her way up a set of marble steps, holding on to Guangxiu and Yiheng's arms. As she approached, she saw the light from within filtering through the tall stained-glass windows, and she heard the sound of the choir singing in English, growing stronger as they got closer.

"I'll be home for Christmas, you can count on me . . ." Jun sang softly to herself, just as she did at the last Christmas celebrated in her missionary school, but now panting slightly as her sons pushed opened the door.

The Past That
Refused to Fade

O N NEW YEAR'S DAY 1987, Party Secretary Dong of the
Women and Children's Hospital paid Zhen a visit at
her home and invited her to attend the next meeting of the
Chinese Communist Party. Secretary Dong had brought with
him a fruit basket for the visit. Despite her work and devotion
to the cause, Zhen had never applied to join the Communist
Party. So this was a bit unusual.

Zhen's neighbor across the hall, Old Zhao, was opening
the door of his apartment when Secretary Dong took his
leave. With Dong barely out of the earshot, Zhao asked Zhen
sarcastically whether Dong had come to consult Zhen, a gynecologist, on behalf of his wife.

Old Zhao was a distinguished physician a few years older
than Zhen. He had spent an entire decade in the countryside
during the Cultural Revolution, what he (and many others)
called the "ten lost years." After being exonerated in 1976,
he was restored to his former position as chief of the endocrinology department. He was a gentle soul whose glasses were
as thick as the bottom of a wine bottle, making his eyes look

perpetually startled, and his arthritis made him so hunched over that he walked like a minesweeper searching for a hard-to-find object on the ground. This harmless man, however, bore an inextinguishable grudge against Secretary Dong, believing it was Dong, then the secretary of the Communist Youth League, who had assembled documents to incriminate Zhao's best friend, had him locked up and beaten to death at the beginning of the Cultural Revolution in 1966. That, needless to say, was bad enough, but to Old Zhao, the worst part was what he believed to be the true motive: that Secretary Dong secretly coveted his friend's good-looking wife.

Decades later, it was hard to verify all the facts, but what was indisputable was that only months after Zhao's friend was put into his isolation cell and murdered, his wife married Dong, who claimed to want "to care for the poor young widow and her young son."

The son of Dong's friend was Jiyue's good friend, while the boy's half-brother, his mother's son by Secretary Dong, was known as a bully. Jiyue called him a "vicious pit bull"; it was he who had threatened Jiyue with a rock years before, in front of the house that used to belong to the Hu-Chen family and now belonged to Dong.

All this unpleasantness notwithstanding, Secretary Dong had never given either Zhen or Hu Xizhong any trouble. He was always courteous and correct in his behavior toward them. Many incomprehensible things had happened during the revolutionary years. Each revolutionary wave swept away a number of the good, the weak, and sometimes the evil, and from each of these waves rose many who were like Secretary Dong, regenerated leaders working and living amid those recalled from banishment after the death of Mao. Given all the moral murk and chaos, who was to judge someone else's actions?

"No, it wasn't about his wife," Zhen said to Old Zhao. "He was just being a good Party man. Happy New Year to you!"

At the Party meeting, Zhen found herself in the guest-of-honor seat right next to Party Secretary Dong, who introduced her as a model leader and a model doctor. A long list of awards and honorary titles from both the hospital and the province was read out, after which a beaming Dong announced that the Party had decided to invite Zhen to become a member.

Now all eyes turned to Zhen, and she tried hard to present the grateful face that, surely, everyone in the room expected to see. It was a huge honor to be invited to join the Party. Many would do crazy things to become members, because it was a golden ticket to career advancement. Zhen accepted the honor graciously, and promised to submit a formal application, initiating the process of the Party's vetting. After the meeting, Dong took Zhen aside to explain the reason for this sudden offer. The hospital was about to make Zhen its director, he said, and in order for her to be in such a position, she would have to be a Party member.

Still, even if it was a bureaucratic formality, Zhen felt vindicated by the gesture. It signaled to her that all her work and accomplishments had wiped out the stains of her family's past and unfounded accusations. It showed that her strategy of cooperation, self-criticism, and effort had been successful. She felt a freedom that she had not tasted for a very long time. For almost the entire duration of the New China, she had been a prisoner of a past that had not been of her own choosing, for which she bore no moral responsibility but which she could never completely escape. Now, with Party membership, she would escape it, finally and completely.

On her first day back at work after the holidays, Zhen's secretary greeted her with a thick medical file. It was, she said, from a patient suffering from ovarian cancer. She had insisted that Zhen be the surgeon to operate on her. Requests for Zhen to handle a case were not uncommon, but they usually came through referrals from other doctors, not from patients themselves. Zhen took a look at the thick file. Her steps slowed when she saw the name on it: Zhang Cuijiao.

"Do you know this person?" the secretary asked, noticing the pause. Zhen nodded. Yes, she did.

Zhang Cuijiao was the high school and medical school classmate who, years before, had falsely accused Zhen of being the head of the Nationalist Women's Youth League in medical school. Though there hadn't even been such an organization in medical school, the charge had clung to Zhen like a burr and had ultimately sent her into exile. Zhen had never confronted Cuijiao; she hadn't seen her since she learned of her charge. Now, she wondered, was Cuijiao coming to Zhen for her medical skills, or was she seeking a reconciliation?

Things had a way of coming full circle all on their own, Zhen thought to herself as she read Zhang Cuijiao's file. For the first time in decades, she started to recall that pretty, delicate young woman in the medical school, with silky long hair and shining eyes. Now, reading her medical record, Zhen saw that Cuijiao had had many health problems before she was diagnosed with ovarian cancer. She'd visited all the major experts, and all had recommended the most radical procedure, removing the entire reproductive system, both the ovaries and the uterus. Of all the surgeons available to her, Cuijiao had chosen Zhen to perform the operation.

Why her? Zhen wondered. Why was a woman whose words

had almost ended Zhen's career choosing her for a last-ditch, desperate effort to save her life? It was hard to imagine that Cuijiao had had a lapse of memory when she told the Party that Zhen was the head of the Nationalist Women's Youth League in medical school. She must have known that there had been no such League, and, moreover, that her statement would push Zhen to the wrong side of the political divide. What was her motive to do that to a classmate? Was there some personal vendetta or competition that Zhen had never sensed? Was it political opportunism?

Zhen read on. Cuijiao's thick medical history, following her from place to place, revealed that she had gone from small towns to smaller villages, including places in Fujian's mountainous regions that Zhen had become familiar with through her own countryside tours. Cuijiao must also have been dragged into the purges and ideological campaigns that swept through the country from the late fifties to the early seventies. She had a capitalist father, Zhen remembered, who owned large companies; almost as bad as Zhen's father having served in Chiang Kai-shek's Nationalist Army. As she reviewed her former friend's life itinerary, new, less hostile thoughts began to creep into Zhen's mind. Perhaps, she thought, Cuijiao had falsely informed on her in a desperate, terrified effort to overcome her own political liabilities? Just as it was hard for Zhen to judge Secretary Dong for the persecution of Old Zhao's friend and his marriage to his wife, she now suddenly found it hard to judge Cuijiao. And, anyway, she had a medical responsibility. A patient was asking for her to save her and she had to make her best effort to do just that.

Zhen closed the file. It brought back too many memories and questions. But as with most of the questions about what had transpired during those revolutionary years, she might never find any answer. Ultimately, maybe, Zhen thought, Cuijiao's choice was her act of reconciliation. After all, what more could one say than to trust someone with one's life?

Seeing Cuijiao on the operating table made a mockery of Zhen's memory of her. The delicate girl with her preference for bows, rouge, lacy blouses, and skirts, the girl of Zhen's memory, was unrecognizable. Here in front of her was a shriveled person, gaunt and hollowed out beyond her years. Her hair was thin, scraggy, and gray. The light that once animated those sparkly eyes had been replaced by sadness.

"Zhen," this sick woman who looked more ninety than fifty-four, began. "It's been a long time."

"Yes it has. How are you doing today?"

"Well, all I can say is, I'm ready." As a doctor herself, Cuijiao knew better than most patients what the risks of this surgery were.

"Very well. So we're taking everything out."

"Yes, everything, and whatever you can find that may have spread."

Not much more needed to be said, except for Cuijiao adding that she was fighting this fight for her daughter, who had lost her father when she was young.

Zhen asked her whether her daughter would be visiting during her hospital stay, and Cuijiao said that her daughter would be arriving from Jianou any time now. Jianou was the mountain town where Cuijiao had spent her years in exile, so apparently her daughter had married and settled there, and without a city registration, was no longer able to return to the city legally. Cuijiao must have been living in the city alone at least for some years now, most likely after her political exoneration. Zhen felt for her, this woman straddling past and present, separated by the distance between city and town; this patient in front of her who used to be a fashionable and likable girl, who had worked hard as a doctor, and had her own share of suffering. She deserved better.

Cuijiao lowered her head, as if it was weighing her down. In her weak voice, she told Zhen that she wanted to thank her for taking her case, and that she trusted her skills and judgment, as she always had.

Zhen looked at her old classmate, and she felt the weight of that trust, rediscovering in it the classmate who had always been loyal and admiring, unfailingly seconding her opinions, defending her arguments. She could well have made her statement naïvely, out of her admiration for Zhen, unaware of its political weight; it was probably true that if there had been such an organization, Zhen would have been chosen to lead it. It was reasonable to imagine that she could not have predicted the fanaticism of the Maoist hunt for ideological error and the gravity of its punishments. It occurred to Zhen that Cuijiao may have avoided connecting with her in the intervening years because of her own woes, not because of her feeling of shame or guilt.

As if to stop these unsettling thoughts, Zhen turned to check the surgical instruments and put on the protective gear. She thanked Cuijiao for her trust and promised to do her best.

When Zhen opened her up, she saw that the cancer had started to spread. After Zhen took out the entire reproductive system, she searched the surrounding tissue for anything suspicious, intent on the task, vaguely aware of the hums and beeps of the machines. She might yet be able to keep her old friend cancer-free, she said to herself. It might not be too late, if she could find the last of the afflicted cells. Let me find the bad guys; let me get them out of here; bear with me, old friend; bear with me and we'll do things again just like in the old days; help me try, help me, my sweet friend of yesteryear; hang in there just a little longer. . . .

"Congratulations, Director Chen!" Secretary Dong said to Zhen, proudly announcing that the Communist Party had accepted her as one of its members. Secretary Dong shook hands with Zhen enthusiastically, beaming with smiles so wide that it seemed as if he was the one being congratulated. Shaking hands with Secretary Dong, Zhen couldn't help but think that after all the years of trying to be on the right side of history, she had finally arrived.

Her friend Cuijiao was not to see such a day of glory. Zhen would learn from Cuijiao's daughter that her mother passed away a year later, her compromised health succumbing to multiple organ failure.

PART IV

Setting Sail

J UN WAS IN HER OFFICE doing her usual Saturday things, checking unopened mail, reviewing the past week, planning the next one. Routine as it was for her, she felt an unfamiliar agitation. It wasn't anything specific, though it came on as she was leafing through a pile of glossy Christmas brochures. The glitz of the images, all that materialistic hype gave rise to an unease. Shouldn't Christianity be about faith? she asked herself. How did the celebration become all about buying stuff?

It was 1975. Since Jun's early days as an entrepreneur, she had always come alone to the office on Saturday when nobody else was there. She'd leave the house before Min and the children had even gotten up, and she'd return at night to find the house asleep again. Now, suddenly, looking at the cascade of ads and product displays, all those pictures of houses, wreaths, glowing candles, families riding on sleighs, she decided that her weekly Saturday return to the office had made her into a kind of zombie. Abruptly, she got up, locked the office door, and quickened her step, trying to catch the earliest bus home.

Jun pushed open the door to the house, happy to find
Guanxiu, now an established public intellectual and a father
of two young children, sitting with Min, who was still in his
pajamas. Guanxiu had been visiting often so he and his dad
could talk about a magazine they were thinking of starting.
The two men were now a well-known father-and-son team of
media commentators on Taiwan, their rise to prominence
due in large part to Richard Nixon's visit to the Mainland
China three years before in 1972.

Guanxiu had been especially vociferous not only about
what he saw as American treachery, but in his adamant belief
that the Nationalists in Taipei, not the Communists in Beijing, embodied the authentic legacy of China. Guanxiu's
scars from the early years of Communist rule in his hometown ran deep. He believed that he had escaped doom for a
reason, and that reason translated into a personal mission—
to defend Taiwan against two threats. One was obvious: the
Communists' insistence, now accepted by Washington, that
Beijing was the sole legitimate government of China, of which
Taiwan was a part.

The second threat was born of the fierce debates that
engulfed the island soon after 1975, when the Nationalist
leader Chiang Kai-shek passed away. Ideas that had been
strictly forbidden until then suddenly started being dis-
cussed, among them the notion, common among the native
Taiwanese part of the population, that the island should be
separate from the Mainland and become an independent
state. Guanxiu wanted to start a new magazine to stand as
a bulwark against both threats, but also to open up a broad
debate about Taiwan's future.

What should this future be? Officially the Nationalist government continued to see itself as the legitimate authority in

all of China, but Chiang's death took a lot of the life out of that assumption. It was now obvious that the idea of reconquering the Mainland was nothing more than an empty slogan. But if Taiwan could no longer pretend to be a kind of alternative China, and if independence would be a kind of treason, what path was open for the island?

Guanxiu and Min believed that there was a possibility of working with the Mainland government to achieve some sort of accommodation. Min had been particularly heartened by Beijing's release, a month before Chiang Kai-shek's death, of his old commander and patron in the Nationalist Twelfth Army, Huang Wei. Huang had been notoriously incorrigible during his years in prison. He had refused to admit any previous fault or to accept the Communist government, and because of that, he had been repeatedly passed over in each of the previous five rounds of releases of former high-ranking KMT officials. Now, just as Chiang's death marked the end of an era, Beijing's release of the last of Chiang's high-ranking generals suggested the Communists' willingness to engage. Guanxiu's magazine would be dedicated to exploring that possibility.

For Jun, the changes in the larger world opened up new fears and new possibilities. Her relationship with the Mainland was different from the men's. For her, the Mainland wasn't a place of horrors from which she had escaped; it was a place to which she longed to return. She knew of the misery her stepsons had suffered under the Communists, but that knowledge was mixed with her longing for reattachment to her old home and especially her family, with whom she'd had no contact now for a quarter of a century. She agreed with Guanxiu and Min that the Mainland and Taiwan were part of each other, but instead of talking in the abstract about legitimacy and the island's future, Jun focused on something more practical: what the shift in world politics meant for her dream of a return to Fuzhou, to her roots, to the family she'd left behind, especially her sister Zhen, from whom she had once been inseparable.

Jun wanted to go home.

Since Nixon's trip to China and its diplomatic aftermath, Jun increasingly sensed that her heart was no longer in her business. She and Min agreed that the company had served its purpose. It had enabled them to raise their family. Now that was done, both she and Min felt a new moment coming when it would become possible for them to listen to their own hearts.

Jun decided to give herself a rare pause to clear her own mind, and her first step was to make a trip to Europe to visit her trading partners, which she'd never done before. Her purpose wasn't to ramp up sales but to eliminate some parts of the business, lessening some of the burden. Min didn't want to go. It was too cold in Europe in winter, he said. Instead, Jun took along a friend of her daughter's, John Ma, a graduate student at Brown University who was studying Taiwan's integration with the world economy. She would pay for his trip; he would research his topic and carry Jun's bags.

The first stop was Berlin, where they visited Checkpoint Charlie, the famous crossing point between the Soviet-controlled eastern part of the divided city and West Berlin. "It's just a wall," John complained, wondering if it was worth the trouble traversing the city, but Jun insisted. "It was the face of separation," she told me years afterwards. Lights on one side, sleepy dimness on the other, two worlds that converged and separated at the same point, searchlights ferreting out the barbed wire atop the wall, like wilted vines with thorns.

The Chinese had long built walls—city walls kept wealth and power within and farms and poverty without. The Great Wall all throughout Chinese history had stood separating "us" in our farms and cities from "them," the "barbarians" who roamed the steppes. Separation always had a face, like the wall in Berlin, like the Great Wall on the meandering mountain ridges. But Jun's separation from Zhen never did have a face. It was a strip of sea in the case of Taiwan and Mainland China, where there was no wall, no gate, no demarcation of any sort, not even a static marker where one transformed into the other. At Checkpoint Charlie, Jun found the image and heard the echo of the pain that she thought was hers alone.

It was Christmas Eve of 1975 when Jun and John arrived in the Black Forest town of Freiberg, to visit the home of Wilhelm Schmidt, whose family had been supplying her with German clocks since the first days of her business. The Schmidts promised Jun that there was a beautiful local church near their house where she could go to Mass after dinner. The family welcomed them warmly, the father proudly showing off the clock fashioned entirely out of Black Forest wood that his son Peter had made when he was just ten years old. Wilhelm's pride in his son's craftsmanship made it all the harder for Jun to explain that she wanted to scale down her purchase of the Schmidt family's clocks, that this was not so much a long overdue visit to get acquainted, but an occasion to say goodbye.

But Jun also understood as she explained this how different her purpose was from theirs, and the difference lay in the rootedness of the Schmidts' versus her own sense of exile, of not fully belonging to the place where she lived but rather to a place where she could not go. For the Schmidts, clocks represented not just a tradition but its continuation, the accumulation of artistry over generations.

"Maybe you could continue for a few years longer, until my son is more established," Wilhelm asked, Peter having just recently taken over the business. The words almost brought tears to Jun's eyes. Her own father would have said the exact same thing had he been in Wilhelm's shoes, striving to perpetuate things, to pass them down from one generation to another. Jun promised to find partners who would keep up and promote the son's business in Taiwan. But things, perhaps paradoxically, had never been clearer to her. She'd gotten into the business of importing clocks because she needed to provide for her own children, she explained. Now her children had all grown and found their own pursuits, and it was time for her to find herself. Jun told the Schmidts about her accidental separation from her family years before, her struggle for survival, and her own brush with death. "I do not have another fifty years," she said. "I need to find a way."

After visiting some factories so John could do his research, the last stop was the beaches in Normandy, France, where the allies' D-Day landings had taken place during World War II. John drove them there in a rented car, while Jun remembered what Min had told her about the landings on the very day he'd proposed to her on Jinmen, the site of another attempted landing, the failure of which had determined the rest of Jun's life. From the two-lane road, Jun saw a low seawall ahead as they approached, keeping the wide-open sea from the steep rise of a hill. Omaha Beach was completely empty that winter afternoon. The rust-colored sand rippled like the water beyond. Jun saw pillboxes on the hill, pillboxes in the woods, and then, there was one right next to her, the gaping gun hole staring at her right in the eye, giving her a start. The inside was just as dark as in the ones standing in Jinmen's beach towns.

The sand was firm, the beach wide and flat. It was a miracle, Jun thought, that anyone coming from the water side had been able to survive, much less seize the defenses on the bluff above. They moved on to the cemetery on a bluff, where the thousands who didn't walk away were buried. Rows of white marble grave markers bore inscriptions recording the lives starting on the other side of the ocean that ended here. "New York June 6 1944," read one marker, "Pennsylvania July 17 1944," another, "A COMRADE IN ARMS known but to God," yet another, row after row.

Jun thought of Jinmen's beach half a world away. Jinmen had no white marble grave markers to honor and remember the young lives lost. History had many faces. People could pay reverence at marble grave markers, or they could gaze at the absence of them. Here in Normandy was peace, a sense of resolution, of a heroic task accomplished. On Jinmen, the highest point of the island was a military outpost where soldiers remained vigilant against another invasion in a war that had never ended.

When she got home, Jun told Min that they needed to go together to visit Normandy the next summer. But before they were able to make plans for their European trip together, Jun received a letter from John's parents. They had immigrated to the U.S. where they ran a Taiwanese restaurant in College Park, near the gate of the University of Maryland. They were relinquishing the restaurant, the letter said, and they wanted to know if Jun would be interested in becoming its new owner. Obviously, they had learned from their son that Jun was thinking of finding a way home to the Mainland, and they explained to her that it would be relatively simple if she made an investment in the U.S. to become a permanent resident and eventually a citizen. With an American passport, it was now possible to travel to China.

Stepping-Stone

J UN WAS PACKING for a trip, and this one was for the long haul. She was crossing the Pacific to take up a new occupation. Once an unlikely importer of clocks and machines, she would now become a restaurateur. Her luggage this time wasn't a small suitcase like the one she took onto the ferry to Jinmen a quarter century before. But she still traveled light. After all, she herself weighed only a hundred pounds and she was still feeling the effects from her colon cancer surgery.

"Only when I stopped getting up at 4:30 to prepare everyone's meals for the day did I realize that I had been practicing cooking for a reason!" she told me decades later, laughing. "God had prepared me all those years for a job that I'd never imagined doing!"

It was the summer of 1976.

Before she left, she and Min had sold off pieces of the New World company, including its clocks division, to different competitors, though they retained the most robust and profitable parts of it. Min would continue to oversee the company's operations in Taiwan, to man its base, they agreed. Deep down, Jun could see that her husband would never make Maryland home now that he was living his civilian dream life on Taiwan: He had taken great joy in managing the company, and he enjoyed the spotlight of being a celebrity talking head on the media. Min said he'd done all his travelling in his army years. Speaking no English, what would he do in America? But he told his wife: "Go; if it doesn't work out, come back, and we'll find another way. If you make it, great! I'll come and spend time there, and the children will have more options."

The Mas put Jun up in their basement studio in their Maryland house, and wanted to take her to see some of the famous sights in Washington, DC. Jun thanked them but declined the tour of the city. She was eager to get to know the business before they left the area. Once she got settled, she would start to explore ways to contact the family in Fuzhou, and she would also start the process of bringing her children to America. Meanwhile, she would have to hold down her new job.

As soon as Jun learned that the restaurant opened daily from 10 a.m. to 10 p.m., she signed up for an 8 a.m. English class at the community college. On the days when she didn't study English, she took driving lessons. She soon learned that running a restaurant was hard even for someone as tough as herself. But she also soon came to appreciate the microcosm of America that passed through her door day after day. Some people hung out for hours, but there were others, students from the University of Maryland, many of them foreigners, who would come in at odd times, working while eating a simple meal. Late at night, Jun often had to wake up those students in order to close. It made her feel less lonely to see them striving so hard for something bigger and better for themselves and their families, and it made her appreciate the opportunities in America. The world here felt far bigger than Taiwan, not just because of the extent of the land but also because there was so much room to turn dreams into reality. It all made it seem right to have come here.

Jun hired a lawyer to start applying for permanent residence status, a requirement both for getting her children to America and for her to travel to China. When the Mas finally moved away, Jun found an apartment of her own and set out to buy a car.

Jun talks to a tools salesman at a Maryland fair, 2013.

"It was a hot day," Jun told me, recalling that first visit to a car dealership, the kind of place that she used to frequent in her street sweeper dealing days. "I test-drove this Honda hatchback, and the air conditioning didn't work. So I took it back to the dealer, telling them that the compressor was shot. Oh, you should have seen the face of that dealer!" Jun still got a kick out of it. "He said, 'What?' and I said, 'The compressor. You know, the part that cools the air that comes out of the vent.' That poor guy, either he had no idea what a compressor was, or he just refused to believe that this tiny Chinese old lady speaking English with an accent would know anything about a car!"

Starting from that incident, Jun liked to show off her collection of technical terms and machine part names when people least expected it. She loved seeing people's jaws drop, which happened often when workmen came to fix things in the restaurant. Chefs and dishwashers, all immigrants like herself, would not mess around with this old Chinese lady boss. To Jun, that was an unexpected but excellent use of her knowledge, except that she had no idea how to fix any of the machines herself.

Busy as she was, she missed home terribly. The mail at the time took two weeks each way between Taiwan and the U.S., and phone calls, costing exorbitant amounts of money, were reserved for emergencies. Jun lived for letters from the family, and she craved the simple dishes she liked in Taiwan—a bowl of hot soy milk, a small dish of mixed pickles, even the aroma of Taipei's streets, the pungent fruity smell mixed with exhaust, the humidity and the heat. Her chefs could not come up with anything even remotely resembling the daily dishes that she craved, and she didn't have the time to cook for herself. There were times when she had to remind herself of the reasons she had come. She had tasks to accomplish, and they were not about her own earthly comforts.

Days and months flew by, her anxieties grew—the children maturing, herself aging, and her parents in Fuzhou—she didn't know how much longer they could hang on, if they were still alive. Yet legal procedures took time. She concentrated on her work. Work had always been her cure.

It was at the restaurant one day that Jun was reminded of

the rapidly evolving world outside. A group of Chinese students, some pro-Mainland China and others pro-Taiwan, were engaged in a heated debate, each side accusing the other of having been brainwashed by their government, and each side insisting that theirs was the real China. Jun just listened in, saying nothing. But she learned that the Republic of China embassy was to lower its national flag on the last day of the year. That was 1978. The first day of 1979, it would belong to the People's Republic of China.

It was a Sunday. The restaurant was completely booked for the evening. But early that morning, Jun decided to drive to the Taiwan embassy in the Twin Oaks neighborhood of Washington. It was cold and rainy. She knew that for most practical purposes, the embassy would continue to function, now officially as a liaison office, not an embassy, really just a change of name. Still, the change signaled a major demotion of Taiwan's diplomatic status, and, out of sympathy, enough people had come to the flag-lowering event, taking up all the possible parking spaces in the area. Jun gave up looking and veered away. She needed to get started with her day.

Many of the restaurant's patrons were from Taiwan, or knew Taiwan, and as Jun circulated among them to say hello and wish them Happy New Year, she heard many expressions of grief and anger at the American "betrayal." "This is a sellout, an assassination, don't you agree?!" Some tried to bring her into the debate. But Jun didn't really care which side of China was the devil and which the saint, and she'd definitely withhold her judgment on America. She just wanted to see a path from one side to the other. She wanted to embrace, not to fight.

And so she worked at making contact with Fuzhou, but discreetly. She knew that even now, though Mao was dead and

China was in a more moderate political phase, her very existence might still cause trouble for her family there. Her first step was to reach out to distant relatives in Hong Kong and asked them to send feelers to Fuzhou.

Early in 1979, as her restaurant still boiled over with political debates, Deng Xiaoping, China's paramount leader, made his historic visit to the United States. The event was the big news of the day. All of America seemed caught up in the enthusiasm of this new relationship with the world's most populous country. Even among the pro-Taiwan patrons of Jun's restaurant, there was a certain pride in the attention being heaped upon Deng, whose very diminutive size exuded so much dignity, dignity that could be shared by all who identified themselves as Chinese. For Jun, Deng's visit reaffirmed her decision to use America as a stepping-stone back to China. If Deng could come to America, so could she go to China. Anxiously, she waited to hear from Hong Kong.

While she waited, Min was set to make his first trip to America. It had been three years of separation. Jun bought a modest home in Rockville, Maryland, about a half hour's drive to the restaurant in College Park. She put in wall-to-wall carpeting, got the fireplace working, and installed a rocking chair beside it. Min could sit there as they chatted about the kids and grandkids and everything she'd missed during their separation. When she went to the airport to pick him up, she intended to duplicate the moments years before when Min had put keys to their new home into her hands. But when she actually saw him, she totally forgot everything, ran straight to him, and buried herself in his arms.

Her tears poured out. It had been so hard doing every-thing alone.

Min brought letters with him, one from her old friend Qingxi, the classmate who'd invited her to Jinmen nearly thirty years before. She was now the principal of a Buddhist girls' school in Malaysia. As she read the letter, Jun remembered their walk on the beach during her first Mid-Autumn Festival on Jinmen, the way Qingxi had let some sand, silvery in the moonlight, fall through her fingers. "They say that Buddha is in every grain of sand," she'd murmured. Qingxi had always urged Jun to see the blessing in everything, even at the lowest point in her life when she'd felt exiled on the wrong side of an impassable body of water. Now, looking at the wintry woods around her suburban home, she imagined palms swaying outside her friend's window, Buddha in every frond.

Not long after that, Min returned to Taiwan. The couple would settle into an annual routine similar to migratory birds: Min would come to the States to escape Taiwan's summer heat, and Jun would return to Taiwan for some winter warmth. But their two younger children, Shi, also known as Chubby, and Yihui, arrived and stayed, making the house full of life again.

It was midnight, the time when Jun checked her mail at the end of her long day, when she saw the letter that she'd waited for all her life. It was an unusually small envelope wedged between two gaudy booklets of ads. The familiar handwriting of her sister Zhen made her heart race so fast that it actually hurt. The unusual envelope was so delicate that she had to turn it around, trying to find a way to open it without tearing the paper inside. Finally she extracted the letter. The paper was almost transparent, so soft that it rattled in her hands and blurred the reading. Jun put it down on the desk, flattened the creases, and tried to make out each word:

"Jun Jie," it started. Older Sister Jun.

Jun's eyes were completely blurred by tears now. Nobody had called her Jun Jie for an eternity. Then she started to pick out the names as if doing a head count: the two mothers, Ah Niang and Ah Nai, her sisters and brothers, nieces and nephews that she didn't know existed. She raced through the letter, and only toward the very end, she found her father. She felt a heavy door, a door that she had so strenuously tried to prop open all these years, slam shut in her face: Father . . . gone . . . 1952. Nearly thirty years before, and she had not known.

She'd suspected it, of course, after such a long time. And yet, only now did she feel the sadness of her father's passing, given permission to mourn.

That Friday night, Jun detoured to American University, where Yihui, now twenty-four, was attending graduate school. She asked her daughter to go to church with her the following Sunday. Yihui remembered being rather curious at the unusual request, but it was midnight then, and she was too sleepy to pursue it further. She almost forgot about it until that Sunday morning when her mother had to wake her up and almost literally drag her out of bed. "Anything the matter?" she asked her mother groggily.

"I received the letter from Fuzhou," Jun started.

Now Yihui was fully alert. She knew how much that letter would mean to her mother: She had started a new life in America just for this moment. Jun told her what Zhen had written in the letter, and that this trip to church was to mark the death of her father, Yihui's grandfather.

But Yihui also knew that the letter would open up a whole new chapter in her mother's life. It would be an effort to bring things full circle, to restore what had been missing for the three decades since her accidental separation, and perhaps most of all, to be reunited with her partner in childhood, her companion in the Garden's generous abundance and through the war years of hardship—her sister Zhen.

"No Tears for Today!"

CLASPING A STACK OF DOCUMENTS, Jun waited in the "noncitizens" line, an irony in itself, she felt. The Luohu customhouse was the gateway to China from Hong Kong, marked by an old trestle bridge, the British flag fluttering on one side, the red flag of the People's Republic of China on the other. Jun inched forward, making sure the papers clutched in her hands were in order: her Taiwan passport and American travel document with the visa of the People's Republic of China stamped on it; her return airplane ticket, and a detailed itinerary of her upcoming stay in Fuzhou, including the addresses and names of her family members and their work units and titles. Through the windows, she could see the late summer sun bleach the concrete esplanade on Chinese soil, making the inside of the customs hall feel doubly dark and muggy. The line was hardly moving.

When she'd left the Mainland thirty-three years before, in 1949, she had not needed a passport to step onto the ferry in Xiamen. She was a fresh college graduate on a short vacation. Now, looking at the photograph in her Taiwan passport, she saw the contemplative face of an aging woman with salt and pepper hair. The eyes in the picture reminded her of her father's quiet confidence, her skin clear, like her mother's, who always tied her shiny jet-black hair up in a perfect chignon. She would soon see her mother again, and Ah Niang too, her father's other wife, even though her father, who had waved goodbye to her on the tarmac of her first flight, was no more. Waiting in line, Jun felt like a girl who was late, very late, returning home.

"Next!" called the customs officer. Jun stepped up to the window.

"You have a green card?"

"Not yet."

"You're an overseas Chinese?"

". . . Yes."

"You're the owner of a restaurant in Maryland?"

"Yes."

. . . . . .

"Going to Fuzhou for —?"

"Going home."

"Visiting parents?"

"Mothers only."

"Anything to declare?"

"Two color TVs for my mothers."

The customs officer threw Jun a queer look, but he let her pass.

Jun picked out her sister right away. The subtropical sun of late summer illuminated her face; the quizzical, bookish look of her youth had morphed into a gaze of confidence. Her authoritative manner bespoke her years of managing the Women and Children's Hospital, but there was also a touch of gentleness that must have come from handling so many newborns and their mothers. Zhen, the sister two years younger to whom Jun had never had the chance to say goodbye, had had the good fortune to singularly pursue her only dream of becoming an important doctor. There she was, waiting for Jun at her journey's end.

"Junjie, you're back!"

"I am."

They locked in a tight, silent embrace.

The boy standing next to Zhen, watching, had to be Jiyue, her youngest son, Jun guessed, a perfect replica of his father. The last time she'd seen Xizhong was on VJ-Day in Nanping when he was still Zhen's suitor, about to attend medical school with her. They had talked about their imminent return to Fuzhou after their wartime refuge, envisioning a postwar peace, weaving dreams of making their contribution to the new post-war world. Jiyue's face shone with the innocence of that VJ-Day.

The plane the sisters boarded the next day to Fuzhou was the same kind of Russian aircraft that Jun had flown on in her first airplane ride. Now from inside of those strangely familiar windows, she pointed Jinmen out to her sister. Zhen knew how close the island was. She had gazed at it from Xiamen. But Zhen didn't want to talk about it, or about Jun's time there, because she knew that an undercover Public Security Bureau agent was most likely on the plane and would overhear them, though she wasn't sure which of the other passengers he was. Before coming to meet her sister in Guangzhou, Zhen had had to tell the local Public Security officer about her sister's return from America, and that she was the wife of a former Nationalist general. She also had to submit a detailed itinerary of her sister's entire stay in China. Seeing how Zhen lapsed into silence, Jun instinctively held back also. The two of them would have to learn the right topics for public conversations.

But many things were going through Zhen's mind. Should she tell her sister that she still had her wedding jewelry? Very likely Jun didn't care. But what she was sure her sister would like to hear, she couldn't say now. She couldn't comfort her over their father's early death by pointing out that, had he not died early, he would have ended up labeled a counter-revolutionary and suffered persecution and torture. She couldn't mention their Bible-reading mothers and how they kept thanking God for bringing home their daughter, Jun, after all those years. And, of course, she couldn't tell her that they were not alone on the airplane. She could still hear the rude kick on her apartment door made by the Public Security officer when he'd come to verify the information in Jun's itinerary that she'd submitted for approval.

These awkward circumstances were one thing; the separation of thirty-three years was another. It certainly left its imprint on the sisters. At this first meeting, Zhen wore a somewhat uncomfortable formal outfit, a white short-sleeved blouse and a black skirt that she'd bought for Jun's visit. She noticed Jun's fitted silk dress, gold-colored with delicate small floral prints. It wasn't flashy exactly; it fit elegantly on her still shapely figure. The discreet light colors in the print picked up the white in her hair and echoed in her eyes. Jun had always paid attention to her looks, Zhen much less so. She'd been happy to get rid of her *qipao*, a style that was rejected at the birth of the new Communist China. She preferred the loose fit and the coarse fabric of the outfits she wore in her years working closely with farmers in the countryside. Both sisters carried themselves just as they always had, however— erect, confident, with an air of authority. Their styles seemed to echo the distinct difference between them: one austerely proletarian, the other discreetly bourgeois.

They wanted to try to bridge the gap created by three decades of utterly different experiences, but both were aware of the elephant in the room, which was the politics of their meeting. Things had changed in China since Mao had died. The country had relaxed some of its controls on everyday life, but the unpredictability of the recent past made people cautious, careful of what they said. The country's paramount leader, Deng Xiaoping, was calling on people to "cross the river by feeling for the stones" to guide them across a river where there was no bridge. To apply Deng's analogy to Zhen's life, Jun had always been a stone for her sister, but instead of one that would guide her to the other shore, Jun had always been an obstacle in Zhen's path, threatening to trip her up. Surely the security bureau had records of those newspaper articles she'd written on Jinmen, of her marriage to a Nationalist general, and of who knew what else that might have been added to her records. And now she had returned, not from Taiwan, a part of the motherland, but from America, China's longtime imperialist enemy. Zhen couldn't fathom the political implications of Jun's return, and she would bet that the security agent she assumed was keeping watch on them didn't know what it meant either.

As it turned out, Jun later told me, the agent introduced himself to her on her return trip to Luohu and cordially invited her to return with her husband on her next visit. The motherland would welcome them, he told her. But on this first plane ride, the sisters were tense and uncertain; the warmth, love, and joy they should both have felt were replaced by an uneasy silence. It was perhaps the best way to protect the tenderness buried deep in both their hearts and to mask the accumulated uncertainties of their decades of separation.

When they arrived at the hospital compound where Jun would stay, people Jun didn't know helped carry her luggage to her apartment. Jiyue was arriving later by train, as plane rides were still a luxury available to the elite few, requiring leadership approval. But Zhen and Xizhong's two girls and Xizhong's father came for the reunion dinner in the hospital dining hall. The host, to Jun's surprise, was the hospital's Overseas Chinese Office, a fact made abundantly clear in the opening speeches of the officers: The office welcomed the sister of one of their best-known doctors and a leader of the hospital, the wife of a high-ranking Nationalist officer (Min) and an overseas Chinese from America. Jun had never imagined that her family reunion would be an official event. The office had clearly done a thorough background check on her. How far this was from her imaginations of the first reunion dinner! In her Americanized vision—played out so often in her own restaurant—she had worried over how much emotion it would be appropriate to show at the sight of her family after all these years. But the actual dinner inspired more awkwardness than emotion. The conversation was suffocatingly cordial, precluding any hint of exuberance. "Even Deng Xiaoping could have fun putting on a cowboy

hat during his first visit to America!" Jun told me later, referring to Deng's ride in an American stagecoach on the Texas
part of his itinerary. Her resentment of the Communist Party
minders and officials who had hijacked her first family dinner was palpable. It was her introduction to the emotionally
cramped life of the People's Republic.

The morning was still relatively cool when the sisters left
the center of the old city to see their mothers across the
river. Jun was accompanied by Zhen in a car with a driver,
courtesy of the Fujian Women and Children's Hospital. The
streets were still narrow, flanked by rows of two-story wooden
houses, shops on the ground floor, living spaces above.
Some of the buildings, in contrast to the modern apartment
and office towers going up, were so tired they needed to be
propped up by poles planted in the already narrow sidewalk.
Here and there was a gap in the row houses, like a child's
missing tooth. Bikes crowded the sides of the streets, the
riders in their drab "Mao costumes" forming two streams of
blurry gray. The Buddhist shrine that the Chen family used
to patronize still stood, in a state of considerable disrepair.
They crossed the Min River bridge over which Jun had left
the city with her father. The traffic was heavy, and the river
was still choked with the slumbering junks and sampans that
she used to see. The air seemed grayer, and the river mist a
bit heavier.

On the Cangqian Mountain side of the river, the consulates, banks, and companies of the former foreign concession
now seemed shrouded with a film of gray, as if to blend in
with the cement matchbox apartment buildings that had
mushroomed all over China after 1949. A red banner saying

"One Child Is Good" was spread across the façade of one brick building. The old racecourse had been turned into a physical education academy. The farmhouse in the fields where Jun last said goodbye to her family was no more; its surrounding fields had shrunk to a few plots squeezed by clusters of cement buildings and interlocking roads. The map of Jun's memory had to be completely redrawn. She rolled down the window, closed her eyes and let the car take her. The singing of cicadas intercepted the breeze. Welcome home.

When she opened her eyes again, the car had come to a stop at the end of a narrow road. Straight ahead was a green hillside rising to the Flower Fragrant Garden. But they didn't go there. They stopped at the foot of the hill and parked next to a low earthen wall. It ringed a detached two-story row house, spilling over with bougainvillea. A thin, bespectacled man emerged at the small door in the wall. He had unmistakable Chen family looks and manners, Jun noticed, but he walked with an uneven gait, a customized high platformed shoe on his left foot.

"Guang?" Jun ventured a guess, remembering her youngest half-brother, who had crawled to her feet when she left that day. What had happened to his leg?

"Junjie!"

Guang was now a balding, nearly middle-aged man standing tall, even with his one shortened leg.

A crowd swelled at the front of the house as word got around that Jun was there, and she had a hard time telling apart new family members from the curious neighbors. She took Guang's extended hand, cold and trembling, and followed him around the end of the house to the backyard. There, she saw a man, bald and sturdily built, step out from the back door. Jun recognized her big brother, Cang. Behind him was his wife.

"Can that be Wenjun!" Cang exclaimed in his typical play-ful tone, a smile rippling his smooth, tanned skin. Father had spent years grooming him to be the next patriarch of the family; he was always the only child sitting at the adults' table, always the one for whom the tutors were hired, the only one to have dental work done to perfection. Father had promised to fix Jun's teeth next, but that was before the family fortunes took a drastic turn for the worse.

Cang took Jun's hand from Guang and led her through the door into a kitchen, where Jun blinked her eyes to get adjusted to the dark interior. There in front of her stood two elderly women. Her two mothers. Still so familiar with their chignons and long gowns, but both now stooped with age.

"Wenjun, you're back," Ah Nai, Jun's biological mother, said, her outreached hands trembling.

"Yes, Ah Nai, I'm back."

Their hands locked in a tight grip, and Ah Nai's whole body, as if electrified, started to tremble, shaking her long gown. Jun stepped up to wrap her arm around her shoul-ders and reached out her other hand to Ah Niang. She heard someone looking in at the kitchen window start to weep. Ah Nai turned to the crowd, partly visible through the door and the narrow window.

"No crying!" she ordered. Dead silence. "No tears today," she said. "This is a day of happiness. This is the day I reclaim my long-lost daughter. This is the day when my family is complete."

Jun then toured the house. Ah Nai was living upstairs, in her own room above the kitchen at the back. Cang and his wife and their youngest unmarried daughter were on the same floor, in the front rooms. Ah Niang lived downstairs with Guang, who was also still unmarried. The only space that they all shared was the kitchen: two iron woks sunk into pits in the stoves, a narrow space behind the stove for feeding the fire, and two large water urns in the corner. Connecting the kitchen and the living quarters was a dark atrium, more of a stairwell really.

From the second-floor balcony at the front of the house Jun could see, through the leaves of nearby trees, the silhouette of the Flower Fragrant Garden. Below, Ah Niang was cutting some roses from her pots on the patio. More flowers bloomed in the raised bed under the hibiscus tree. Later that day, the family would gather there for a photo. They stood in three rows, the two grandmas on chairs flanked by small children in the front row, the younger women on a stone ledge behind them, and the men in the back row on the raised flower bed.

Standing with the family against the low earthen wall as she looked into the camera, Jun recalled all those years when she lived in the Flower Fragrant Garden, looking down the hill. She vaguely remembered seeing this shabby row house that her mothers now called home. It was there then, part of the scenery, though partly screened by the earthen wall around it, and by the hibiscus tree and the bougainvillea branches that now were about to frame the photograph. Smile! Smile! the photographer reminded everyone. Do not look back, do not look away, smile, smile for this photo, the image of home, of family, the happiness of "whole family luck," as family photos are traditionally called.

• • •

Jun was happy to be there, finally, but is there any happiness unalloyed with melancholy? At the dinner table that night, set up in the kitchen, spilling over into the atrium, the children were confused over which of the sisters, Jun or Zhen,

My Downstairs Grandma (Yan Ruibao), Upstairs Grandma (Lin Ruike), and Jun, from a family photo taken by my father.

was their legitimate "Big Aunt." They had known Zhen with that title throughout their entire lifetimes, when they didn't even know that an Aunt Jun existed. Seeing the consternation on their faces, Jun thought it best to let the children keep their familiar Big Aunt. "I'm your Aunt Jun who has been away too long, so you can call me just Aunt Jun, Tardy Aunt Jun," she said.

It was the small, unexpected things that touched her the most. Biting into the dessert, Jun tasted her childhood favorite ingredient of roasted soybeans in the place of the usual peanuts and sesame seeds. The children complained about the substituted main ingredients in their most important course. Jun realized that her mother must have orchestrated that special treat for her. She felt sorry for the children, who certainly had no idea why they were cheated out of the ingredients that they'd expected. Should she apologize to the children for their disappointment? But where would apologies end? Should she apologize for not being there for them as their true Big Aunt when they grew up? Or to the family for her long absence? But who was to share with her the guilt, the helplessness, and the pain—the torment, when during all those years she could not—despite her ardent wishes—take up her share of the family burden and be with them?

When the children were sent to bed, and the adults gathered, Jun thought of her father. He would have been happy to see everybody together again. He had presided over so many feasts in the grander setting of the Flower Fragrant Garden and had dedicated himself to caring for everyone in the family during the hardest times. There wasn't a whiff of that past in this dingy stairwell crowded with his descendants. Those children, by now asleep, certainly did not have any idea about him, or the family's past. To them, having two grandmothers seemed as perfect and natural as one grandma and one grandpa. And as for her own siblings, they all agreed, "He was fortunate to have gone so early." When she evoked their father's memory, her two mothers sat silent. She felt a stab of sadness like a knife in her heart, and no one there seemed to share that pain.

But she hadn't been there when he died. She had been absent when everybody else suffered the hardship and humiliation of her family's descent from wealth to poverty. She hadn't contributed to the struggle to survive. By dint of random timing, she had escaped the political indoctrination, the terror of class warfare, the re-education, the hardships, and the humiliations that Zhen had undergone—unbridgeable differences in their life experiences.

Jun had missed a lot, but it wasn't her fault. What else could she have done? Could she now, somehow, try to make up for it? It was Zhen who had suffered what she as the older child would have suffered, and done what Jun had been unable to do, and therefore, it was Zhen who now commanded the love and respect of the rest of the family, who occupied the seat of honor.

Jun saw that there would be no going back. No restoration of her position in the family, and no undoing of that accidental separation. She saw it in her baby brother Guang's deformed leg limping toward her, and in her awareness that he had grown up struggling with his disability entirely without her. She saw it even in her big brother Cang's rows of even white teeth that she would never have, and in her mother's demand to the sniffling crowd of spectators, "No crying! No tears for today!" She saw it in my mother Xiang's deference to her instead of constantly seeking her big sister's indulgence as she used to do. Jun's memories were of a life entirely unknown to the new generation, the young nieces, nephews, and cousins who had been told nothing of the wonders of the Flower Fragrant Garden, of Father, of the family's lost prosperity. The world that Jun had fought all her life to return to had slipped into a new reality. She was now a "returned overseas Chinese" instead of a homecoming native daughter.

To survive in China after her accidental departure, Jun understood, the rest of the family had had to pledge their unwavering loyalty to the Communist Party, the archenemy of the Nationalist Party in Taiwan. To demonstrate this loyalty, Jun was starting to see, the Chen family clan had dropped inconvenient facts—her father and her husband's service to the Nationalists, her own existence—down a kind of black hole, so that the memories that Jun had nurtured during her years on Taiwan were purposefully forgotten here in Mainland China. Her world had disappeared, and so had she herself. She had not figured in the New China's family lore. Out of sight, she had been out of mind as well. Now she could see the discomfort that her sudden appearance was causing, the way everybody tiptoed around the black hole as if afraid to fall in. Jun never even got to see the Flower Fragrant Garden on that first trip home, except for quick furtive glances from down below. It was a gated compound, she was told, reserved for senior members of Fujian Teachers University, her alma mater, and no one else could get in; why bother to try?

What would speak louder than an apology, Jun decided, would be a generous helping hand. She announced that she would sponsor two young family members to study at an American university, one from Downstairs Grandma's side of the family, the other from Upstairs Grandma's family, provided he or she could gain admissions to their chosen schools. This would be a serious financial commitment for any middle-class American family like Jun's. But she was perhaps unaware that at the time higher education in China was free. So while Jun's offer was welcomed, nobody quite understood how generous and costly it would be for her.

When she felt she was still being kept at arm's length, she tried to find reasons. She wondered if it had something to do with her status as a merchant. The only one in her generation to have received the best traditional education, Jun was acutely aware of China's traditional Confucian disdain for merchants. She wasn't clear how restaurateur would rank in the family's esteem, but no doubt if Jun had returned bearing the title of university professor, she would have inspired more admiration. The parents would have told their children, "Study hard, and maybe someday you'll be a respected scholar like Aunt Jun." They did hold up Zhen, a physician after all, as a model to follow.

"Where do you live?" Ah Nai asked, prompted by Jun's talk

of family members going to school in America. When Jun answered, "Near Washington, DC," Jiyue, Zhen's son, perked up. His father, he said, had visited there just the year before. Zhen explained that Xizhong had been on one of the first of the province's medical friendship tours to the U.S., representing his hospital, but nobody had known at the time that Jun was living in Maryland. For all they knew, she might still have been on Jinmen.

It turned out that during his Washington trip, Xizhong had stayed very near Rockville, the suburb where Jun had bought her modest home. He had been there just at the time she was wracking her brains to find a way to reconnect with the family. She might have driven right past his hotel on her way to her lawyer's office to discuss the legal implications of visiting Fuzhou. Everybody was stunned by this coincidence. These two members of the same family had passed each other like strangers in the night.

Jun and her mother, Lin Ruike, whom she called Ah Nai, my Upstairs Grandmother, in the mid-1980s.

————

On the last night of Jun's visit, Ah Nai retrieved the Bible that she shared with Ah Niang from a small basket secured to the windowsill at the turn of the staircase. Jun sat by her mother's side on the edge of her woven wicker bed. A cool summer breeze came through the window, ruffling a loose strand of hair from her mother's unfailingly neat but greatly diminished chignon.

Ah Nai found the passage she was looking for, pointed at it with a shaky finger and read: "In my anguish I cried to the LORD, and He answered me by setting me free . . ." Jun chimed in when the passage started to come back to her: "The LORD is with me; I will not be afraid. What can man do to me? The Lord is with me; He is my helper. I will look in triumph on my enemies."

They exchanged other passages from memory.

"So do not throw away your confidence; it will be richly rewarded, you need to persevere so that when you have done the will of God, you will receive what He has promised."

"Let no debt remain outstanding, except the continuing debt to love one another, for he who loves his fellowman has fulfilled the law."

Then Jun bid her mother good night.

"Let no debt remain outstanding . . ." Jun repeated those words to herself as she boarded the plane on her way back home to Maryland.

• • •

Yihui remembers finding her mother subdued upon return-ing from that first trip, and she was sad for her. Yes, there was a reward for her mother in having engineered her reunion with Zhen and the rest of the family in Fuzhou, but she didn't get the warm embrace of her dreams. Jun told her daughter about how at that dinner she'd ceded the title of Big Aunt to Zhen, though it took a while for the symbolic importance of that gesture fully to sink in. Jun hadn't given up her traditional place in the family willingly. She'd simply recognized the reality, and reality is sometimes not what one wants it to be. It wasn't terrible, she told Yihui. Nothing had gone disastrously wrong. And yet, nothing fully made sense, nothing truly fit. The fulfillment that Jun had so ardently wished for gave way to a melancholic resignation that this was the way it was, and this was the way it had to be.

Still, Jun's visit, and especially her promise to foot the bill for American educations, made a big difference. Jiyue, Zhen's youngest, came first in 1984, matriculating at Montgomery Community College to improve his English before enrolling at the University of Maryland.

Two years later, it was my turn. I went to Georgetown University thanks to Jun's generosity, and from there I embarked on a well-worn path of so many Chinese students in America—getting degrees, finding a job, having a family, now working as a professor of linguistics at Brown University, where I write these words. When my parents got the news of my admission to Georgetown and my impending trip to America, they triumphantly declared: "We've arrived in the new global age." Aunt Jun had single-handedly created a pathway for a family once targeted for political prosecution to become the envoy of a new modern era.

Into a New World

IT WAS AN UNUSUALLY BRILLIANT spring day in Seattle in 1993. I had just passed my dissertation defense and was putting some finishing touches on the text before the final submission. My phone rang. It was the most unexpected call in my entire stay in the United States: Aunt Zhen was calling from a hotel right down the street from me. She and Xizhong were in the city to attend a medical exhibition at the University of Washington where I was getting my Ph.D.

During my seven years of graduate school—after the first year in Georgetown funded by Aunt Jun, I got a full scholarship at UW in Seattle—home had felt like the farthest place on earth. My modest scholarship barely covered my basic expenses, making trips to China impossible. Even phone calls home were rare. Now the family's most revered couple—the de facto heads of the clan—was at my doorstep! I was glad I actually had something to show for my time here, and for Aunt Jun's generosity: I would be receiving my Ph.D. degree in just a couple of months.

But most of all, I was dying to see someone, anyone,

from my Mainland home. So much had happened there—
particularly the June 4 student movement on Beijing's Tiananmen Square in 1989 and the Communist Party's violent
suppression of it—and all of it had deeply affected me even
as I looked on from afar. Then there had been China's
resumption of its economic reforms, its move toward a capitalist economy (Mao would be rolling in his grave) that was
rapidly turning the country into a rich and powerful global
power. Not that I could expect Aunt Zhen to clarify the political developments back home, but at least, maybe she could
give me a sense of what it was like for her and the rest of the
family to have lived through it all.

I ran the few blocks to the hotel, and Aunt Zhen sat me
down in her room. She and Xizhong had just had their first day
at the exhibit, and their eyes lit up talking about it, competing
with each other to tell me what they had just seen. "IVF technology!" Aunt Zhen exclaimed, in vitro fertilization. "That's the
future in my field." She'd already arranged meetings with the
UW medical school to discuss a potential joint program with
her hospital to make IVF technology available to Fujian women.

"But don't we have enough people as it is?" I asked,
remembering the policy of family planning, which had been
at its height when I left the country.

Aunt Zhen was patient with me. "Different people and different families have different needs. Some need help in con-
traception and others in getting a child. As a doctor, my job
is to help each woman to have her rightful chance to achieve
what she wants."

"And the children today are growing fatter." Xizhong said,
eager to share his excitement. "Adults who suffered from hunger for much of their lives are indulging themselves in their
new wealth and abundance, eating a lot, becoming obese,

unaware of or ignoring their slowing metabolism. America has the technology to fix many of these problems."

They were both sixty-eight years old that year, but both were clearly thinking about the next stage in their careers and the brand-new world that they hoped to bring into being in China.

The reform had brought about a sea change, Zhen was quick to point out. Longdi, the village of her exile, had been accessible by car for years, she learned on her first visit in twenty years. When her car rounded the bend and onto her favorite bridge, she saw glimmers of electric light blinking through the leaves in the descending dusk.

"The villagers ambushed me with firecrackers and gongs at the shed by the bridge!" The scene was still vivid to Zhen. "They said that it was a ceremony reserved only for emperors! As if Emperors frequented that place!"

We all had a good laugh. But Zhen may have been better than any emperor as far as these villagers were concerned, because she had fulfilled her promise to set up a clinic there. In the new village hall that night, a five-table feast was laid out in her honor, and everything was a local specialty of Longdi, including the glutinous rice and peanut dessert.

She had brought with her, as personal gifts, a clock for the village, books and student supplies for the school, a bell to mark the beginning and the end of each class, and sacks of candies for everyone. She saw watches on many arms, a sweater on every back, and a healthy glow on all the unfamiliar youthful faces around her. Yet she searched in vain for many of the faces she had missed all the intervening years. Life expectancy had not improved much for the older generation.

Zhen's next destination was the clinical meeting of the American College of Obstetricians and Gynecologists in Washington, DC, where she was going to present two papers, one on her team's effort to bring down an unusual rise in infant and maternal mortality in Lianjiang, and the other, on an almost parallel endeavor to gain UNESCO accreditation for her hospital in Fuzhou as a Baby Friendly Hospital, which would mean that it had reached international standards. And she had successfully accomplished both projects in the record time of two years.

The first paper reported on her dealing with a medical crisis that occurred in Lianjiang, a town on the Min River about half an hour's drive from Fuzhou. What happened there had threatened to undo the progress Zhen had made in getting care to poor women who'd never had it before. Once a poor farming and fishing center, Lianjiang had boomed, thanks to the growth of light industry. But while greater prosperity usually meant fewer birth-related deaths, reports coming in to Zhen indicated just the opposite. Deaths among birthing mothers were going up, from 12.7 per ten thousand to 22.2 in a single year, from 1987 to 1988. By 1989, the number was 31.8 per ten thousand, and it showed no signs of abating.

A close study of the medical records showed failures in two stages. They first discovered that sepsis—a bacterial infection that gets into the bloodstream and invades the vital organs—was the chief cause of death. It turned out that most of these cases could be traced to a single midwife, locally known as Amah Lin. And it was the visit to Amah Lin that helped unwind the mystery for Zhen and her team. Amah Lin told them that she had assisted at many births over her long career, until three years earlier, an eighteen-year-old girl from a nearby village started to hemorrhage after delivering a baby. Rushed to the hospital, the young woman's life was saved, and Amah Lin learned the problem: A small bit of placenta

had stuck to the uterus wall and she had not noticed it. After
that, she started to do something she hadn't done before—
manually check the uterus after every delivery. Still, there
were more cases and more deaths. After they'd delivered
their babies, women would experience an abrupt spike in
their pulse, their breathing would become rapid, red patches
would appear on their skin, their fever would soar, and they
began talking so wildly that nobody could decipher what they
were saying. After a while, the fever would give way to chills
and the women's limbs would turn blue, and by then, even if
they were rushed to the hospital, it was too late. Only a couple of the stronger and older women had survived. The local
grannies blamed the increasingly casual sexual relationships
women were having, which, they said, attracted the attention
of evil spirits. But Zhen could see these symptoms were actually postpartum infections, probably caused by Amah Lin as
she palpated the women's uteruses with her bare hands, looking for fragments of placenta. Zhen arranged for the local
midwives to get some needed extra training in her hospital.

Once the patients arrived at the hospital for emergency
care, the new fee-based policy became another obstacle: The
patients and their families had to pay the fee upfront for emergency procedures traditionally subsidized by the government.
Few of these women could afford such fees. But such fees
were crucial to the hospital's own survival in the government's
push toward a semi-free market. Fee-based structure was also
blamed for the increased birth-related deaths in clinics newly
set up in remote areas, but for somewhat different reasons.
These revenue-starved clinics were reported to have pushed
caesarean sections over natural births for more profit, sometimes even without the women's consent. But C-sections were
inherently more dangerous for birthing mothers. These small

clinics, ill-equipped for emergency cases when things went awry, also contributed to more birth-related deaths. So in the rush of economic reform, these vulnerable women whom Zhen had spent her entire career helping once again got short shrift.

Zhen's response was swift. She worked with the health ministry to make new rules, including waiving fees for life-threatening emergency situations and punishment for unnecessary C-sections, she expanded training programs to include local TBAs, or traditional birthing assistants like Amah Lin, and she made trips to monitor the progress. In the two consecutive years after Zhen's team's intervention, there were zero cases of birth-related deaths. Zhen wanted to tell the story of that success to her international colleagues.

Lianjiang's case made Zhen see the importance of leadership in the new reform era. She wanted to lead rather than chasing after problems. To lead, she enthusiastically embraced the BFHI, or Baby Friendly Hospital Initiative, sponsored by UNESCO. The initiative promoted breastfeeding and educating young mothers, whose immediate benefit, Zhen felt, would be in reducing postpartum hemorrhage, a major cause of maternity deaths. Breastfeeding immediately after birth could stimulate the system to contract, thus reducing bleeding. In the longer term, she saw the hospital as a perfect setting to educate young mothers, especially rural women, about their own health and childbearing. These were taboo topics for women in general, but the knowledge women would gain would help them make better decisions to take control of their own bodies and better protect themselves. Zhen applied for the two-year fast-track certification for her hospital. Accreditation by UNESCO would have the added benefit of enhancing China's place among the advanced nations of the world.

One day, while working on the Baby Friendly Hospital application papers, Zhen got a call from the province's health minister. She thought she was in for some political refreshment session. But no, it turned out that the mayor of Fuzhou and his wife were expecting a child, and they had asked for Zhen and nobody else to deliver their baby. Zhen did, not knowing at the time that the mayor, Xi Jinping, would, years later, become China's president.

Then, in the midst of what she had anticipated as the exciting but straightforward challenge of accreditation, unbelievable tragedies struck. Five newborns sent to the very state-of-the-art nursing room built to meet the BFH specifications suddenly stopped nursing. Their hearts raced, their breathing intensified, and then they died, all in a single day. The same thing happened in the weeks that followed. In all, sixteen babies died suddenly and inexplicably. A storm of yelling, howling, and blame broke out, to the point where Zhen, fearing for her life at the hands of some grief-stricken families, hired bodyguards for protection. She thought briefly of resigning, but soon dismissed the idea: how could she leave such a mess for someone else to clean up?

Then one day, after finishing an English article in the medical library, she jumped up and dashed to the new neonatal room. She called in the electricians, located the AC unit, and asked about its filter, and what she was told jolted her like a charge of electricity. The filters had been removed after the first week of use. Why? Because removing them got room temperatures down more quickly, something the nurses had demanded. Zhen ordered samples to be taken from the air duct, and what she suspected from reading the journal article turned out to be right. The air ducts contained Legionella pneumophila, the bacteria that caused Legionnaires' disease.

It was first discovered in the United States in 1977, when a mysterious infection led to thirty-four deaths at a 1976 American Legion Convention in Philadelphia.

"And you're going to tell about all of this at the conference?" I asked, a bit incredulously, imagining how much courage it would require to explain that many losses. "Certainly." Aunt Zhen was calm, without a strand of doubt. "We reported every detail to the UN certifying committee, and we still got the fast-track Baby Friendly Hospital certification within two years from the time we applied. If our record was good enough for the certification, it should be good enough to discuss in a conference, perhaps especially so."

Presenting these two papers at an international conference would be a kind of glorious climax to the first long stage of Zhen's career, and would help her to open a new one. The Two Ailments campaign, she told me in Seattle, had been taken off the books, brought to an end because it was no longer deemed necessary. According to her memoir, a total of 26,616 cases of uterine prolapse had been treated, with a cure rate of 83.3% and "no major complications or fatalities." Of the 1,060 cases of obstetric fistula treated, the cure rate was 86.32%, which meant that the program she devised and directed had rescued nearly 900 women who would otherwise have had lives of misery and exclusion.

Sitting in her hotel room that day, I felt pride just to know this remarkable woman, much less to be her niece. But I was also somewhat disappointed. Zhen and Xizhong's world, as exciting and consequential as it was, had always seemed singular and insular to me. Their medical work—the setbacks and achievements—had always been the prism through which they viewed and measured the world outside their labs and offices. Training their eyes on the next goal and the next prize in their medical field, they constructed narratives of their lives and work free of the dissonance of China's political disorders—like the Tiananmen student movement and its brutal suppression on June 4, 1989. It was as if by averting their eyes from the dark side of politics, they could obliterate the repression taking place around them. But then again, who am I to judge these two prominent doctors who had dedicated their lives to saving and improving others' lives? Their passion had always been to use the new science and technology—with the support of China's government, however flawed it may have been in other areas—to rescue ordinary people from age-old medical afflictions, and in this they had admirably succeeded.

Zhen and Xizhong proceeded to Washington a couple of days later, and they paid a visit to Jun's home in Rockville, Maryland. Min was about to arrive from Taiwan for his annual summer months' stay in the U.S., and the sisters and their husbands would be together for the first time—it would turn out to be the only time—outside China. Their memories of that visit, however, were distinctly different. Jun remembered fondly hosting the couple: "It was such a wonderful time together," she recalled to me later. Jun's personal endeavor over the past years of helping family members acquire American college educations—which she called "advancing meritocracy"—was at its height then, having expanded from her initial pledge to support just two young people from the Fujian clan, Jiyue and myself. Others from Taiwan followed, the difference being that the relatives from Taiwan, including her own ever-expanding cohort of grandchildren, could afford to pay their own tuitions. All they needed from Jun was sponsorship. To accommodate the increased trans-Pacific traffic, Jun had bought a larger house near the old one.

Zhen and Xizhong arrived right in the middle of many happy events: Jiyue (their son) had found a job as a research scientist following his graduation with a degree in chemistry from the University of Maryland. Jun was getting ready to fly to the West Coast to attend my commencement at the University of Washington in Seattle. Things all seemed to have worked out as Jun had planned. She felt that her hard work was bearing fruit that would be passed down the generations.

Jun showed her sister and brother-in-law her new house, not as a material display, but as a way to explain her life to them. "Min is arriving tomorrow" she said, showing her husband's study on the first floor, dominated by a framed picture on the facing wall, of a younger Min in full military glory standing next to a seated Chiang Kai-shek. The Nationalist

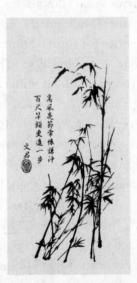

書籤詩

沈敏

2003 年 10 月

世局紛紜冷眼觀，
魚龍變幻見多端。
閒來方覺天機妙，
靜坐自然大地寬。
執政無能累百姓，
台灣亂象震三方。
榮枯得失雲煙過，
一夢黃粱不復遷。

Jun's painting and calligraphy printed on one side of a bookmark, Min's poem on the other side of the same bookmark. Jun's gift to the author in around 2010.

flag took up the entire background, its white sun beaming over the two men.

The photograph had always been in Min's study, in the old home and in the new. Jun must have been so accustomed to it that she wasn't thinking of the effect it might have on Zhen and Xizhong. But it clearly did make an impression on Zhen—that was what she brought up when she talked to me about that first visit: "Your Uncle Min was a handsome young man standing next to Chiang Kai-shek," she commented, saying nothing about the house, several times larger than her own apartment, or about the tree-lined, clean suburban streets, or the cars or other possessions she had never had, but mentioning only one thing, the photograph of Min in uniform standing next to the man Chinese propaganda treated as the "running dog of American imperialism."

She must have used her physician's training to keep her composure.

When Min arrived the next day, Zhen must have seen how the youthful angular face in the photo had softened with age. Min's piercing gaze, that of an ambitious rising military star, had given way to a more mellow, contemplative, and often smiley look. He charmed his sister-in-law with a poem, composed on site to commemorate their first meeting. Zhen was duly impressed by the handsome young officer turned poet general. Still, Zhen and Xizhong didn't seem to engage with Min in a meaningful way. As Aunt Jun commented to me: poetry and military matters were not their cup of tea.

Or perhaps Jun was more preoccupied with her own agenda. She was eager to learn from her sister about the death of their mother, which had happened since her last trip to China. She'd known about Ah Nai's final illness and had wanted to go back, but she'd been suffering from deep vein thrombosis, and her doctor had forbidden her to take any international flights. She'd learned the news in a letter sent by their brother Cang.

But Zhen didn't know much herself. Their mother had been living with Cang in an apartment in Fuzhou that Jun had bought for him. Zhen didn't see her mother often while she herself was completely consumed by the two concurrent battles in Lianjiang and on the BFHI. She hadn't even been told of a serious fall Ah Nai had taken, until Ah Nai complained of chest pain a few days later and Cang sought Zhen's help. Zhen brought her in for an examination and found a broken rib, but by that point, infection had set in. There was not much the hospital could do, given Ah Nai's age at ninety-three and her compromised immune system from the chemotherapy for her tumor.

"Ah Nai's lifelong wish was to see you again, and she did," Zhen said, attempting to placate her sister's guilt. "You made her happy."

Zhen declined Jiyue's offer of a Maryland sightseeing tour—oblivious to her son's eagerness to show off his newly acquired driving skills and local knowledge—and shopped for medical books instead. Her heart had already flown back to the new projects she wanted to start at home. She and her husband made a quick stop at their nephew Shi's new restaurant on their way to the airport. The last thing that caught Zhen's eye was a photo prominently displayed at the entrance. In it, Shi, his wife, and his mother, Jun—all beautifully dressed—stood with the newly sworn-in President Bill Clinton, also in suit and tie. It was a souvenir from a donor event.

• • •

A couple of months later, Jun flew to Seattle to attend my commencement as I received my Ph.D. diploma. "When you were in Fuzhou," Aunt Jun asked me at dinner that night, "did you ever watch a local Fuzhou opera called *Chen Ruolin Gave the Prince a Death Sentence*?" I shook my head. I had never heard of it, and I hadn't a clue why it should be brought up on the day I received my degree. "It has everything to do with you," she said, smiling.

The story was about one of our family's ancestors, Chen Ruolin, Jun started to tell me, who was the minister of justice under the Qianlong Emperor in the late eighteenth century. The emperor's son, coveting a beautiful young woman, issued a fake edict to bring her to his chamber in the palace. When the young woman jumped into a well and died rather than losing her honor, Justice Minister Chen, after investigating, ruled that the prince be sentenced to death. That was the law of the land, but the emperor, torn between his son and his favorite minister, chose to spare the life of the former and to offer the latter an honorable suicide, by swallowing gold.

In fact, the tragic death of Chen Ruolin in the opera appears to have been a theatrical invention, because, in historical fact, he lived till his retirement and died of illness on route returning to Fuzhou. But he was nevertheless a historical figure, and a direct ancestor of mine, the second *jinshi* degree holder in the Chen family lineage. The opera is a local classic, and it burnished the Chen family lore with a touch of glamour. "Now you're the first woman in the family to hold such a high degree," Jun told me, referring to my newly minted Ph.D., making the connection between me and our illustrious ancestor who also had the land's highest degree. But of course, she chose to overlook the fact that the high degrees of my ancestors were awarded to only a handful of candidates each year, unlike the hundreds and thousands of Ph.D.s generated in America each year.

Aunt Jun never got tired of talking about Fuzhou and the people that populated her childhood there, even when the facts hurt. I understood her. To me, Aunt Jun was like my seven-year-old-self trying to push open the heavy door of the main building inside the Flower Fragrant Garden: the cool air of the courtyard seeped through the door and enveloped me on that hot summer day as I leaned into it. But the grinding sound from the hinges startled me. I ran away, and never did get into the courtyard.

Aunt Jun leaned into her house of memories too. But she did not run away as I did. She leaned into it, pulled out strands from that past, and gave them a new life. Zhen, on the other hand, crafted a narrative suitable for the new Communist China, and behaved as if that part of their shared lives had never existed.

In our conversations, Jun rarely talked about Zhen. Instead, I became a kind of go-between, reporting to Jun about my frequent visits to China after I started teaching. Jun always seemed genuinely proud of her sister when I told her of Zhen's latest achievements. They inspired the pride that she had derived from her ancestors and the confidence that the family would rise again, despite the obstacles hurled in its path. And so, in her own way, Jun tried, step by step, often at great financial cost to herself, to give her relations a leg up in the new reform era.

It was years after the fact that I learned how Jun's emotional commitment to her mother had pushed her to the brink of financial crisis. When she returned to Fuzhou to celebrate Ah Nai's ninetieth birthday, Jun was already paying full tuition for Jiyue and myself. But only days after the celebration, the sisters found out that their mother had stage three melanoma. So when her mother asked Jun to help their big brother Cang to buy an apartment in the center of Fuzhou, Jun readily agreed. As a mother herself, Jun could see that Ah Nai—who had been living with Zhen after she was reassured that Guang and Yu would bring their Ah Niang to live with them in the city—didn't want to leave her firstborn son behind, in the dilapidated house at the foot of the hill below the Garden that everyone else had abandoned. Moreover, this request might very well have been her last. But when Cang decided to buy an apartment soon after Jun returned to America, Jun found herself short of cash. She had long before cut out family vacations and much else of what she deemed nonessential spending, and so had to dip into her long-term investment accounts, accepting exorbitant early withdrawal fines to pay for everything. None of us coming from the Mainland had any idea about cash flow or the financial risk Jun took to help the family leapfrog into the modern era.

Against her own doctor's advice not to take long flights due to the danger of blood clots, Jun returned to celebrate the Chinese New Year just months after having made the same trip to celebrate her mother's ninetieth birthday. She felt that her chances of seeing her mother were running out, and that she owed Ah Nai a heavy debt of gratitude. It was Ah Nai—whose own prospect of an American higher education had been replaced by her marriage to Jun's father—who reminded her girls that knowledge was something no one could take away from them, and that they were destined for things bigger than being what she called "decorative vases" in their husbands' homes. It was her mother's words and her deeds of perseverance, and of magnanimity toward all in her large and complicated family that had given her the strength and courage to recover from her devastating separation from her family decades before. Jun would do anything to make her mother happy, no matter what the financial cost, or the cost to her own health.

So it came as a shock when her mother enlisted her help in moving out of Zhen's home and into Cang's new apartment. "But Zhen's home is your home," Jun said to her, thinking of all the advantages her ailing mother would have living in the hospital compound surrounded by doctors who cared deeply about her. It took her a while to realize that medical treatment was no longer on her mother's mind. What mattered to Ah Nai was the traditional importance of the first-born son: it was proper for a mother to end her life with her son, and not with her daughters.

Jun knew better than to contradict her mother's wishes, mindful that at this point every wish could be her last. As Zhen said calmly, their mother had always done things her own way. But it was deeply sad for Jun that her mother, at the end of her life, seemed to betray her convictions about the equal worth of women in choosing to leave Zhen's home and her attentive care. She had, Jun felt, taken advantage of Jun's own financial generosity to buy Cang an apartment to help him fulfill his filial duty, affirming the tradition of hierarchical male dominance that she had taught her girls to defy.

One disappointment followed another. After Jun helped her mother settle in to Cang's new apartment, Jun learned from Cang's daughter that plans were underway to demolish all the buildings inside the Garden to make way for a cluster of new apartment buildings.

If Jun was going to visit the Flower Fragrant Garden ever again, it had to be now. Cang, she knew, had no interest, so Jun found eager companions in her half-sister Yu and baby half-brother Guang. But the Garden, when they got there, was unfortunately still off limits to nonresidents. Neither Yu nor Guang had the connections to get permission to enter a gated community owned by the university. My parents who used to teach there had long moved to another city, and it didn't matter that the university was Jun's alma mater. She'd never even received her diploma because the school was so broke the year of her graduation that it couldn't afford to print diplomas. Jun walked away dejected and wondered out loud: "Big Brother Cang doesn't like to talk about the Garden. I've always wondered why."

"Of course he doesn't want to talk about the past!" Guang's response was swift and ready. He launched into a speech that seemed to have been prepared and practiced just for this day: "For years, our old family ties put us in the wrong social class, and we don't even know any of those people!"—those people being the illustrious ancestors whose images had graced the halls of the Garden, images that Guang had never seen, of people he had never known. "The political background checks even went to the next generation," he continued, his vehemence a surprise to Jun. "As the oldest son, Cang was forced to confess the family's stinking class background over and over again, at every political meeting, literally for decades. Why should he want to make a sentimental trip when finally, no one bothers him any longer, his family ties don't matter anymore, and he doesn't have to live with worries of stumbling onto yet another political land mine? Why should he go back, even just for one more time?"

Jun was deeply affected by Guang's speech, knowing that he himself had had an especially rough time even compared to his brothers and sisters. His disability had kept him from being sent down to the countryside during Mao's revolutionary years, but it had also disqualified him for jobs and even from taking university entrance exams when they were first reinstated in 1977. Guang was the last in his generation born in the "old society," and he'd never had a chance in the new Communist China, though not for any lack of talent. Jun had learned from her sibling that he had an incredible memory and used to come home from the movies reciting whole monologues and conversations verbatim; and during high school, he'd produced blueprints that an engineer neighbor claimed to be the best work he'd ever seen. It was only in recent years that his life had started to turn a corner. He had finally found a regular job and married a college graduate, which was something even if his wife's main interest had been to acquire a city registration certificate by marrying a Fuzhou resident. It wasn't a passionately happy union, though they'd just had a baby, a girl.

"Just think," Guang continued that day, "people used to stand in line for hours just to get a tiny ration for what now seem like small things—rice, cooking oil, sugar, down to the fabric for clothing. Now we have no lack of any of them. Not only that, you can grow your own vegetables in the backyard, you can start your own business, or go abroad, and no one can accuse you of being a capitalist roader or a traitor and ruin your life and your children's lives by association. So what has changed? What has changed is that the political trip wire has been removed, and the guarantee of individual freedom to pursue one's own destiny is now enshrined in the constitution."

Jun, in going to the old neighborhood, had intended to rekindle a sliver of the past; instead, she'd learned how her little brother wove Communist teachings into his own life to make sense of it. He had embraced a freedom and prosperity that he had never known and believed that they were built on a clean break from the very past that Jun had wanted to recover. In this new light of understanding, Jun gained a deeper appreciation for her family's resolute turn away from the past, their embrace of the new era, and Zhen's almost frenzied effort to seize every possible opportunity to live her life's dream of being a doctor.

When they got back to Cang's new home and told him where they had been, Cang, to everyone's shock, exploded in rage, as if simply mentioning the Garden had touched a kind of third rail: "I just moved out of that damn neighborhood," he roared in his thunderous voice, seeming to be angry at Yu, though his words were clearly meant for Jun. "We're done with that hill! What do you mean you went back there? What do you want there?" Yu was by now shaking, whether from rage of her own or from Cang's intimidating manner, which Jun had known well when he was the bullying big brother.

"It was my idea," Jun said, taking a step forward, shielding her little sister and brother as she thanked them and sent them home.

The aroma of the New Year's Eve dinner was drifting out from the brightly lit new kitchen of Cang's apartment. Modern appliances glinted amid the cacophony of cutting, chopping, stirring, and sizzling. Their mother was hard of hearing and in her own room.

Jun turned and went straight to the bathroom. In the mirror was the gleaming white porcelain toilet. No more chamber pots for Cang's family. The hot and cold running water faucets stood as almost comical impressions of the two water jars that used to stand side by side in the old kitchen, holding water drawn from the common well of the past. The sweep of the family's history seemed to flit by on the mirror. Cang's own children would in their way now enjoy a sliver of the good life that Jun had known in the Flower Fragrant Garden, decades before their lifetimes. Jun had played her part in moving the clan into these much better times. She'd striven to forge a connection between past and present, to bring things full circle, and to show that love, forgiveness, and prosperity could all be woven into a new narrative. But in the end, she still found herself alone. Her solitary effort was no match for the Communists' powerful propaganda, in the case of Guang; or the comfort of returning to the old ways, as in the final choice that her own mother had made. The gate to the Garden was locked, literally, and the door to collective memory had been angrily slammed in Jun's face.

Jun understood, as she perhaps never had so keenly before, that the separation resulting from her accidental exile was permanent. With that realization, her tears fell, plopping into the modern new porcelain sink.

• • •

The world's first live IVF baby emerged around the same time that China embarked on its era of Reform and Opening, though it took China a decade to achieve its own first live birth. When Zhen's hospital's lab failed to make meaningful progress in mastering the new technology, she announced that she would get IVF training herself and then lead her team to achieve live births within two years, by the century's end.

Zhen was seventy-two that year, and perhaps the most decorated doctor in Fujian Province. She had also achieved national prominence, having been chosen to represent China at the World Women's Conference in Beijing in 1995. Still, she faced challenges, including the fact that she was twelve years older than the cutoff age for IVF training. She solved that problem by putting down her age as sixty on the application form, a little lie that was "overlooked" somehow by the province's health ministry. During the session in Guangzhou, she had to share a dorm room with classmates decades younger than she was and already trained in cutting-edge fields such as genetics, endocrinology, and molecular biology. Like them, Zhen had to sleep in a bunk bed.

But she was determined to achieve her goal, and to make a statement in the process. She wanted to validate the dreams of poor couples and give them an equal chance for a family. A quarter century of Reform and Opening had created a yawning disparity between the haves and have-nots. Money seemed to be able to buy and dictate everything, even in the medical field. The caesarean-section skills that many local health workers learned during Zhen's training sessions were reportedly being abused to make profits, endangering lives. Registrations to see specialists like herself, which were supposed to be free, were being scalped for 200 to 300 *yuan*, a small expense for the rich, but several days of wages for many of the poor. To have a child was a miracle for infertile couples, and Zhen was determined to show that it could happen for the poor just as it would for the rich.

In the first year and a half, however, Zhen's team treated seventeen couples, and all seventeen failed to develop viable fetuses. Their eighteenth case was that of a couple named Lin, another modest pair from the countryside with a typical story. Mrs. Lin had been subjected to a forced tubal ligation after giving birth to her son. When the young boy died, her doctor was unable to reverse the ligation, leaving her no way to try for another child, unless Zhen and her team could finally master the IVF technique.

One night, just as Zhen was about to wind down for the day, the phone rang. Mrs. Lin had started her contractions. An epidural had been administered, and dilation was progressing. Zhen rushed to the hospital. The room was exceedingly quiet, save for the occasional clinking of the instruments and the constant beeping in the background. The twins were taking their time. Finally, seven hours after labor began, in the early morning of January 5th, a round head matted with pitch-black hair appeared, then another. The brothers leaped straight to the morning newspaper, page one: "The first test-tube babies in Fujian Province were born early yesterday morning at 1:07 a.m. and 1:27 a.m. respectively." There was a large picture of two swaddled bundles with raw faces, the sleepy older one in Zhen's arms, the naughty younger one, flashing a mischievous grin, being held by her colleague.

The successful births of the first IVF babies, significant as it was, marked but another milestone in Zhen's long career. To her, the case that better showcased her lifelong work was one of a young woman named Xiaohua.

Xiaohua had come to Zhen when she was eleven. She had been run over by a car three years before and would surely have died had the driver of the car not delivered her immediately to a nearby military hospital. Starting from that day, Xiaohua had undergone surgery after surgery to reconstruct her various organs, since the car had run right over the middle of her body. By the time she found Zhen, she needed help to reconstruct her uterus and to fix a severe and extensive case of fistula. It took years, since each of a succession of necessary procedures required time for healing before the next one could be performed. "I practically saw her grow up!" Zhen said to me. When she learned that the young woman had married and was happy, she thought the case was closed.

But soon after the news of Zhen's team's IVF success got out, Xiaohua showed up once again. She had been unable to conceive and she wanted help. The treatment took almost two years, and when the time came, Zhen volunteered to deliver the baby, even though by then she rarely handled normal deliveries. "Just imagine," Zhen told me later, "a baby born out of a womb that was damaged beyond recognition when the mother was only eight years old! If the live birth of the Lin twins was a milestone, Xiaohua's baby was a testament to a woman's determination to claim a normal life after unimaginable trauma." Aunt Zhen had seen many cases of life and death revolving around the creation of babies, but she had always maintained a professional emotional distance. In this case, she did not try to hide her emotions. Who could blame her, seeing Xiaohua's miracle baby boy emerge from the womb that Zhen had reconstructed?

Then the baby developed a severe case of jaundice, and both he and his mother were back in the hospital. Xiaohua was inconsolable, seeing her baby suffer. Zhen explained that jaundice in newborns was a common occurrence, and it could be treated.

"It's so hard for me to see my baby suffer," Xiaohua said, "harder than if I was suffering myself."

"I know," Zhen assured her, speaking from long experience. "You're learning the first lesson of being a mother."

On the last day of 2008, I flew to Fuzhou from Boston. Aunt Zhen and Xizhong were unwell. They had both spent most of the past year in their separate hospital rooms, and things were getting worse. When I arrived on New Year's Day I learned that Uncle Xizhong had died just a few hours before. My intended visit now turned into a condolence call to Aunt Zhen, if the hospital granted me the permission to see her.

She had been hit suddenly by a severe case of aplastic anemia a year before. The hospital had flown in the nation's top doctors for consultation, and once they arrived at a diagnosis, the prognosis was three months. But Zhen was fighting back.

"My platelet count has reached 30,000," she told me when I arrived at her bedside, with the hospital's special permission. "I promised Xizhong I'd come to see him as soon as I reached 30,000, and now . . ." Her voice caught, her hand trembled, and she looked away momentarily.

I was thinking how to comfort a strong woman like Zhen when she resumed our conversation: "You want to write a book about me," she said. "I'm going to give you some contact information, people you can call to learn more if you want." She then pulled out her cell phone, and with her swollen thumb, stiffly scrolled down a screen, writing down names and numbers on a piece of paper with her right hand. "I haven't written anything with a pen in the past year, and now my handwriting is shaky," she explained almost apologetically. I watched her concentrate, bending and pushing her puffy fingers, her chest heaving, her lips pressed tightly together, using all her strength to make her rebellious body obey her commands.

"Read it back to me," Zhen said as she handed me the sheet of information, "just to make sure that you can read my handwriting." The sheet was almost full, and I obediently read out the names, job titles, and phone numbers, to Zhen's approving nods.

Aunt Jun happened to be in Taipei when the sad news about her brother-in-law reached her. Just two months before, she'd gotten an urgent call at home in Maryland telling her that Min, her husband of almost sixty years, had had a heart attack and was in a Taipei hospital. All he wanted was to see his wife. Not any nurses or doctors, only Jun. "He basically threw a temper tantrum even in the midst of a heart attack," Aunt Jun later told me. "He'd always hated hospitals."

She got to Taipei in time to see Min, but then he passed

away, leaving Jun so drained that she twice delayed her planned return to the U.S. In the depth of her sorrow, she'd held an elaborate funeral for Min, a major event in the island's capital, attended by Taiwan's political and military luminaries including its vice president. Then she underwent the onerous task of sorting out the estate. Jun had decided that she didn't have the stamina to go to Fuzhou, but now hearing of Xizhong's death, coming so soon after her own loss, reminded her of what really mattered. She decided to delay her return trip to the U.S. one more time in order to be with her sister.

The night Jun arrived in Fuzhou, Zhen got permission for one short trip out of her hospital room so she could have a special dinner at home with her sister. Jun took me along to assist her unsteady steps. The taxi dropped us off at the gate of Zhen's hospital residential compound in the chilly dusk. The cement apartment buildings inside the compound were already fading into the evening, their edges smudged. Aunt Zhen's apartment was on the fourth floor of a six-floor walkup.

Jun insisted on slowly making her way up the stairs on her own. The bare bulb in the landing cut her features into sharp relief: the impeccably styled but thinning white hair that barely concealed her scalp, the high cheekbones that now seemed hollowed by the years. Jun's usually bright, friendly eyes were tinged with the sadness of Min's passing, and now further clouded by Xizhong's death. She was eighty-six and Zhen eighty-four, and they had been widowed within two months of each other, a shared experience of old age, echoing in its melancholic way the shared experiences of their childhoods. Jun must have realized that this would most likely be the last time they would be together.

The apartment door had been left ajar in anticipation of

Jun's arrival. As she walked in, she saw Zhen struggle to stand up, and rushed to help her. The two women steadied each other.

"I've dragged myself out of death's jaw," were Zhen's first words. "I thought I would never see you again."

"But Xizhong has brought us together."

They settled down in their chairs in the small room, Xizhong looking on from inside the black bunting of a picture frame. The candles flickered; there was a smell of incense and fresh flowers.

"Here we are, two sisters again," Jun said. She had always been softer than Zhen in tone, but not soft by any other measure. "Single girls, like we were when we parted company."

"How uncanny," Zhen said. "It was exactly sixty years ago."

In the middle of a small table for two, where Zhen and Xizhong had eaten for years, sat a tureen. "We'll have Buddha Jumping Over the Wall tonight." Zhen said, as she took off the lid. Steam puffed out along with the rich aroma of the soup, so named because it was infused with delicacies from the sea and the mountain that even Buddha would escape his temple to taste. Sitting there in their thick layers of clothing, the two women must have felt as if the years had evaporated like that puff of steam. It was the tremendous force of will they had in common that had powered them to survive, to succeed, and to reach this day. They had both climbed mountains, and yet they knew that they would remain on their separate mountain tops, Jun the devout Christian, Zhen a member of the world's most enduring and powerful Communist Party.

"Let's eat!" Zhen said, and both sisters dipped their spoons in the soup.

Epilogue

THE FLOWER FRAGRANT GARDEN HAS made way for apartment high-rises. Only the old encircling wall remains, marking its original footprint, keeping visitors out.

Aunt Jun passed away in her Maryland home in 2017, at the age of ninety-four. She never returned to Fuzhou after that last meeting with her sister. Before Min died, she had planned to purchase a pair of burial sites in Fuzhou next to her parents' graves—Min having said he didn't care where he was buried, as long as it was beside her. But she scrapped that idea after Min's funeral, when it became clear to her that none of the people who came to pay their respects—former or current military men living in Taiwan and America, as well as prominent figures in Taiwan's political and social establishment—would visit his gravesite if it was in Fuzhou. So she purchased her own family plot in Maryland instead, and buried Min's remains there. A video of Jun's funeral was beamed to Fuzhou, where Zhen had called together the family for a commemorative meeting, treating all to a sumptuous dinner in honor of her sister afterward.

Aunt Zhen survived her year-long ordeal of aplastic anemia, spending most of 2008 in an isolation ward. She returned
to work after two years of bumpy and painful convalescence,
and continued to see patients three days a week until a month
before her passing on September 18, 2022.

• • •

The Chen family that I've come to know—my two grandmas and all their children—possesses no family photograph
from before 1949, the year the Communist Party came to
power on the Mainland. Photography was invented in 1826,
twenty-two years before the birth of Chen Baochen, China's
last emperor's tutor. But the family has no photographs of
him—indeed not a single photograph of any of its ancestors who lived in that era of photography. Jun remembered
that there used to be some pictures. Faces of the ancestors
once hung in the Garden's front hall, looking out from their
frames over the altar table. There were other pictures in her
father's library, documenting everyday life in their majestic
family compounds and homes across the empire where these
scholar officials had lived and served. But all of the drawings
and photographs of the past that the family ever possessed
were burned, shredded, or dispersed, along with the contents of their library. The images of the past were obliterated,
the family memories and legends sealed tight behind the lips
of the generations that were born before 1949, all deemed
incriminating evidence that threatened the family's survival
in the new Communist China.

But the family has survived the revolutions, as did the
Bible that my two grandmothers had shared. My Downstairs
Grandma used it every night before bedtime. Once, I helped
her pick up a photo that had slipped out from between its

pages and saw a handsome foreign face on it. He had wavy shoulder-length hair and beautiful penetrating eyes. I asked Downstairs Grandma who he was. She gently placed the photo on the cover of the Bible, brushing off invisible dust. "This is Jesus Christ," she said. "A photographer took a picture of a beautiful piece of cloud one day, and in the dark room when the photo was developed, he found this face instead." No one else in the family remembered that photo or had heard that story. It seemed as elusive as that beautiful piece of cloud.

The first house of the Chen clan in their ancestral village of Luozhou, thirty kilometers south of Fuzhou City, survives as well—a double-courtyard house that marked the clan's heightened status in its place of origin. When I visited in 2015, it had been turned into a family shrine. A new plaque had just been added to the shrine in honor of Aunt Zhen. It says: "A Good Doctor of the People." The generous peristyle that rings the courtyards had important ancestors' official pictures hung on its walls. I walked past the ancient court paintings toward modern photographs, and for the first time, came face to face with my grandfather, identified by name and by a short biography, accompanied by the image that had been missing in my entire life until then. The photo must have come from some official records, since the family did not keep any images of the past. He was wearing a Western-style suit with a wide striped tie and was sitting slightly sideways, looking out as if he'd heard my approaching footsteps. I could see in his eyes that he knew me, and I knew him. I saw my aunts and uncles in those eyes; I saw my own mother in that frame. My heart was pumping his blood. And that hint of a smile playing on his lips suggested that he was holding back words that he would have said, to Zhen, to Jun, and now to me, in a voice that had rung in Aunt Jun's dreams and that had pulled her home.

Grandfather looked peaceful and calm in the sole surviving photograph of him. He had never lived here in Luozhou. The home he loved was the hilltop aerie he had designed and built, the Flower Fragrant Garden. On that day so long ago, in the warm sun of the verdant south, as he watched the workers dig into the mountaintop to lay the stone foundation, he would've smiled as he looked out to the greenery on the slope below, dotted with the red-roofed Western-style villas of the foreign concession. The Min River meandered on the bottom of the hill, and the ancient port city of Fuzhou stretched out along it to the sea. Home. It must have felt eternal, this pinnacle of the illustrious Chen clan.

Acknowledgments

Writing this book has been a big part of my personal journey in America. I had come to America to study for a PhD in linguistics. But more than a degree, I've found this story. Through writing this book, I have come to reclaim a big piece of the past of my mother's Chen family that I never knew, and to gain a chance to reflect on a country split and a family torn asunder. Along the way, I have benefited from insights, encouragement, and help from many people.

My deepest gratitude, of course, goes to my Aunt Jun, who passed away in 2017, and her younger sister, Chen Wenzhen, whom I called Aunt Zhen. Their lives inspired me to write this story; their memories, explanations, and help in locating people for interviews have made it possible for me to comprehend the magnitude of what they have lived through and what they have achieved.

I'm also grateful to my parents in Xiamen, Li Rulong and Chen Wenxiang, as well as many members of my extended family in Mainland China, Taiwan, and America—aunts and uncles, cousins and nephews, and relatives from my mother's Chen family to the related Shen and the Hu families who live on different sides of the divided China and across the great Pacific. They have all generously shared with me their memories, helping fill in many details of a story that spans continents and extends across a century. Each in their own way helped me understand things I never would have otherwise. I remain in awe of their determination not just to endure, but to strive time and again, over centuries and across different cultures.

Writing in my second language and in a genre that I'm not trained for, I've benefited from the extremely generous advice of many people over the years. It's impossible to name all of them, but the story may not have been able to see the light of the day without a few important early supporters. My dear late mother-in-law, Barbara Steinfeld, lent me her confidence when mine faltered. The well-established writer Nicole Mones, whom I still have not met in person years after we first communicated, painstakingly explained to me the intricacies of the craft of writing and affirmed the value of the story that I tried to write. Alan Lightman, whose writings I adore, has been a very kind teacher and friend. And the veteran journalist Richard Bernstein, with his deep understanding of China and rich experience in journalistic writing, was instrumental in my final completion of the story.

But the story would never have become a book without my wonderful agent, Peter Bernstein, and his wife, Amy Bernstein. With a keen sense of history, they from the very moment I met them appreciated the literary value of this story. Alane Salierno Mason of Norton brings in her deep editorial expertise, and worked with the Norton team to turn the story into this beautiful book.

What has sustained me over the years is my family. My husband, Edward Steinfeld, has never for a moment doubted that I would bring this writing project to fruition. My two sons, Daniel and William, have so greatly expanded and enriched my life with their youthful wisdom, and they are constant reminders for the need to record the memories and the paths their predecessors have come down from very different times and places.

I'm profoundly grateful to them, and to many more beyond the scope of this page, who have enabled me to reach a once impossible goal.

DAUGHTERS OF THE FLOWER FRAGRANT GARDEN

Zhuqing Li

READING GROUP GUIDE

DAUGHTERS OF THE
FLOWER FRAGRANT GARDEN

Zhuqing Li

READING GROUP GUIDE

DISCUSSION QUESTIONS

1. In telling the story of Jun and Zhen, Zhuqing Li's *Daughters of the Flower Fragrant Garden* imparts an enormous amount of historical and political information. How does focusing on an individual's story change or reconfigure your understanding of political and historical events?

2. In Longdi, Zhen's son, Jiyue, stops eating when he realizes that each mouthful of food that he eats is one mouthful less for the impoverished villagers, that "kindness to him demanded a huge sacrifice from these poor people" (p. 210). Does kindness always demand a sacrifice? Why were the villagers willing to deprive themselves for Jiyue?

3. What preconceptions about China, Taiwan, and their histories did you have going into *Daughters of the Flower Fragrant Garden*? How has your perspective changed? Did reading this book raise new questions for you? If so, what are they?

4. The idea of a complete or whole family comes up again and again after Jun becomes trapped in Jinmen by the new border between China and Taiwan. What does a "complete" family mean to Zhen? To Jun? To their two mothers? What is a "complete" family to you?

5. How do you view or judge Zhen's choices to work with the Communist government, join the Communist Party, and become a leader of the "family planning" sterilization effort in mainland China?

6. At the end of the book, Zhuqing Li writes about Jun and Zhen's last meeting, "They had both climbed mountains, and yet they knew that they would remain on their separate mountain tops, Jun the devout Christian, Zhen a member of the world's most enduring and powerful Communist Party" (p. 346). What about these "mountain tops" separates the two sisters? How are they able to connect despite their vastly different experiences? Why does Li write this about their final meeting?

7. Is there someone in your family who embodies your family story in the way that Jun and Zhen do for Li and the Chen family? If so, how?

8. Are you surprised by the ways in which both sisters embraced the political ideologies of their respective homes? Is this something you notice people doing in the world around you?

9. When Jun finally returns to Fuzhou, she is forced to cede her traditional title of Big Aunt to Zhen, who filled that role in Jun's long absence. What is Jun's new role? How do you think the author would describe the role of Jun and Zhen in her and her family's lives?

10. Which of the two sisters in *Daughters of the Flower Fragrant Garden* do you relate to and identify with most? Explain.

11. Li describes a profound sense of recognition when she sees the only surviving photograph of her grandfather in his ancestral village of Luozhou. Have you ever felt something similar? Describe your experience.

12. What positive lessons do you think Zhen learned from the ideology of Communist China? What positive lessons do you think Jun learned from nationalist Taiwan and the United States of America?

13. The course of Jun and Zhen's lives were shaped by enormous political events beyond their control. What large political and historical events have shaped your life?

14. After being offered membership in the Communist Party, Zhen "felt a freedom that she had not tasted for a very long time" (p. 279).

How would you characterize the freedom Zhen felt? Does it match your understanding of freedom? Explain.

15. In different ways, Jun and Zhen are motivated by their concepts of family and tradition. What ideas about family and tradition do you carry with you? Where does your understanding of family and tradition come from?

Diana Abu-Jaber	*Life Without a Recipe*
Diane Ackerman	*The Zookeeper's Wife*
Michelle Adelman	*Piece of Mind*
Molly Antopol	*The UnAmericans*
Andrea Barrett	*Archangel*
Rowan Hisayo Buchanan	*Harmless Like You*
Ada Calhoun	*Wedding Toasts I'll Never Give*
Bonnie Jo Campbell	*Mothers, Tell Your Daughters*
	Once Upon a River
Lan Samantha Chang	*Inheritance*
Ann Cherian	*A Good Indian Wife*
Evgenia Citkowitz	*The Shades*
Amanda Coe	*The Love She Left Behind*
Michael Cox	*The Meaning of Night*
Jeremy Dauber	*Jewish Comedy*
Jared Diamond	*Guns, Germs, and Steel*
Caitlin Doughty	*From Here to Eternity*
Andre Dubus III	*House of Sand and Fog*
	Townie: A Memoir
Anne Enright	*The Forgotten Waltz*
	The Green Road
Amanda Filipacchi	*The Unfortunate Importance of Beauty*
Beth Ann Fennelly	*Heating & Cooling*
Betty Friedan	*The Feminine Mystique*
Maureen Gibbon	*Paris Red*
Stephen Greenblatt	*The Swerve*
Lawrence Hill	*The Illegal*
	Someone Knows My Name
Ann Hood	*The Book That Matters Most*
	The Obituary Writer
Dara Horn	*A Guide for the Perplexed*
Blair Hurley	*The Devoted*

Meghan Kenny	*The Driest Season*
Nicole Krauss	*The History of Love*
Don Lee	*The Collective*
Amy Liptrot	*The Outrun: A Memoir*
Donna M. Lucey	*Sargent's Women*
Bernard MacLaverty	*Midwinter Break*
Maaza Mengiste	*Beneath the Lion's Gaze*
Claire Messud	*The Burning Girl*
	When the World Was Steady
Liz Moore	*Heft*
	The Unseen World
Neel Mukherjee	*The Lives of Others*
	A State of Freedom
Janice P. Nimura	*Daughters of the Samurai*
Rachel Pearson	*No Apparent Distress*
Richard Powers	*Orfeo*
Kirstin Valdez Quade	*Night at the Fiestas*
Jean Rhys	*Wide Sargasso Sea*
Mary Roach	*Packing for Mars*
Somini Sengupta	*The End of Karma*
Akhil Sharma	*Family Life*
	A Life of Adventure and Delight
Joan Silber	*Fools*
Johanna Skibsrud	*Quartet for the End of Time*
Mark Slouka	*Brewster*
Kate Southwood	*Evensong*
Manil Suri	*The City of Devi*
	The Age of Shiva
Madeleine Thien	*Do Not Say We Have Nothing*
	Dogs at the Perimeter
Vu Tran	*Dragonfish*
Rose Tremain	*The American Lover*
	The Gustav Sonata
Brady Udall	*The Lonely Polygamist*
Brad Watson	*Miss Jane*
Constance Fenimore Woolson	*Miss Grief and Other Stories*